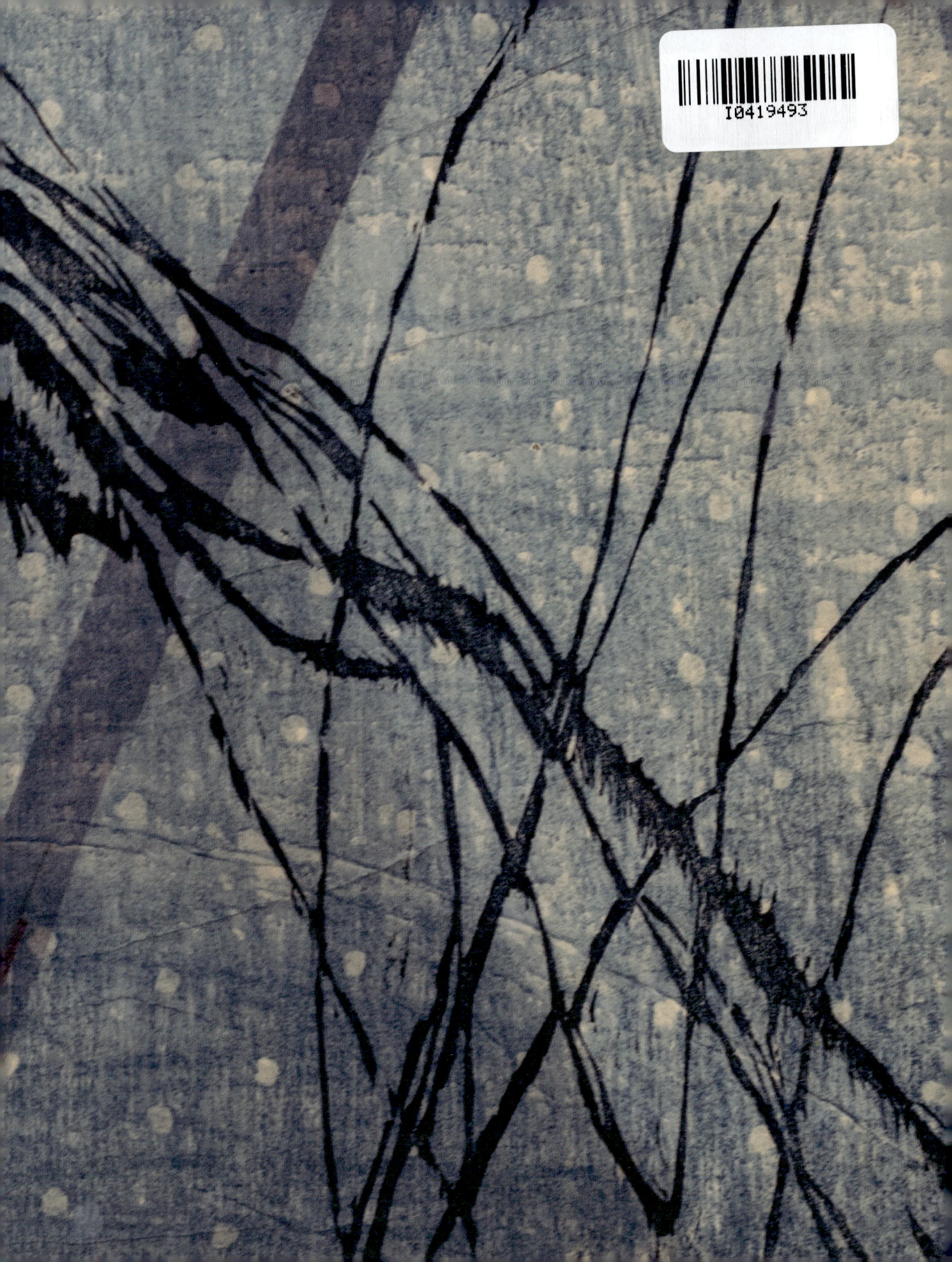

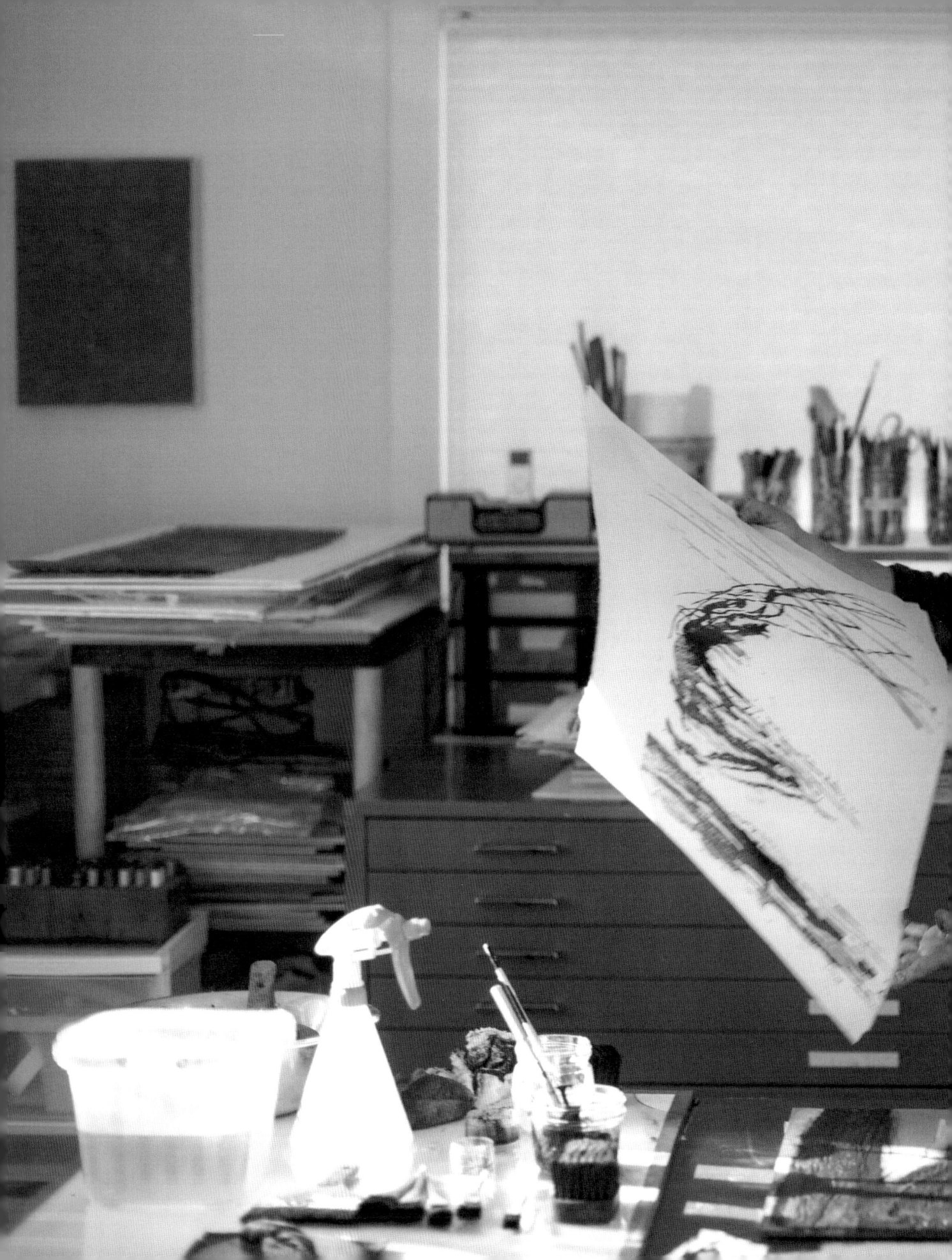

KEIKO HARA

FOUR DECADES OF PAINTINGS & PRINTS

Linda Tesner | Ryan Hardesty

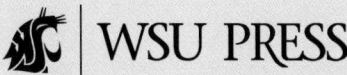

WSU PRESS

JORDAN SCHNITZER
MUSEUM OF ART WSU

Washington State University Press
PO Box 645910
Pullman, Washington 99164-5910
Phone: 800-354-7360
Email: wsupress@wsu.edu
Website: wsupress.wsu.edu

Jordan Schnitzer Museum of Art WSU
PO Box 647301
Pullman, Washington 99164-7301
Website: museum.wsu.edu

This publication was produced in conjunction with the exhibition *Keiko Hara: Four Decades of Paintings & Prints*, organized by Ryan Hardesty for the Jordan Schnitzer Museum of Art at Washington State University from May 24, 2022, through March 4, 2023.

© 2022 by the Board of Regents of Washington State University
All rights reserved
First printing 2022
All works are courtesy and collection of the artist unless noted as otherwise.

Printed and bound in the United States of America on pH neutral, acid-free paper. Reproduction or transmission of material contained in this publication in excess of that permitted by copyright law is prohibited without permission in writing from the publisher.

Library of Congress Cataloging-in-Publication Data is available.

The Washington State University Pullman campus is located on the homelands of the Niimíipuu (Nez Perce) Tribe and the Palus people. We acknowledge their presence here since time immemorial and recognize their continuing connection to the land, to the water, and to their ancestors. WSU Press is committed to publishing works that foster a deeper understanding of the Pacific Northwest and the contributions of its Native peoples.

Graphic design by Tracy Randall
Cover design by Debby Stinson
Previous spread: Keiko Hara in her Walla Walla studio. Photo: Amahra Leaman

On the cover and on half title and end pages: *Verse · Ma and Ki · Memory* (detail) | 2017
Mokuhanga monoprint with collage, silk gauze, two panels hung back-to-back | 84 x 24 inches
Photo: Sean Sullivan

contents

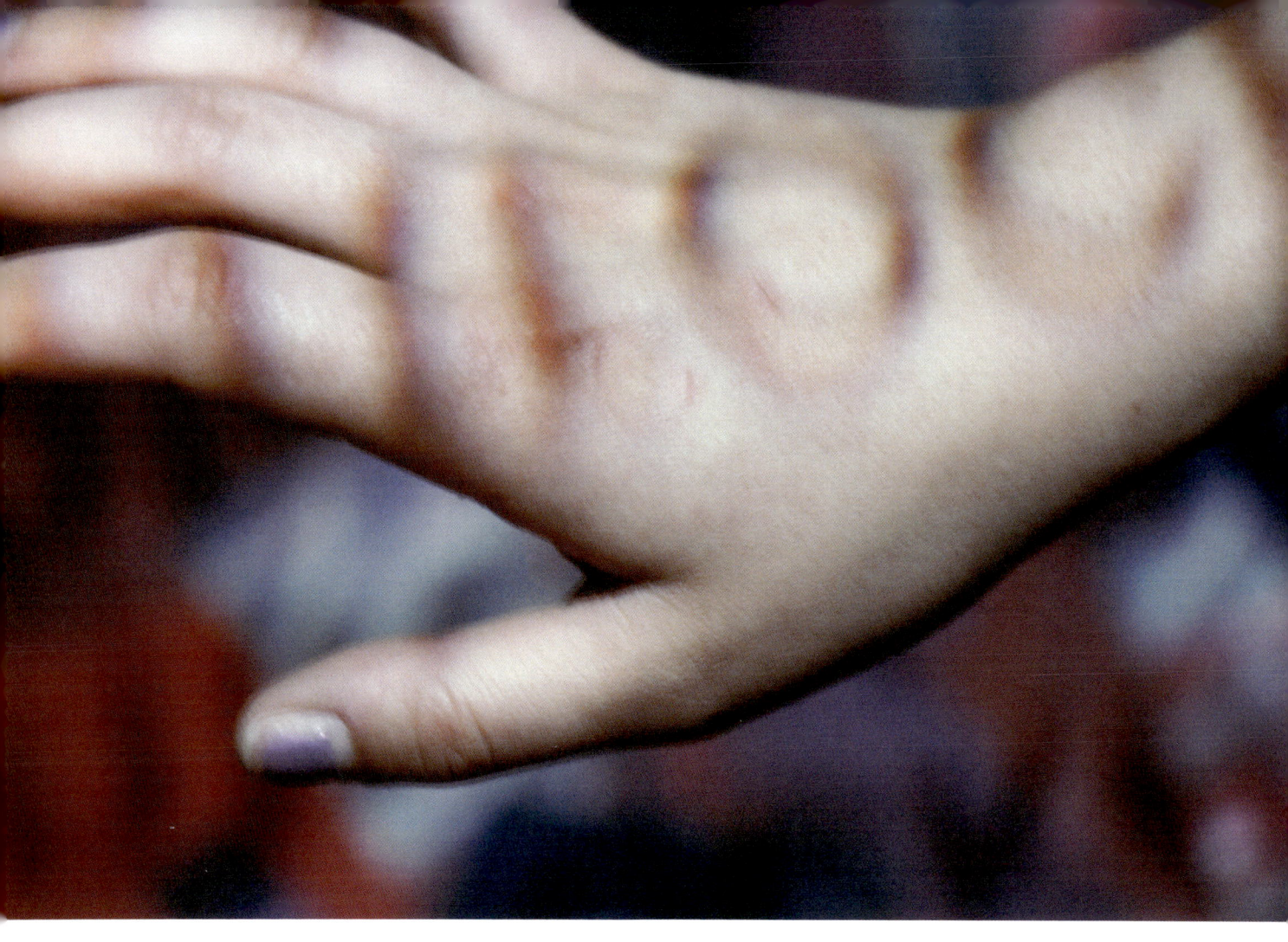

Topophilia · Imbuing Seasons | 2004
Installation at the Northwest Museum of Arts and Culture, Spokane

introduction

Ryan Hardesty,
Executive Director
JSMA WSU

I have had the immense pleasure of knowing artist Keiko Hara for just shy of twenty years, and our first project together set the tone for the many years that have followed. When we met in 2004, Hara was preparing for a major installation at the Northwest Museum of Arts and Culture in Spokane, Washington, where I served on the project as co-curator. The exhibition's centerpiece was a multi-media, four-room "house," its exterior covered with hand-worked rice paper. Stepping inside, visitors were bathed in a kaleidoscopic environment of color, light, and projected pattern. It was a transportive experience.

During our visits leading up to the installation, I learned two simple facts about the artist: Hara's creative spirit and ambition are insuppressible, perhaps even unmatched within our region, and while she is an introspective person, her default impulse is one of generosity, which makes sense given her twenty-eight years as a teacher. She is also the most generous host in her adopted home of Walla Walla, Washington. My numerous studio visits with Hara over the years typically involve her whisking me around town to see her various studios, to visit the Walla Walla Foundry, and to retrieve fresh produce from the valley farms, with countless stops and introductions along the way.

We are exceedingly proud to originate and present *Keiko Hara: Four Decades of Paintings and Prints* at the Jordan Schnitzer Museum of Art at Washington State University. Our project represents Hara's first full-scale museum publication alongside a survey exhibition of her painting and printmaking practices. Hara's boundless artistic vision and production are remarkable and enormously deserving of our attention and careful study, especially as we draw upon the power of art as a window into human thought and as a provocation of emotion to raise awareness. In fact, throughout her career, Hara has been guided by the concept of topophilia, exploring its meaning of "a strong love of place" in large multi-media installations as well as in paintings and prints. She believes each of us holds essential connections to places of meaning, beauty, and power, whether these "places" be external or internal.

Born in what is now North Korea to Japanese parents during the Second World War, Hara moved to Japan in 1945 and was raised and educated there. In 1971, she left Japan for the United States to further her education, imagining America as a progressive cultural environment that would challenge her artistic development.

For an artist moving between lands and cultures, Hara's work shows an artist stitching together many memories and navigating radical life transitions brought on by partings, loss, and making new homes. While personal memory and longing have been central to the artist's work, over the years Hara has increasingly focused her projects toward a collective universality, writing, "It is our individual topophilia that unites us as human beings." I propose that Hara's practice may be seen as an attempt to bridge the gap between physical worlds, connecting us across timeless currents flowing through human life in all places.

This publication required a community effort and would never have been possible without the dedication, love, and collaboration of colleagues, supporters, and friends—all of whom played their respective roles in bringing this very special book to life.

Our appreciation begins with Keiko Hara, who kindly provided the beautiful images, captions, and reference materials in this retrospective. Her lifetime of poetic paintings and prints are meticulously documented, and we are grateful for her vision and creativity that have enchanted us all.

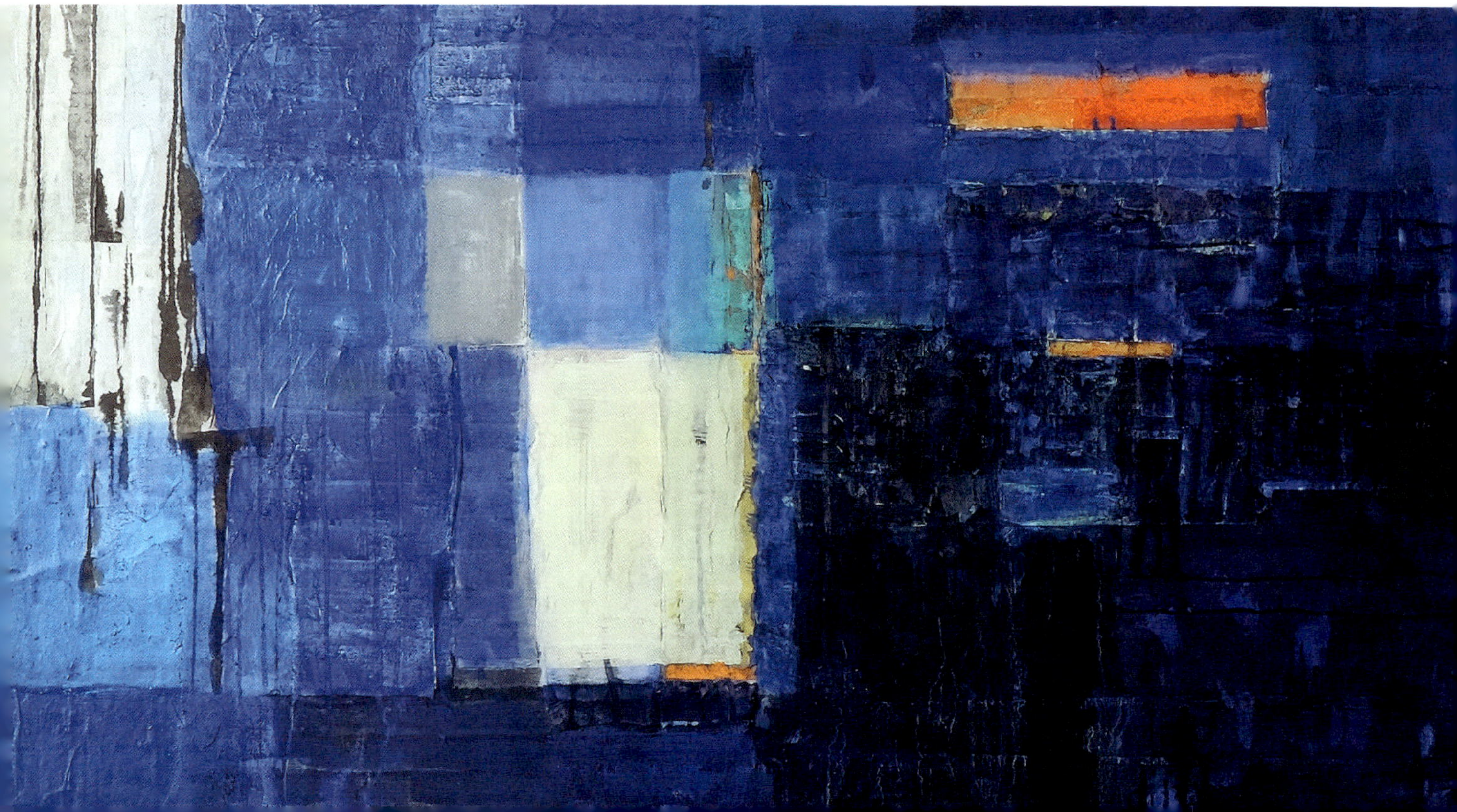

We wish to thank independent curator and writer Linda Tesner for her insightful essay. We are appreciative and honored that she enthusiastically accepted our invitation to provide the lead essay chronicling Hara's life and engagement with painting and printmaking across a span of four decades.

Thank you to the museum staff for their support, encouragement, and helpful contributions throughout this process. In particular, I wish to acknowledge Debby Stinson for her timeless cover design, valuable insights, and significant contributions in keeping everything on schedule.

To the team at WSU Press—thanks to Linda Bathgate for her buoyant nature, faultless ability to schedule multiple pieces into manageable tasks, and guiding hand in bringing this book to press. Jessica Schloss gracefully facilitated the design and printing stages, and a special thanks goes out to Tracy Randall for her beautiful graphic design and her talent of coaxing order and harmony into every element of this wonderful publication.

Lastly, and perhaps most importantly, a very special set of recognitions goes out to our publication's donors. We begin with Ainslie and Keith Peoples, Hara's longtime supporters and friends who graciously underwrote the publication through a major gift. Additional and valued support for our publication came from Barbara Johns and Richard Hesik, Patricia Watkinson, and an anonymous donor. Thank you for your belief in this idea, bringing it so generously to print, and making dreams come true for admirers of Hara's artwork across the globe.

The corresponding exhibition to this publication also benefited from the generosity of many, including Samuel H. and Patricia W. Smith, Nancy Spitzer, Patricia and Lisa Anderson, and the Walla Walla Foundry. We thank you all for your enthusiasm for Keiko Hara and support of this museum.

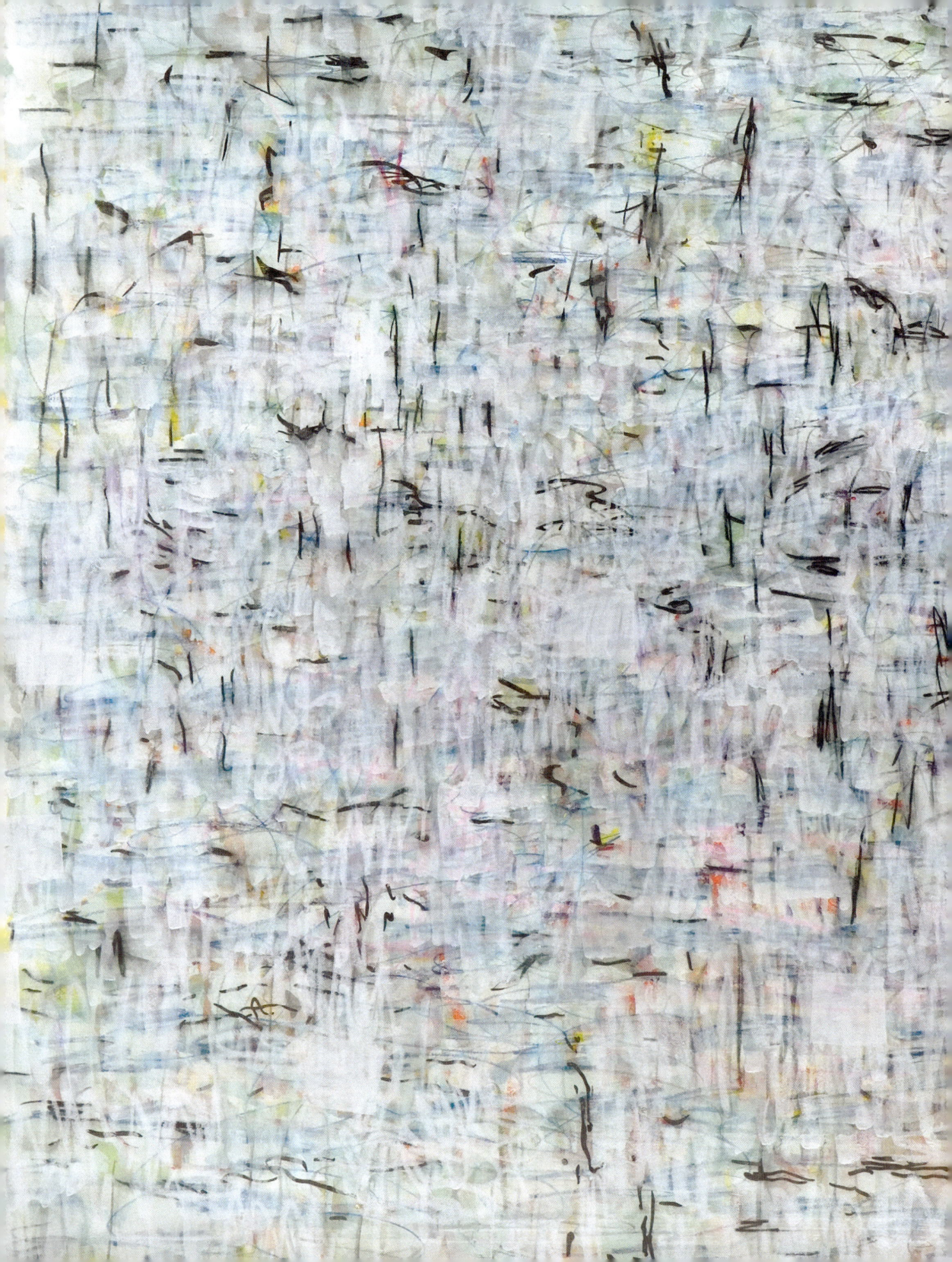

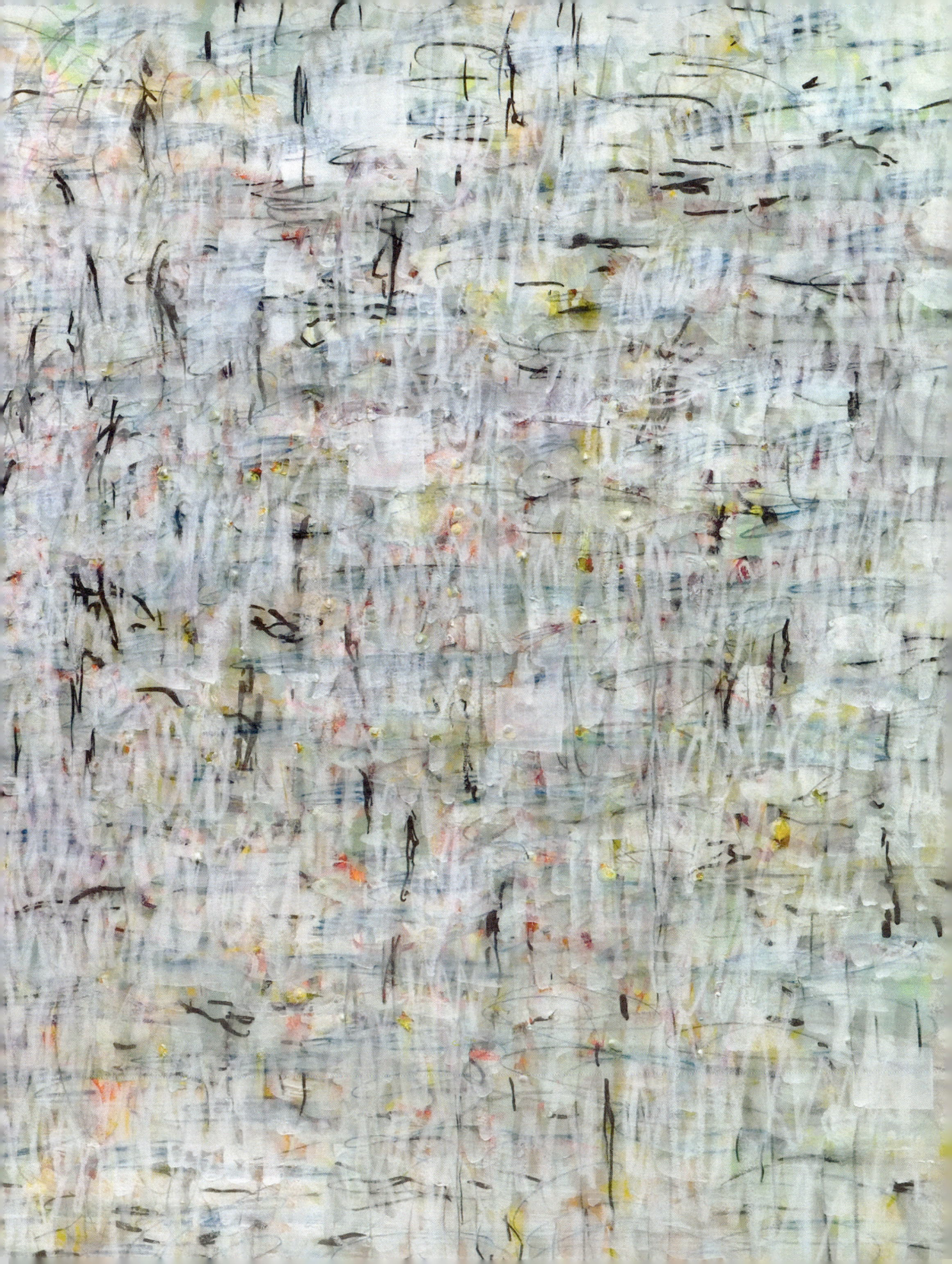

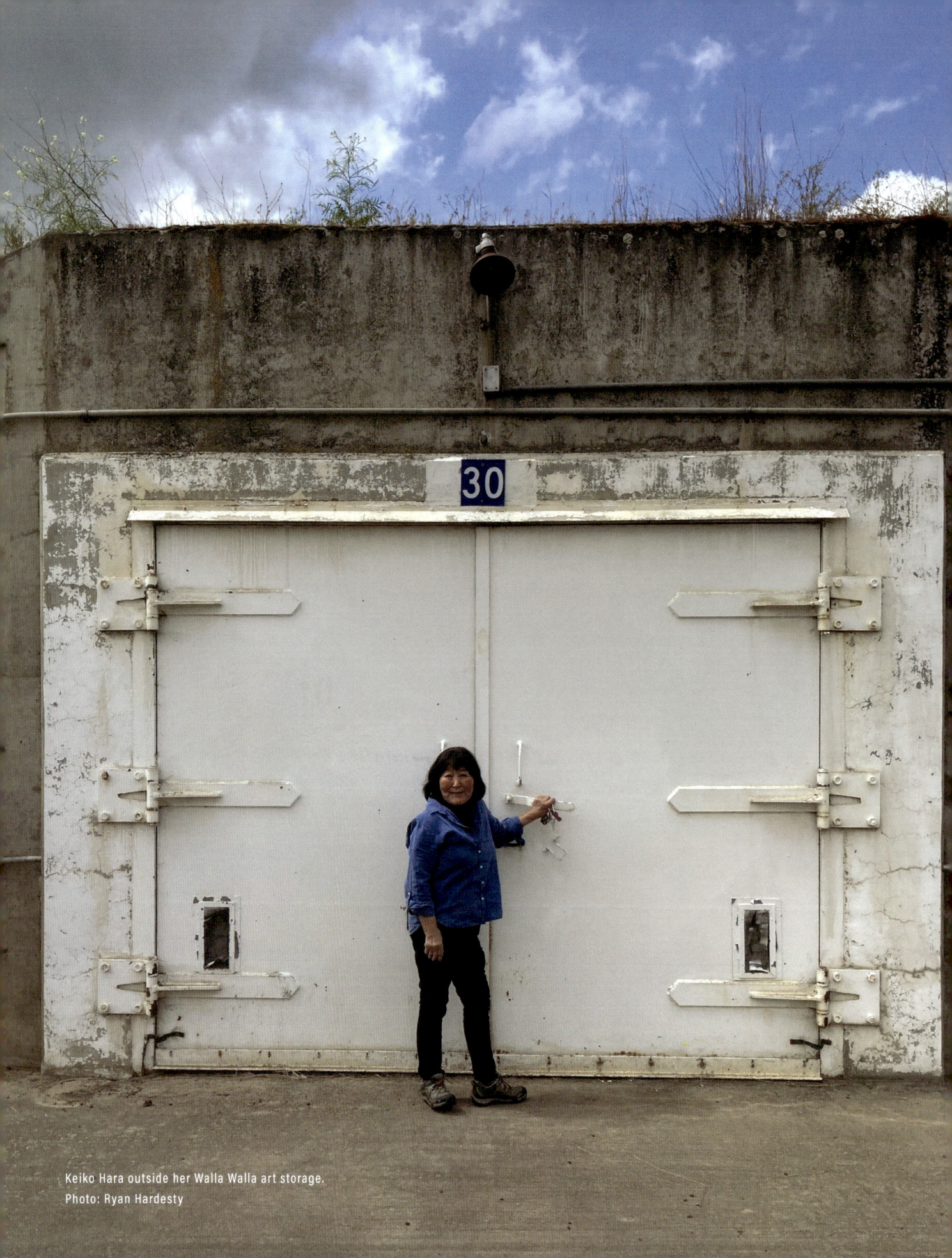

Keiko Hara outside her Walla Walla art storage.
Photo: Ryan Hardesty

essay

Imagery at the Edge of Imagination

Linda Tesner
Independent Curator and Writer
Portland, Oregon

On the very outskirts of Walla Walla, Washington, near the city's small airport and surrounded by uncultivated fields, is Keiko Hara's studio. The building is an old Army barrack; inside, the space is devoted to various areas that support Hara's complex working processes. There is equipment for printmaking, supplies of paper, and space for painting. Hara does not limit herself to one medium or one technique. Her materials and process are hybrid and determined by her innate curiosity.

Juxtaposition, contrast, and interrelatedness are lifelong themes that are interwoven into the oeuvre of Keiko Hara. Now celebrating her eightieth year with a major exhibition at the Jordan Schnitzer Museum of Art at Washington State University, one might say that Hara's visual poetry explores themes of yin and yang—of light and dark, calm and turbulence, volume and void, absence and presence. Her own dual nature as Japanese American and her roles as both teacher and studio artist underscore these dichotomies. But much more than that, her work also elegantly and subtly articulates a sense of in-betweenness, the liminal and slippery space that exists in the untouchable interstice between cerebral and emotional, between image and the imagination.

Keiko Hara was born in 1942 to Japanese parents living in what is now North Korea. By 1945, her mother and the children had returned to Japan, where Hara would spend her childhood in the Yamaguchi prefecture. But Hara's early years were marked with anxiety, as her father, who worked for a Japanese-owned company in Korea, was captured by the Chinese and imprisoned for eight years. Hara's childhood was spent on the Seto Inland Sea, where she was soothed and mesmerized by the ocean and the ever-changing still lifes that washed to shore. She says it was as if the tide continually spat out compositional elements—shells, seaweed, driftwood, the flotsam and jetsam of the ocean—that mysteriously arranged themselves into tableaus that she read as works of art.

As a young woman, Hara studied at the Gendai Art School in Tokyo and the Oita-Kenritsu Art College in Oita. She then taught art to children, all of whom had disabilities,[1] at the Kenritsu Yogo School in Kagoshima. She was interested in the relationship with their minds and emotional aspects of their development through the arts. The experience led Hara to imagine a career in art therapy which, in 1971, she decided to pursue in the United States. Her research in America made her realize that this career path would require consummate dedication to evolve the nascent profession of art

---

[1] This was an important moment for Hara, as she was fascinated by the art made by children with disabilities. She recognized the therapeutic opportunities that art-making provided for these children.

Keiko Hara: Four Decades of Paintings and Prints | Essay

therapy in Japan—at the detriment of a robust studio practice. She decided, instead, to earn a bachelor of fine arts degree at Mississippi State University for Women, then graduate degrees in art from the University of Wisconsin (1975) and Cranbrook Academy of Art in Michigan (1976). After teaching in Wisconsin for several years, she was lured to Whitman College in Walla Walla, Washington—at first under the assumption that a college in Washington must, in fact, be in Washington, DC—where she taught painting, printmaking, and book arts. Hara has made Walla Walla her home since 1985 and is now an emerita professor. When asked if she yearns for the sea of her childhood, Hara says that the abundant wheat fields of the Palouse—which stretch into the horizon as far as the eye can see—have become her adopted "ocean." In the east wind, the wheat stems undulate and shimmer like a simulacrum of tidal waves.

Hara's studio practice can be grouped not into specific periods, but into themes that she revisits repeatedly, delving deeper and deeper into concepts that intrigue her. In the cyclical nature of Hara's work, repetition means something new with each successive work. *Image · Space* (1977–1978) (p. 20) is the earliest painting in this exhibition, yet even at the distant vantage point of forty-five years, the painting portends themes that Hara has revisited over her entire career. The painting is a field of colorful orbs, drawn and painted onto Hara's hallmark *washi* paper. Hara's hand is vividly evident in the array of marks and gestures that pattern the painting from edge to edge. Hara had just been in Japan, where she met a traditional papermaker; she brought him threads and pigments to use in making papers she would later use in her work. Interspersed between the lifesaver-like shapes are seemingly random drawn marks and gestures that might remind one of the threads and fibrous bits one finds in handmade paper.

An abiding theme that has engrossed Hara is topophilia, a term she has returned to in numerous works over decades. Past scholarship on Hara has credited the British poet Sir John Betjeman as having coined the term, but it was W. H. Auden, in an introduction to a selection of verse and prose by Betjeman called *Slick but Not Streamlined* (1947), who attempted to define it. The etymology of the word comes from the Greek *tópos* (place) + *philia* (like or love for something). It is a word that has been invoked by many other creatives and thinkers.[2] In general, the term describes "a longing for special places either for their beauty, for their fascination, for their ugliness, or even for their indescribability."[3] To Hara, the term further conjures the Japanese word *aware* which, according to Hara, refers to "an artist, poet, or person's ability to grasp the beauty and sadness of life's passing moments in the context of a single, often trifling (ephemeral) event or image."[4] Hara's work gives shape to fleeting shards

[2] Notable among these are French phenomenologist Gaston Bachelard (in *The Poetics of Space*, 1958) and human geographer Yi-Fu Tuan in his essay and book *Topophilia* (1961 and 1974). *Topophilia* (2015) is also the name of a documentary by Peter Bo Rappmund, an exploration of built and natural environments along the 800-mile length of the Trans-Alaska Pipeline.

[3] Terri Hopkins. *Japanese/American: The In Between, Keiko Hara and Michihiro Kosuge, 1998.* Portland: The Art Gym, 1998, 5.

[4] Ibid., 6.

of memory or momentary glimpses of nature. It is these delicate and almost imperceptible fissures of experience that intrigue Hara.

The first work to which Hara ascribed the title "topophilia" is *Topophilia 1* (1981) (p. 36–37), a series of twelve lithographic prints on handmade Japanese *gampi* paper (twenty-four images, as the prints are viewable on both front and back). The prints are hung from dowels to create a suspended "curtain" of images that can be viewed from innumerable perspectives. Added into the lithography are collage elements and machine sewing, both of which add new forms and lines to the compositions. A central image in this series is a seashell shape. Hara says that she is less interested in what the shape represents than in how the form exists in/on the picture plane, but the "shellness" of the silhouette is a visual cue. The lithographs, in radiant and deeply saturated hues, are full of patterns from nature. Some suggest seaweed or coral, whirlpools and tidal pools, fish scales, fronds and other herbage, sand patterns, refracted sunlight seen through a rippled veil of water, and even a sense of saltiness in the very air. Other imagery looks like Japanese *kanji* brushwork, as if the prints were literary pages of an unknown narrative.

Included in Hara's exhibition is a series of four works titled *Topophilia 7 · Grey, Blue, Green,* and *Red* (1996) (p. 48–49). The series is an excellent example of Hara's master abilities with printmaking, specifically *mokuhanga* (Japanese woodblock printing). As a schoolgirl in Japan, Hara learned to make woodblock prints—an artform that is commonly taught to pupils. Later, in her academic studies, she mastered other printmaking techniques—lithography, screen printing, and intaglio—which she often combined with other elements, such as collage, papermaking, and glass. Her interest in *mokuhanga* specifically, however, was rekindled when a 1987 faculty fellowship took her to Kyoto for a semester of teaching and research. There Hara plunged into the art of *Ukiyo-e* or "pictures of the floating world," the genre of Japanese woodblock printing that flourished from the 17th through the 19th century.[5] Common *Ukiyo-e* themes included views of courtesan life, narratives of the merchant class, and scenes of nature. Back in her Walla Walla studio, Hara began to incorporate woodblock prints into her work in her own idiosyncratic way, combining them with other media. She appreciated the way in which pigments either absorbed deeply into the fibers of paper or, through screen printing, sat viscously on the surface of the paper. She used these techniques to create both richness of line and moments of translucency. Hara's dedication to the art of *mokuhanga* led to the establishment of the Mokuhanga Project Space, where this art form is taught and preserved. She continues to curate *mokuhanga* exhibitions, program workshops, and other events.

In 1996, Hara met Tadashi Toda, a fourth-generation *Ukiyo-e* master printer. Toda was already distinguished by his printing work of Western artists such as Chuck Close, Francesco Clemente, Helen Frankenthaler, and Anish Kapoor. Hara invited him to Whitman College and he, in turn, invited Hara to work with him in Kyoto.

---

[5] *Ukiyo-e* was elemental to the West's perception of Japanese art in the late 19th century, particularly the landscapes of Hokusai and Hiroshige. Japonisme had an enduring influence on the French Impressionists, Post-Impressionists, and Art Nouveau artists.

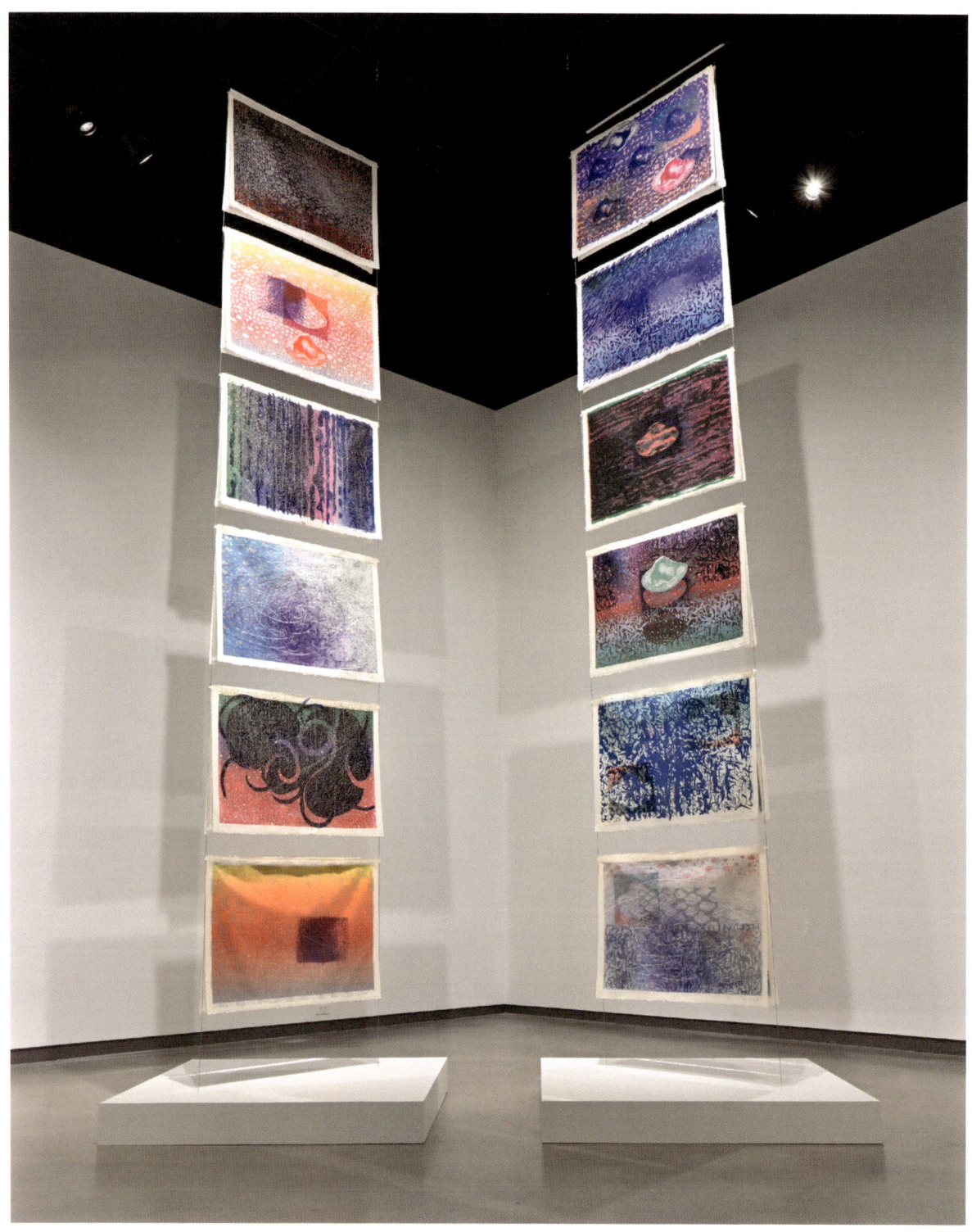

Topophilia 1 | 1981
Installation at the Jordan Schnitzer Museum of Art WSU
Photo: Bob Hubner, WSU Photo Services

Toda printed the series *Topophilia 7 · Grey, Blue, Green,* and *Red,* remarkably using twenty-one woodblocks and twenty-three colors to translate Hara's original black and white drawing into the lush prints. Using Toda's richly toned prints as a base, Hara added in stencil, collage, and language fragments. The Japanese words refer to a specific Noh play in which a mother is searching for her son along the banks of the Sumida River; the son's ghost evaporates within the mother's embrace. The central form in each print feels both solid and ephemeral; the nonspecific shape mysteriously and almost simultaneously comes into focus and dissolves into a void. It looks eerily like a high dive platform in undefined space, but it could also be imagined as a waterfall, a fragment of a geological ledge, or part of a gate. This nebulous trope, that of fugitive and temporal sensations, is a leitmotif of Hara's work.

Another example of Hara's amalgam of process is found in *Verse from Sea* (2002) (p. 28 detail, 62–63), a portfolio of twelve prints using *mokuhanga* woodblock printing, stencil, and collage.[6] This series is Hara's paean to the sea of her heritage and her memories of growing up at the ocean's edge. Each print is a lyrical, visual prose poem, condensing innumerable impressions and sensations of being at the beach—the tumble of rocks in the waves, the water-on-water of a cloudburst over the sea, the patterns humans and animals make on the wet sand. One important thing to note about Hara's multiples is that she never creates exact reproductions. This is a joyful aspect of the print-making process that Hara uses to great effect. Each print is individuated by slightly changing the registration of the woodblock, or using ghost images from previously inked-and-printed blocks. Thus, even a multiple is a one-off, imbued with the hand of the artist.

Topophilia Ma and Ki in Memory (2015) (p. 88–89) is monumental—a 24-foot painting in oil and collage on canvas. Simply by virtue of scale, viewing the painting frontally and by peripheral vision, one is enveloped by the work. Divided into quadrants, the painting presents four distinct environments—or perhaps more accurately, four separate sensations. These are not representations of landscape or of the seasons; they are more answers to the questions: How does one describe a feeling? What do concepts of time and space look like?

Of this work Hara writes, "My idea was a dream, in the way we all have dreams. Dreams are so vivid, but when we look at our dreams, we only have bits and pieces left, not a whole, no matter how complete they seemed before waking." The words in the title, *ma* and *ki,* refer to two important Japanese concepts. *Ma* refers to a seeming paradox in Japanese art and design, where void can be as important as presence—it roughly translates as "negative space," but the word evokes a more subtle sense of "an emptiness full of possibilities." *Ki* is a Japanese word meaning spirit or energy (*chi* in Chinese), an elusive term, yes, but pregnant with possible interpretations, depending upon the viewer. Hara points out that *ki* is often combined with other syllables in Japanese, such as *kibun* (feelings) or *genki* (energy).

---

[6] This complete series is found at Harbor View Medical Center in Seattle.

A watershed work in Hara's oeuvre is a monumental, room-size installation called *Topophilia Ma and Ki · Memory* (2016) (p. 13) that was shown at the Kentler International Drawing Space in Brooklyn.[7] The installation was an immersive experience for the viewer, as one walked through the installation between fifty double-sided *mokuhanga* monotype prints that hung from the ceiling like Japanese scrolls. Each panel was made of two sheets of semitransparent Japanese *washi* paper backed with silk gauze, hung so that the viewer meandered around the panels which moved ever-so-slightly in the ambient air. Interspersed within the installation were fifty shiny aluminum cutouts, shaped in a stylized floral pattern—or are they cloud forms?—which were strung horizontally onto cords like beads threaded through and between the panels.[8] Then, the panels were individually lit with *washi*-wrapped light bulbs, choreographed to create both brilliance and shadow within the installation. The floor was an expanse of aluminum tiles, sandblasted to suggest the wind pattern on sand, the evanescence of the sky, or ripples on the surface of water. The panels were hung at differing heights, ascending into the shape of a Fibonacci spiral, the pattern based on the golden ratio that is structurally inherent in all living things. Additionally, Hara collaborated with New York-based artist and musician Donald Groscost, who conceived a four-minute loop of collaged electronic and sampled tracks—gongs, chimes, seagull cries, and dreamy storm sounds. The moodiness of the soundtrack set an emotive mood of reverence and contemplation.

Topophilia Ma and Ki · Memory is an important project in Hara's oeuvre because it marks a moment in which Hara's focus shifted subtly from the personal to the collective. Hara stated that the installation was dedicated to the memory of her parents and the end of her family's name in Japan, a name that spanned more than 350 years. But she also made the piece as a memorial to the devastating Tōhoku earthquake and tsunami in 2011, which resulted in the meltdown of the Fukushima Daiichi nuclear reactors. Such a staggering tragedy is difficult to comprehend—the fact that the events caused nearly 16,000 deaths is oddly specific, but ultimately vague and abstract. Hara visited Tōhoku soon after the catastrophe to see for herself what the annihilated landscape looked like. Seeing only one lone pine tree standing in a landscape of sheer devastation, Hara was moved to want to preserve the sense of tremendous loss of human beings, each with his or her own story.[9] In Hara's words, "The unthinkable loss of life and land in natural and manmade disasters touches my soul deeply. As my life evolves, my art too has evolved from a more personal approach to being concerned with the universal human experience."

---

[7] See keikohara.com for a video of this installation.

[8] Lilly Wei. *Keiko Hara: Topophilia Ma and Ki · Memory*. Kentler International Drawing Space, New York, 2016. Wei wrote that the aluminum forms "might be stylized chrysanthemums, a flower that signifies the Japanese imperium, or lotus flower, emblematic of Buddhism, Hinduism, and more."

[9] Coincidentally, the Kentler International Drawing Space is located near New York Bay, which suffered its own flooding and storm damage during Hurricane Sandy in 2012.

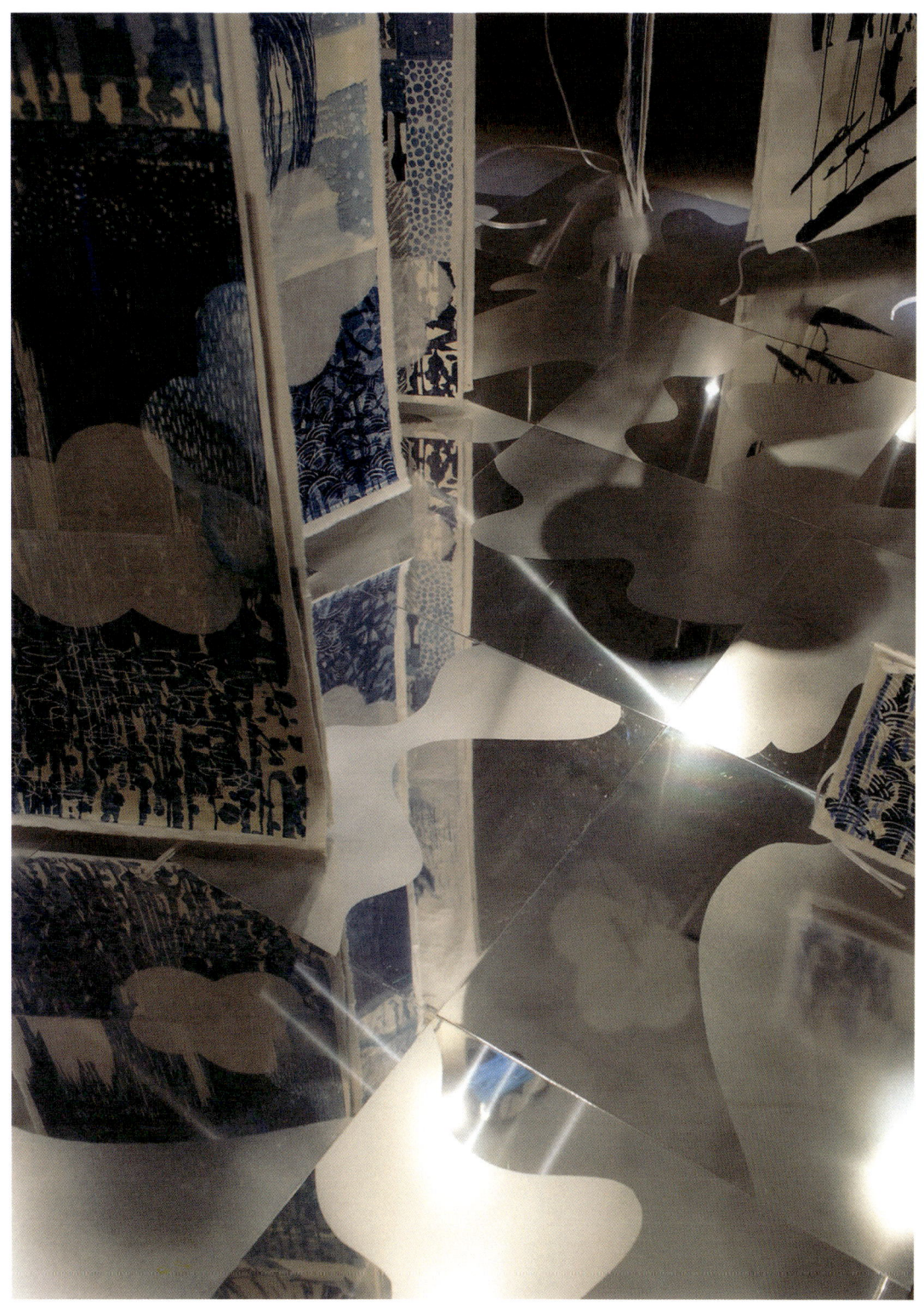

Topophilia Ma and Ki • Memory | 2016
Installation at the Kentler International Drawing Space, New York

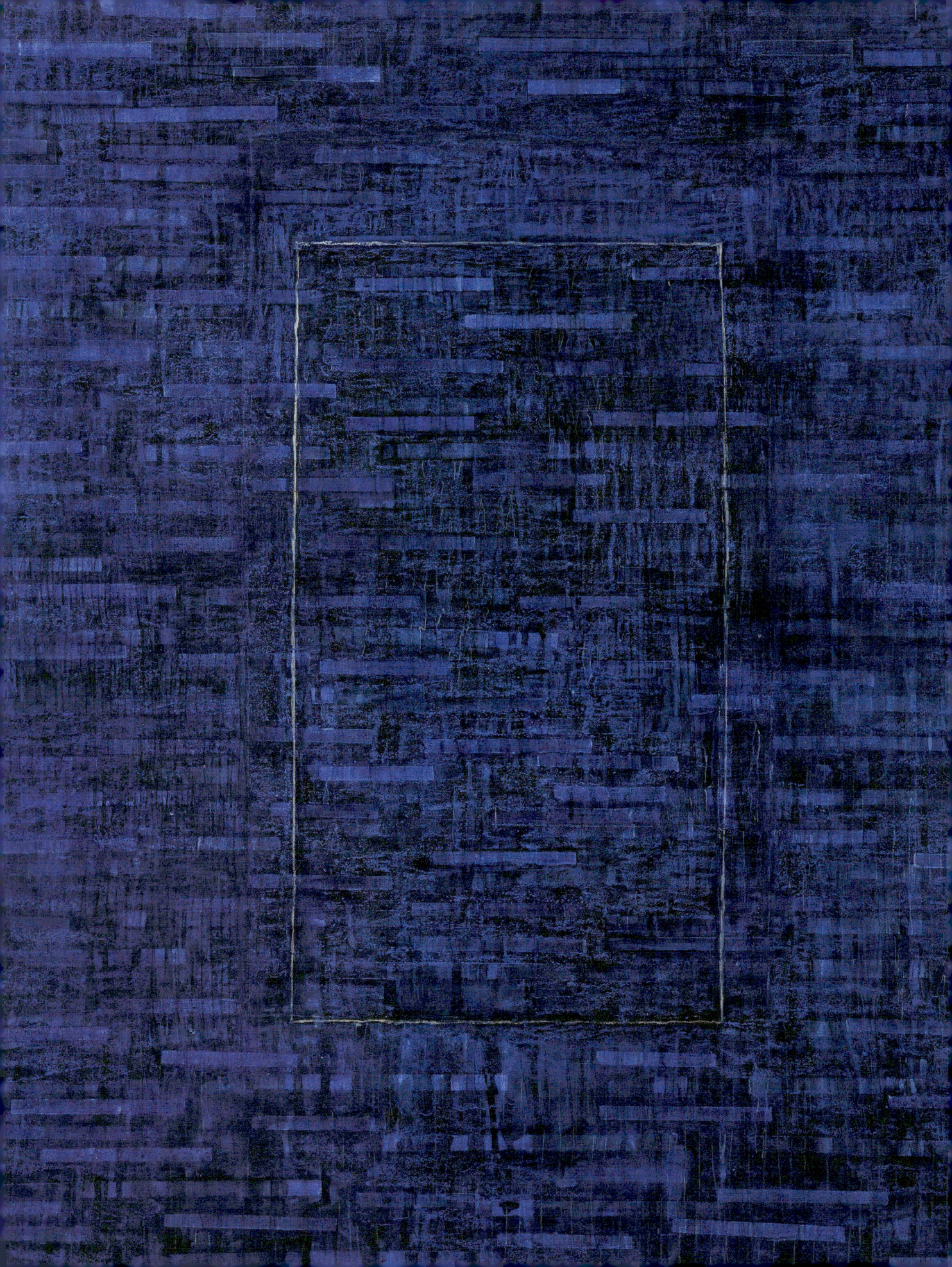

Mokuhanga, in Hara's hands, establishes the gravitas of this multi-paneled installation. The imagery on the fifty panels is wrought primarily in varying shades of indigo, balanced by white, gray, and black. The abstract forms conjure all manner of natural processes, from the volatile eruption of the earth's crust to rain showers, falling snow, ocean waves, and the flickering dappled sunlight seen through foliage. Her images are evocative, not definitive, as if seen from the very edge of consciousness.

The woodblock printing method allows Hara to either intensify colors or dilute them by creating ghost images, depending upon how aggressively she inks the woodblock. When printed on *washi*, the viewer sees both the primary image on one side and the penumbra of an image on the other side. The screens are, in fact, palimpsests in which the imagery builds upon, obscures, or enhances others. There is a saying that memory is a palimpsest that is continually being written over, but never perfectly so. This is a concept that Hara embraces.

It would be a mistake to limit a discussion of Hara's work to printmaking only. She also has a robust painting practice. When pressed to describe the difference between painting and printmaking, Hara says that "Painting is more like jumping in the ocean and swimming around to find everything. Printmaking is about certain ideas that I want to test and explore further." Both are important processes to her and are reflected in her titles. Paintings with titles such as "Verse" and "Space" are almost like preparatory sketches or thought experiments that might lead to a deeper investigation in a print series. Examples of this are four paintings in the exhibition, *Verse—Space in White, Blue, Green, and Black* (2019) (p. 14 detail, 103), in gouache, graphite, and collage on paper. From even a slight distance, these paintings look like color field paintings, each with an elemental vertical white rectangle drawn onto the surface. But, when viewed at very close range, one experiences Hara's nimble hand with mark-making. The picture plane is enlivened by splotches and lines, underlying colors, pulsating explorations of light and dark, and the ever-so-slight sculptural element of collage. One other comment that should be made about Hara's materials: she is assiduously devoted to using nontoxic, water-based materials; many of her pigments are handmade by the artist. She eschews acrylic as a somewhat garish and "flat" medium, while her layers and layers of gouache, graphite, and collage create such depth that one feels as if one could step into her paintings.

This essay would be incomplete without mention of Hara's significant achievements in public art. Her first public commission was inspired by her exhibition, *Topophilia 5 · 100 Gates* (p. 45), that was installed at the Tacoma Art Museum in 1994. The installation included one hundred simply constructed wood arches; Hara's works on paper created translucent posts. Like Hara's later installation in Brooklyn, the viewer experienced the artwork kinetically, by ambling through and between the gates. A question was posed to Hara: Could these elegant gates be reconceived to exist out of doors?

Facing page
Verse · Space in Blue (detail) | 2019
Gouache, graphite, and collage on paper | 48.75 x 33 inches

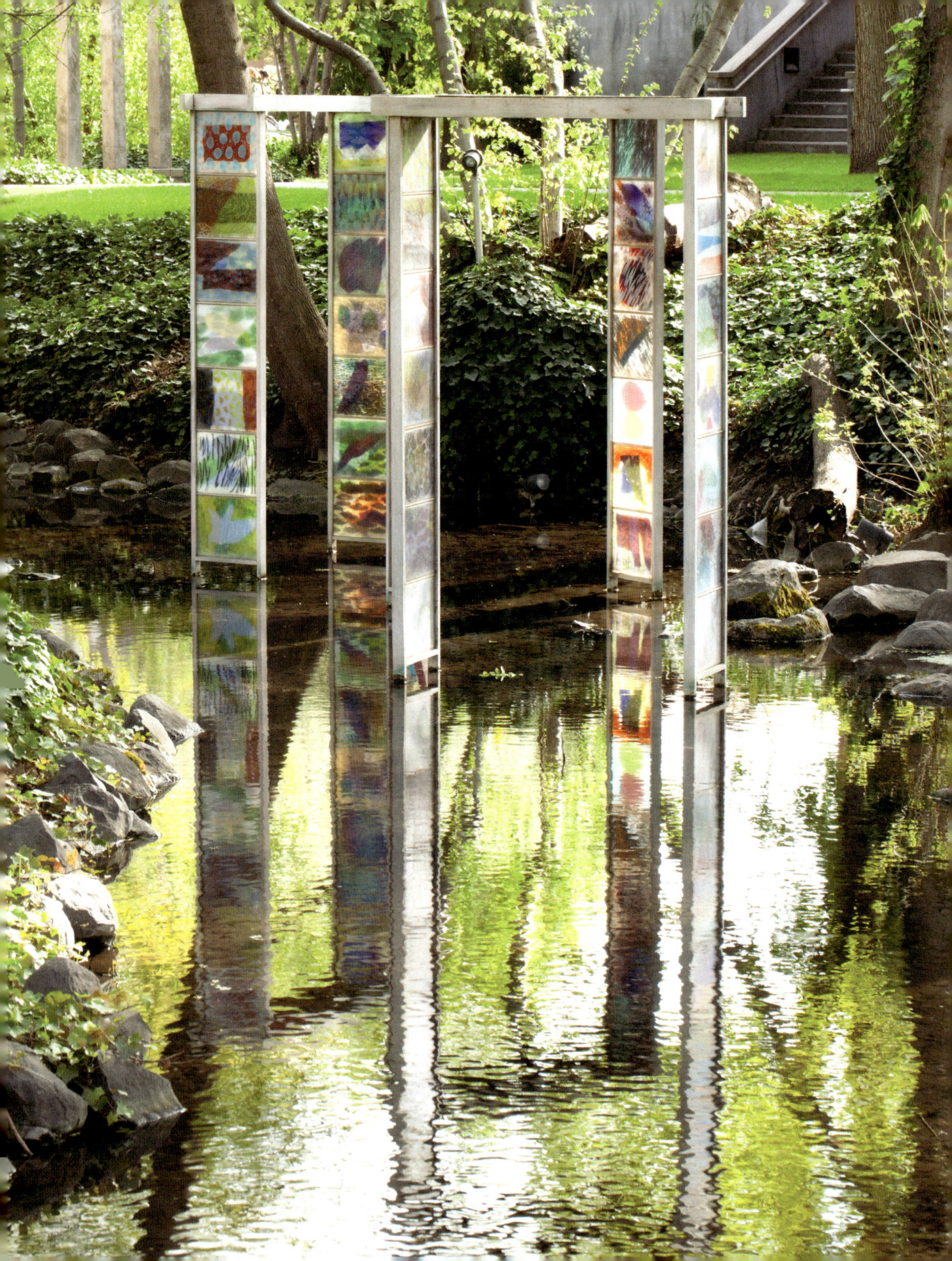

The resounding answer was "yes." Hara's first public art commission was made by Whitman College, where she created a site-specific work called *Topophilia Gates* (1999) (p. 16) in glass and bronze. Sited in a gentle creek at the base of a lush ravine on the Whitman campus, three simple gates are constructed of posts and lintels made of colorful glass panels. The gates are reminiscent of Japanese *torii* gates, which traditionally symbolize the passage from mundane to sacred space. Hara's bronze structures were designed by the artist and the Walla Walla Foundry, an organization with which Hara shares a great affinity. Each post comprises seven multi-layered screen-printed and stenciled fused-glass panels, each a distinct and colorful composition reminiscent of Hara's paintings and prints. Like her *mokuhanga* screens, in which each side of the same print reveals distinct but related imagery—each recto is composed of ghost images of the verso—the translucency of the glass panes offers the same opportunity to blur the boundaries between one side and the other. Of course, being sited in a natural setting, the changing light conditions and reflection from the running water cause the colored glass to sparkle and transform. The idea that there is no front or back to the gates—no specific way to pass through them—suggests that the entire environment enlivened by the artwork is, in fact, sacred. Undoubtedly, members of the Whitman College community find the sculpture to be a hallowed environment for reverence and contemplation.

Since *Topophilia Gates*, Hara has completed other important site-specific public works, including *Topophilia—Imbuing in Maru* (2006) at Seattle Central Community College and *Verses—Reflected and Reflecting* (2010) at the City Archives and Record Center in Portland, Oregon.

"My interest is in spatial qualities," says Hara. "I am a sculptor working with finite space."[10] These words seem paradoxical, given that Hara works primarily in two dimensions. However, even within the flatness of a print or painting, Hara's deft abilities create literal and metamorphic topography— time and space—in layers of ink, collage, drawing, paint, and sewn line. Using the language of abstraction, Hara captures the relationship between things and ideas. Not overly concerned with the pictorial depiction of nature, she delves much deeper than that with the courage to give image to the imageless. She achieves the seemingly impossible, capturing the evanescence of feelings, memories, and subtle sensations with a transcendental sense of mystery and otherworldliness.

---

[10] Patricia Watkinson. *Keiko Hara: Mokuhanga/A Selection of Woodblock Prints*. Sammamish, WA: Sammamish Arts Commission, 2017, 3.

Facing page
Topophilia Gates | 1999
Collection of Whitman College, Walla Walla

Following pages
Verse · Space Yuukyuu (detail) | 2019
Work on paper | 20 x 24 inches
Private collection

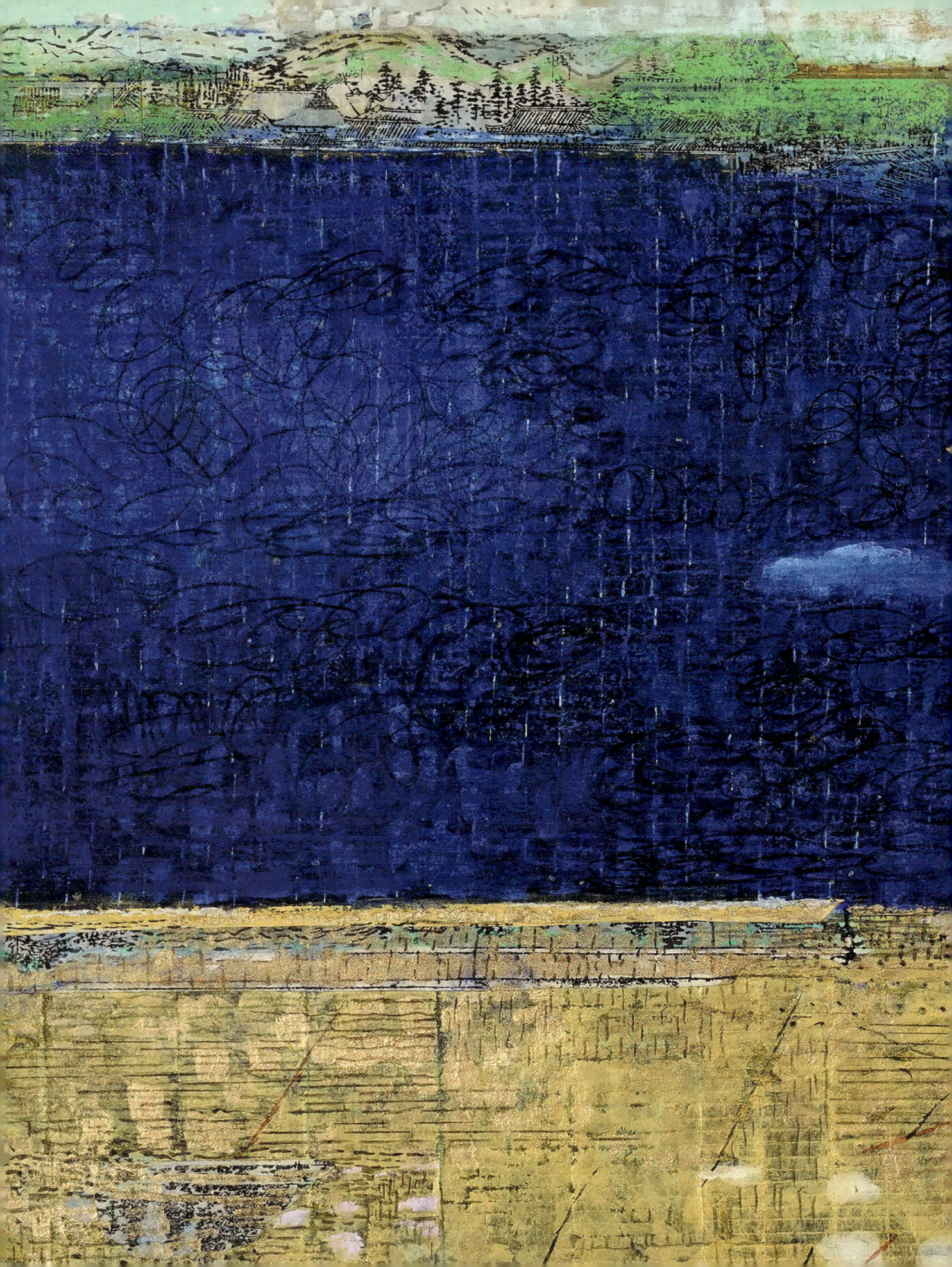

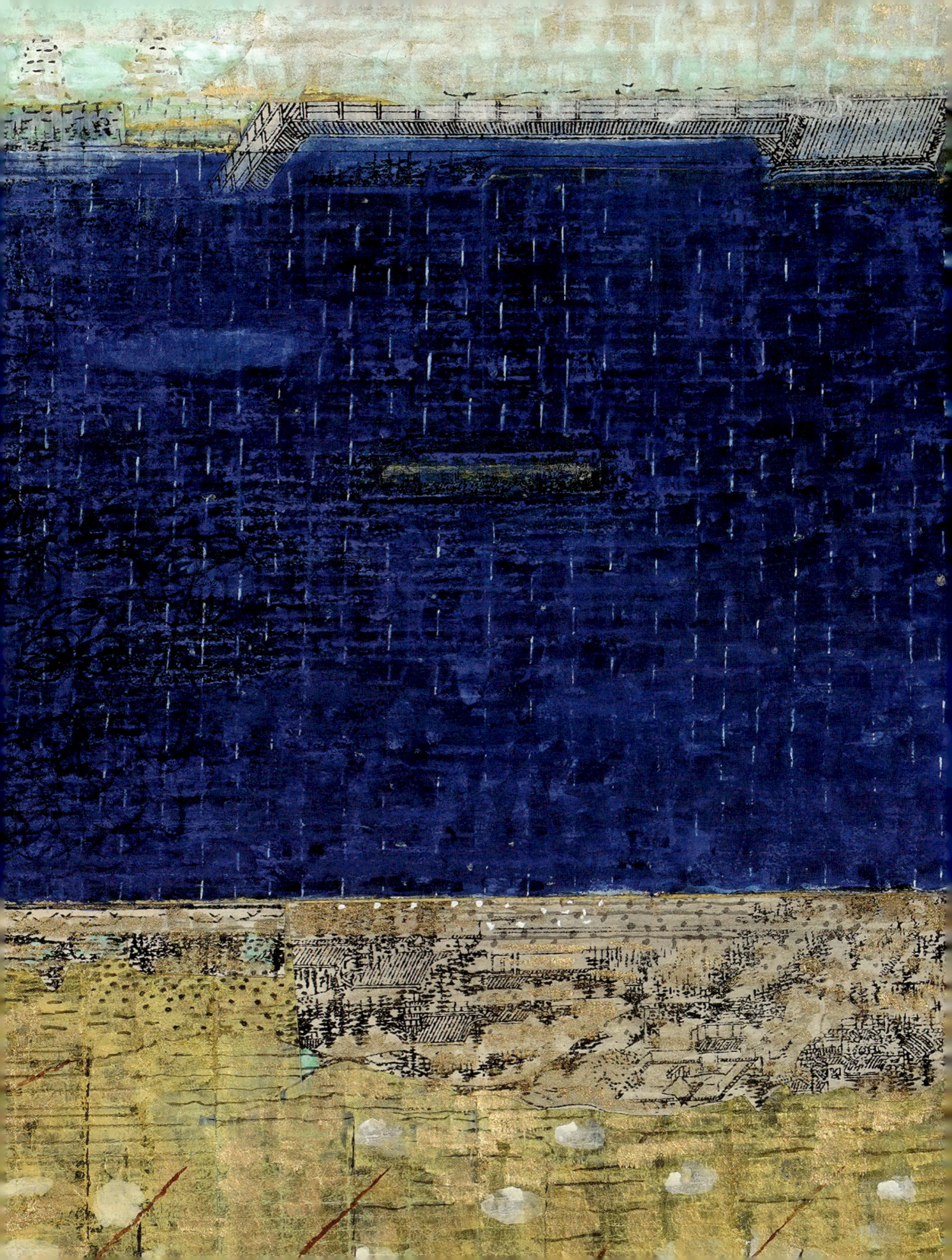

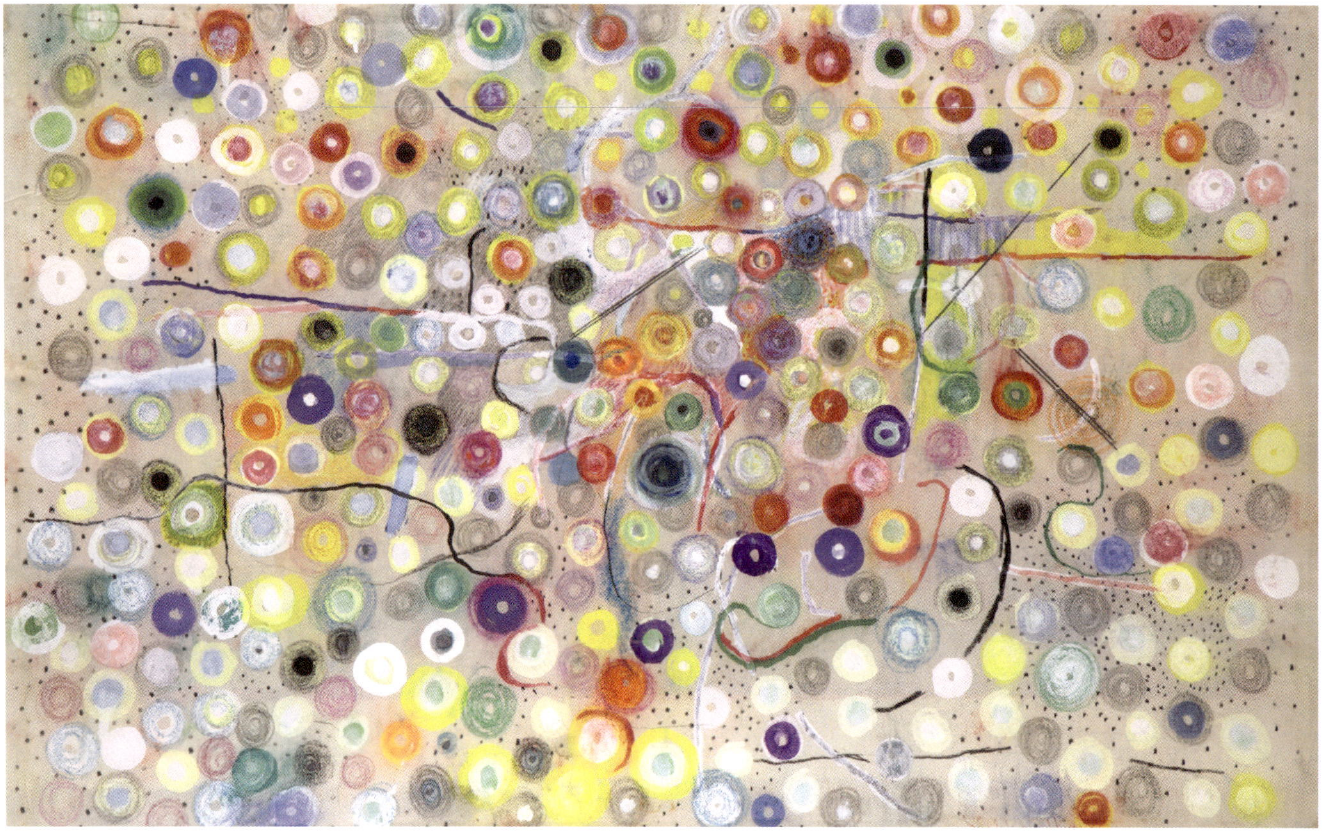

Image · Space (front above, back below) | 1977–78 | Gouache and drawing media on handmade washi paper | 22 x 37 x 1.12 inches

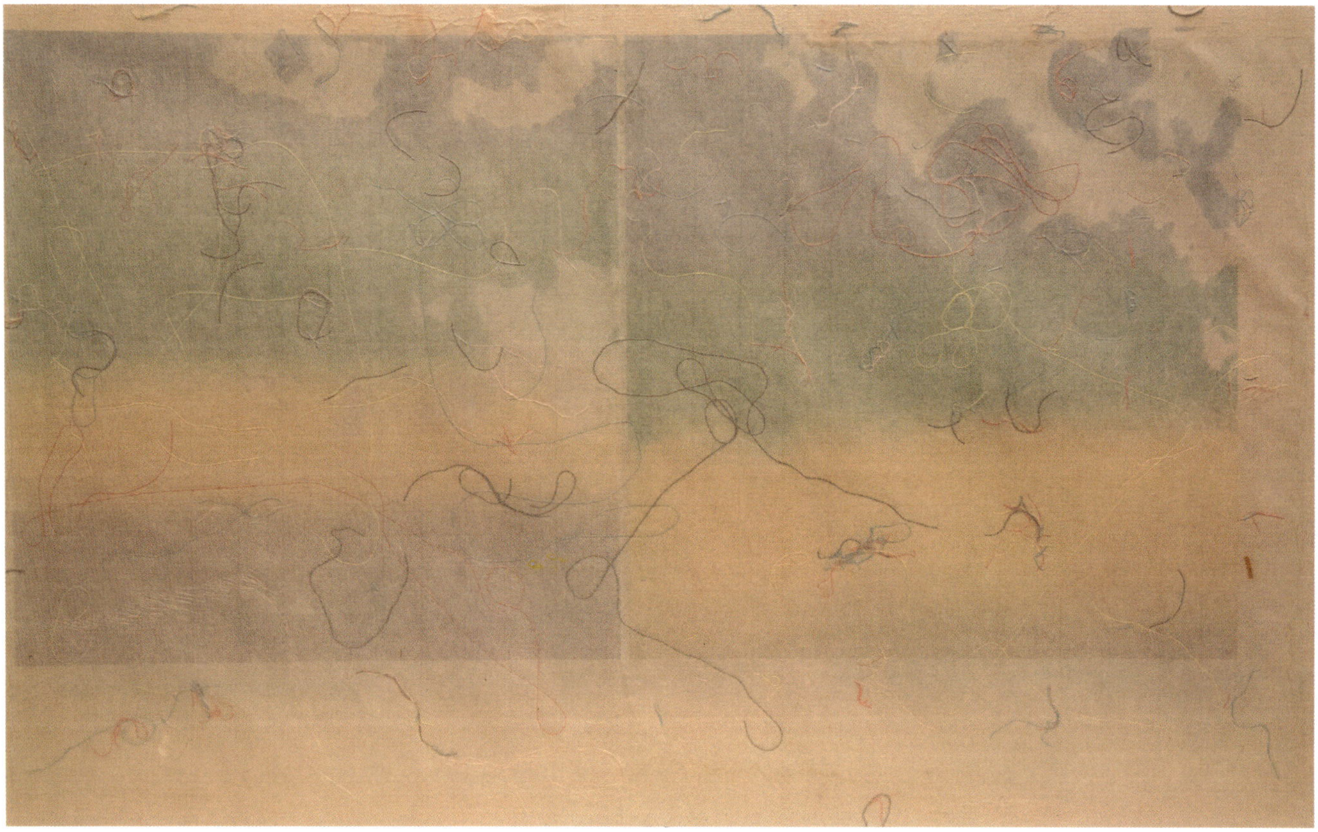

interview

Ryan Hardesty,
Executive Director
JSMA WSU

Ryan Hardesty: Our exhibition begins with an early work from 1977 to 1978 titled *Image · Space* (p. 20), which presages numerous themes and motifs that you would continue for the next forty-five years. For example, I believe it is the first time you used handmade *washi* paper to incorporate a semitranslucent support. You also established the use of circular motifs to imply cycles of life, remarking about this work, "Expecting a new birth in me is a part of the rhythm and beat of the universe."

Keiko Hara: Yes, that particular artwork began during my pregnancy. I was looking at the whole sky and I was listening, but also, the universe was making living sounds. I felt I was part of the universe. I understood my existence in a profound way for the first time in my life as a presence across space and time. I had to do something with this experience and my art, and so, I made the painting on rice paper that you are referring to.

— · —

RH: Perhaps you could also share with us your introduction to handmade papers from an artistic perspective. I also believe there is a story behind how you sourced the *washi* paper used on the verso of *Image · Space*.

KH: At that time, I was introduced to papermaking in the United States at Cranbrook Academy of Art because they had a papermaking mold. And they had the first papermaking conference [North American Hand Papermakers, formerly Friends of Dard Hunter] in Appleton, Wisconsin, where there was a beautiful museum [Dard Hunter Paper Museum] with all sorts of papermaking equipment, and paper from all over the world was displayed in this museum. I began to experiment with papermaking alongside my printmaking, and I had so many ideas that I couldn't stop...I remember an assistant lying on the floor, saying, "No more, Keiko!"

My father died on Christmas Eve, and I could not go back to Japan because I was pregnant with my daughter, who was born on New Year's Day. When we made the trip, she was six months old. I was the only one left in my family, and I had to take care of the house. I needed to build a fence around the property, and the carpenter I hired said, "My father is a papermaker." The father was one of the last traditional papermakers left in the region. Past generations of his family made rice paper for a samurai lord. I was excited, and I went to see him; I offered to pay him to make paper as I wanted it. I brought him pieces of thread and different fibers to incorporate; it was untraditional, but it was my own way. This papermaker was very old and accomplished, yet he really enjoyed it! This was the first time I ever worked with a papermaker in Japan. After returning to the United States, I constructed the wood frame for *Image · Space* and mounted the papermaker's *washi* to the backside.

— · —

Keiko Hara in her Walla Walla studio. Photo: Amahra Leaman

RH: As a related question, perhaps you could trace your relationship to printmaking for us, speaking to your experiences with *mokuhanga* as well as traditional Japanese *Ukiyo-e* printmaking as a cultural influence.

KH: *Mokuhanga* is a very common and available practice. For instance, the Japanese art education system is well organized, and I taught within it for five years before I came to this country. Printmaking is always taught to elementary and junior high school students. Many people who are not artists make *mokuhanga* New Year's cards because they've already have had these experiences in their schooling. While it's a common craft, until recently there was no professional printmaking education available, nowhere you could go to develop as an artist within the educational system. Historically, you would go to a special *Ukiyo-e* printmaking shop to work as an apprentice under a master. If you really know Japanese history, *Ukiyo-e* in its time was not considered fine art: They were affordable prints made for common people of the Edo period, depicting beautiful scenery, geishas, or kabuki. For the cost of a cup of soup, people could buy these scenes which they did not have access to previously.

— • —

RH: Keiko, would you be willing to share a memory of your first artistic experience as a young child? I would guess you were an imaginative young person.

KH: Well, when I was very young my father was taken by the Chinese as a prisoner. He was a scientist and inventor; he couldn't come back for eight years, and my mother had to work to support us while she awaited his return. My little sister and I were left by ourselves, and I used to go to a little, beautiful creek. There were soft, colorful stones that I could gather to scratch on the street outside our house. It was fantastic; I would draw all day on the best canvas I've ever had…it was dark and very smooth asphalt, with no cars at that time. I would draw from morning until nighttime when my mother came home. I still remember how excited I was, how fun it was to make marks on the street. Then the rain would come and clean it off, giving me a new canvas. I had plenty of space to work.

RH: This makes for a perfect segue to my next question. Many of your works are of dimensions that foster an immersive experience as space becomes enveloping. While printmaking is traditionally produced at modest scales, limited by press and plate size, your press-less woodblock prints are at times pushed into the realm of room-filling installations, matching the range of your monumental paintings. I am curious about your use of scale and the experiences you hope to create for potential audiences.

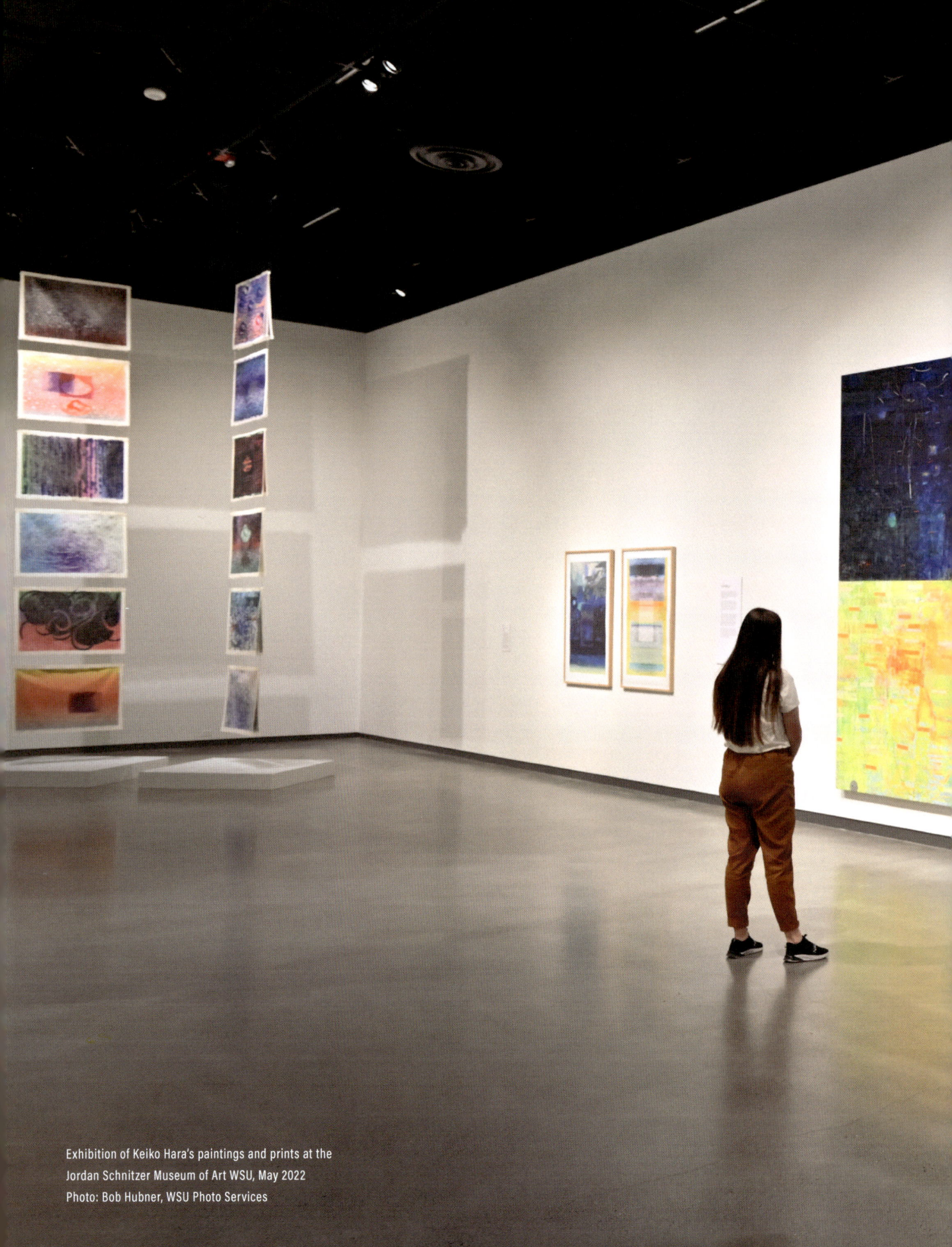

Exhibition of Keiko Hara's paintings and prints at the
Jordan Schnitzer Museum of Art WSU, May 2022
Photo: Bob Hubner, WSU Photo Services

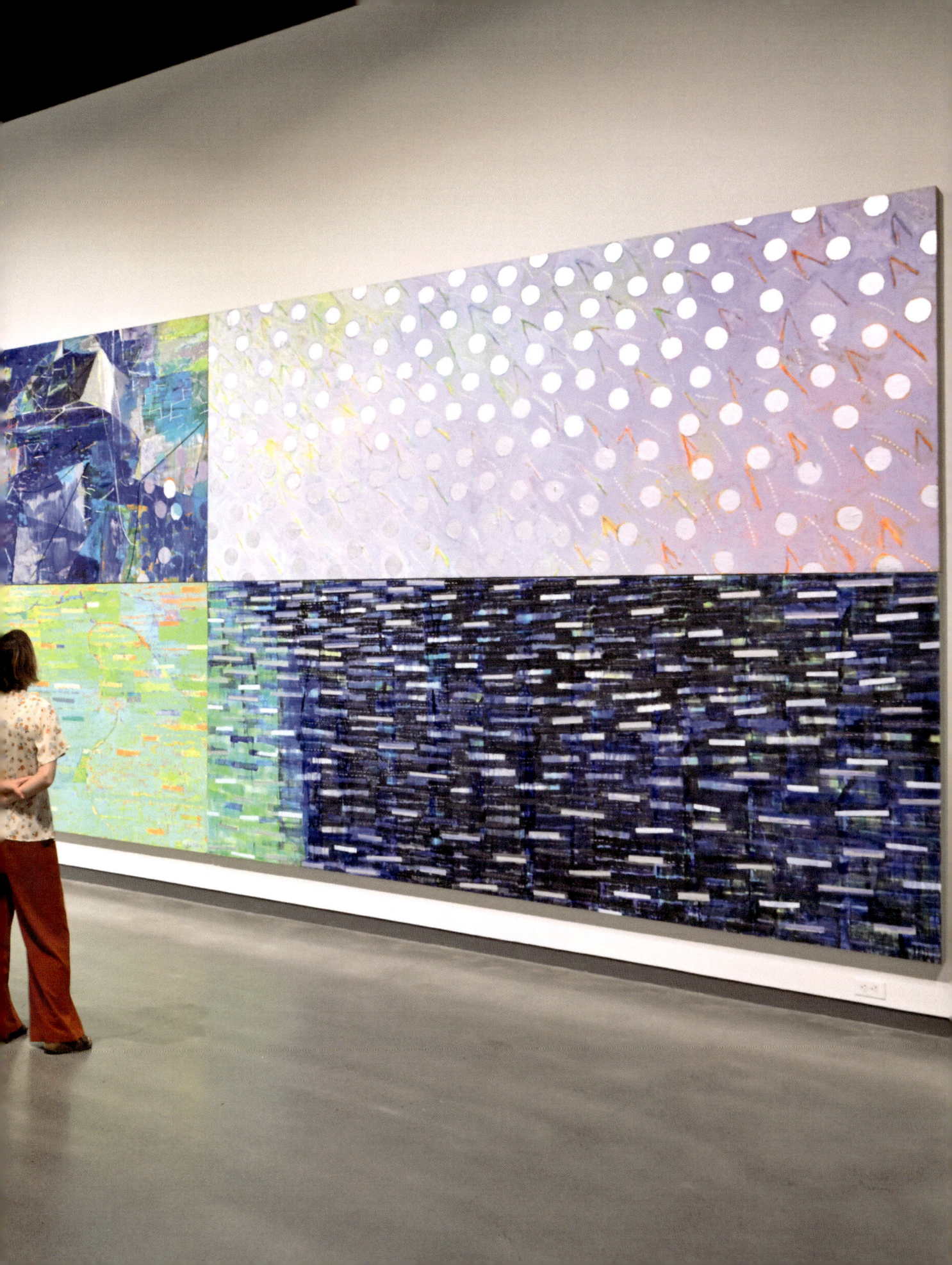

KH: Yes, I have worked on many small works, but when I get interested in working on large-scale pieces, my main goal is to have the viewer go *into* my art, to be able to move around inside the work to experience the space and not just the surface. It is also something I have done with hanging prints or sculptural gates with panels that are double-sided, where the viewer can move *through* and *out* and *in*.

— • —

RH: This publication and its exhibition celebrate four decades—actually closer to four and a half decades—of your painting and printmaking practice. You've moved between these mutually informing fields with seeming ease, yet the genres are distinct, containing their own histories, conventions, opportunities, and challenges. Can you speak about your relationship to both: how do they inform each other, and when does one precede the other?

KH: I think painting is something of an unknown place for me. It inspires me and I've just jumped in and tried to find out what it can be. Printmaking is a little different. I have a fairly good idea what it is. I use techniques and processes to make images I then examine and respond to. Then I push ahead to discover something I haven't experienced or found before. Actually, I need both printmaking and painting [laughing]!

— • —

RH: Many of your recent works feel informed equally by methods you've developed through both painting and printmaking, sometimes showing evidence of your engagement with water-based media and handmade papers carried over from your *mokuhanga* practice. Can you talk about these efforts to combine collage and *washi* paper into the realm of painting? You've even at times mounted paper to panels much like a painter would mount canvas or linen to a stretcher or panel.

KH: Oh yes! It has become my main vocabulary. That's why I think printmaking gives me a chance to reexamine what I am doing with process, and I have gained many possibilities in my paintings as a result. For instance, I have paintings in which I've incorporated rice paper onto the linen support, or I've used my own water-based printmaking pigments and binders as a first layer for paintings, followed by oil-based pigments after treating the surface. Oil pigments give me luminosity and vivid colors, and yet I've found ways to create brilliance and depth in my printed surfaces as well. Printmaking is an exploration and I like to make many variations of a print—I am more interested in the process, and I don't have time for editioning!

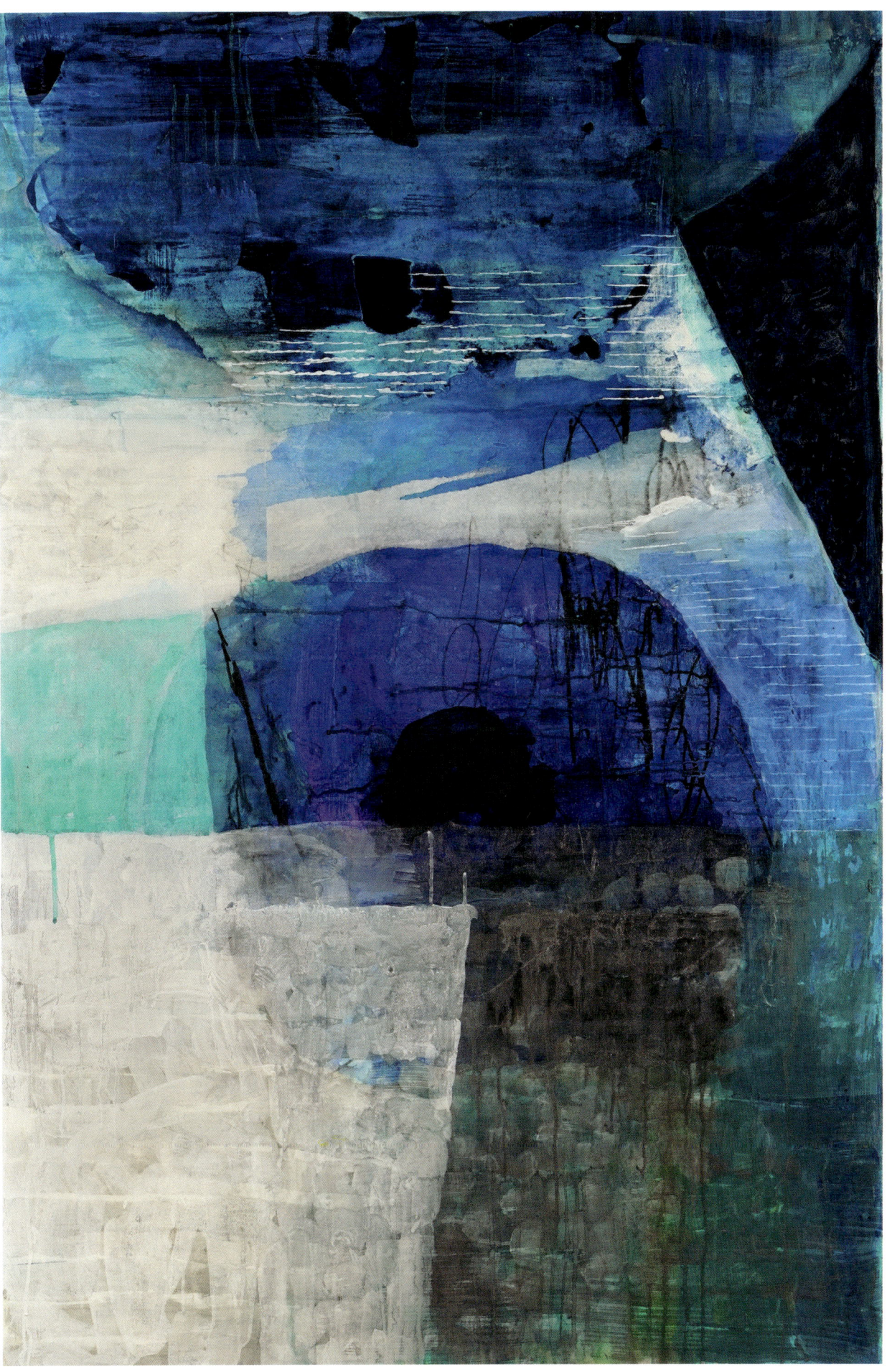

RH: I would love for you to speak about the role of memory, or even dreams, in your life and artistic process. It seems to me these cross-temporal and subconscious links provide power from the past to shape and influence the future.

KH: You know, my dreams are very strange. At one point I was a shell collector. I was very interested in the shapes and colors, sometimes my shells would come from far away. I started dreaming every night about new shapes and colors of shells—I would wake up in awe and my mother would say, "You are a crazy girl; why don't you dream of candy or something?"

Memory is so important in our lives. Memory is not just something in our personal past, but memory stretches back through ancestry and human histories. Memory is alive and active and informs the present and future. We can live again and again in memory through time.

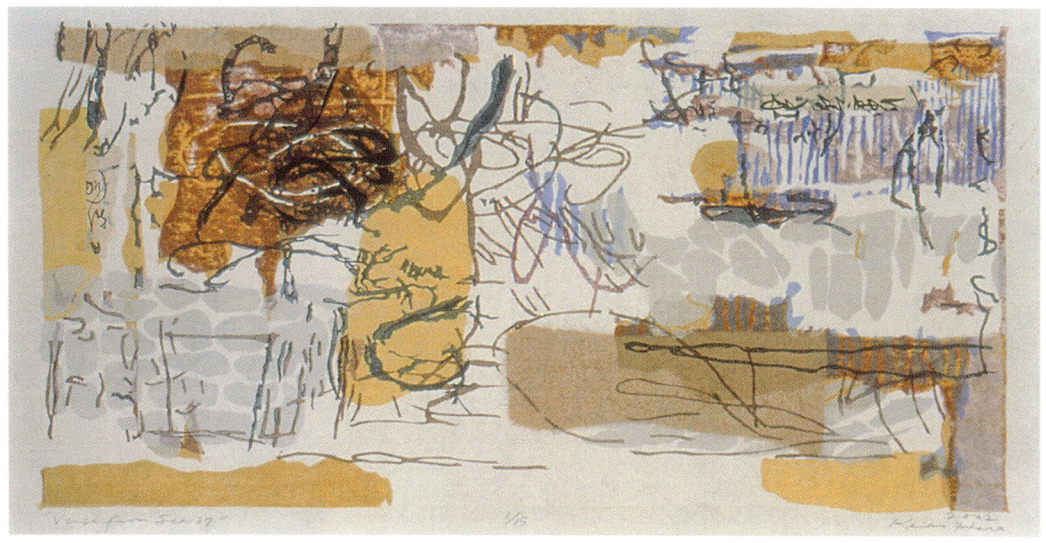

Verse from Sea (detail) | 2002
Mokuhanga woodblock, stencil, and collage print | Edition 15
10 x 20 inches

— • —

RH: Relatedly, while personal memory and longing have been central to your work, over the years you've strived for a collective universality, writing, "It is our individual topophilia that unites us as human beings." Could you speak to this desire to bridge worlds?

KH: Topophilia as a concept comes from very old stories. There is a well-known Japanese writer named Sei Shōnagon of the late 10th century who wrote about nature and life. She frequently used the Japanese term *mono no aware* [translated as an empathy toward things or an awareness to ephemerality and impermanence], which is similar in meaning to topophilia [a love of place]. Topophilia is personal and based on individualized life experiences. No one can take that from you. Yet, cultural and political discord is a threat to this unless we can value in others what we value in ourselves.

— • —

RH: Keiko, is there anything you want to say about your life in Walla Walla—the home you've made there and what it has meant for you to live in that beautiful valley?

KH: You know, I never would have stayed for so long unless I really loved it. I like the skies, the wide-open spaces. Sometimes in the evening, I just drive out into the fields…it is almost like when I used to walk on the beach in the morning back in Japan. The fields have a similar sense of space and scale. I thought I was going to miss the ocean, but now I think this is the ocean for me.

— • —

RH: It's almost cliché to say, but you are one of the hardest working artists I've ever known. You simply never stop. Our exhibition is up, and this publication is nearing completion. What's next for you?

KH: I think getting older is fantastic, because I have so much more to draw upon and use in brand new ways. Every day is something new.

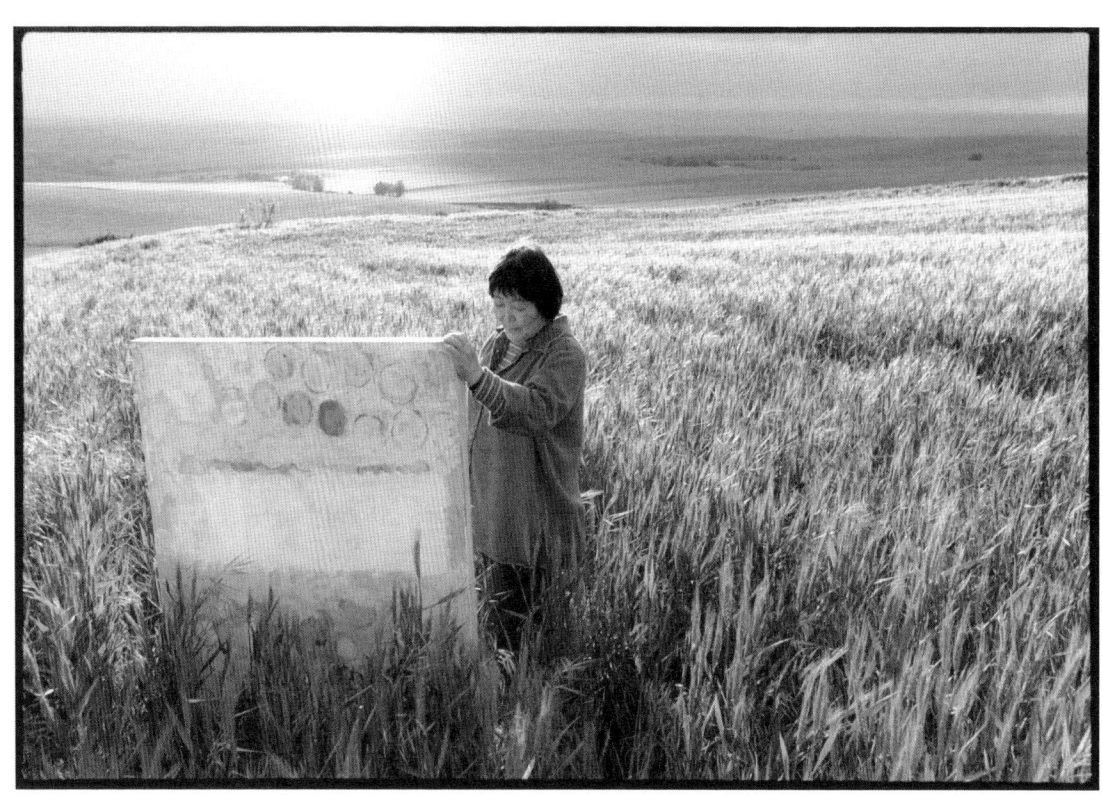

Keiko Hara outside of Walla Walla. Photo: Aaron Johanson

plates

Four Decades
of Paintings
and Prints

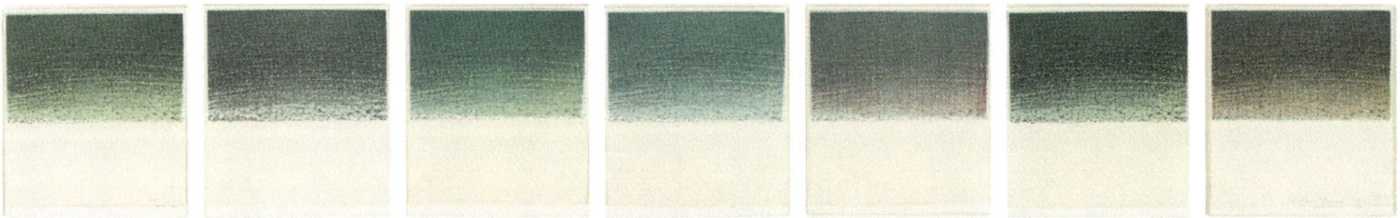

Ra'Ra''Ra'''Ra''''Ra''''' | 1976
Lithographs on seven sheets mounted on an accordion-fold mat board | Edition 10
8.12 x 7.625 inches each, 8.5 x 54 inches total
Collection of the Detroit Institute of Arts, Drawing and Print Club Purchase Prize, F76.39

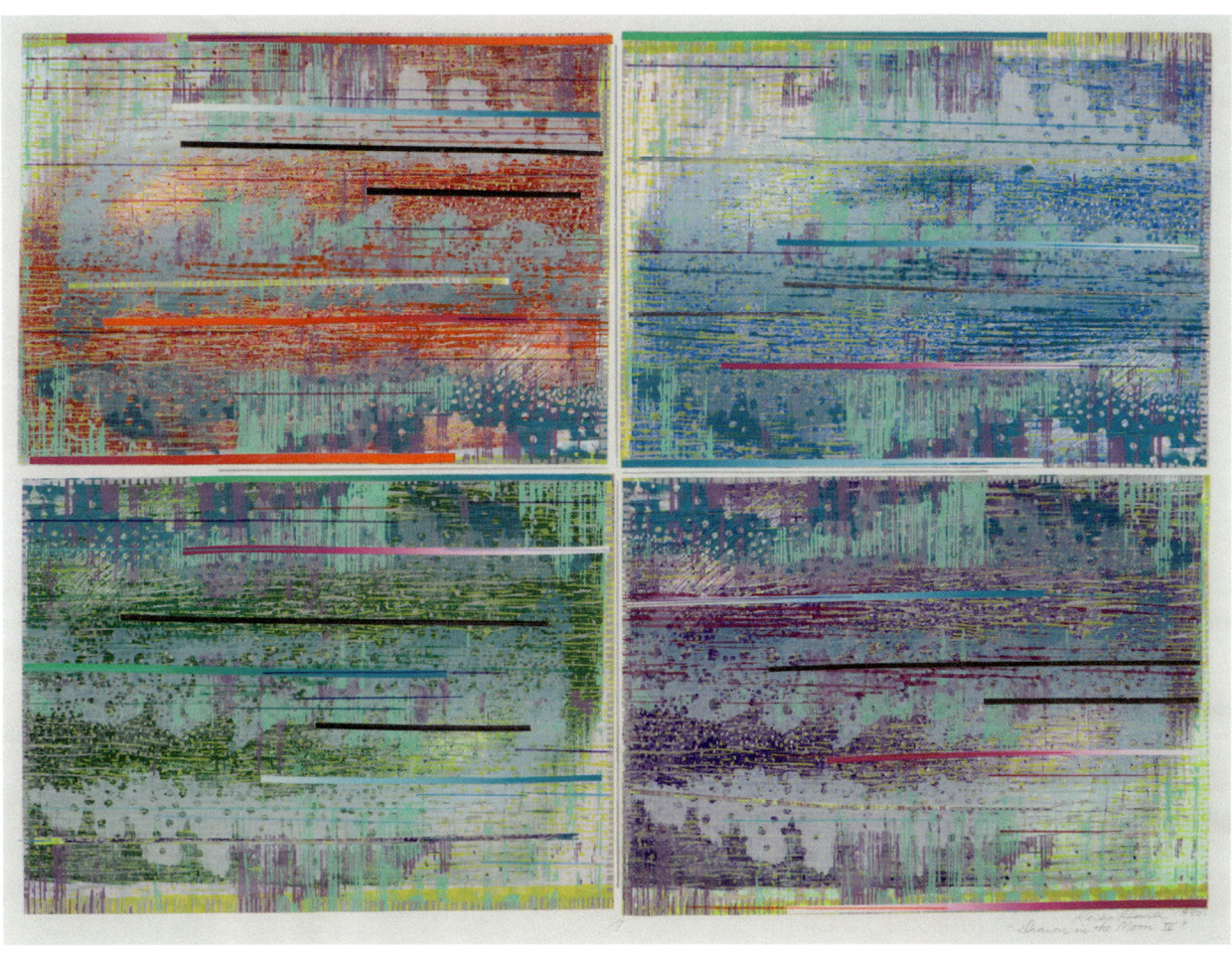

Drawn in the Moon IV | 1980
Screenprint, lithograph, collage, silver mylar tape, and wax pencil | 22 x 30 inches
Collection of the Detroit Institute of Arts, Stewart and Stewart Archive.
Museum purchase, Cleo and Lester Gruber Fund, 2021.108

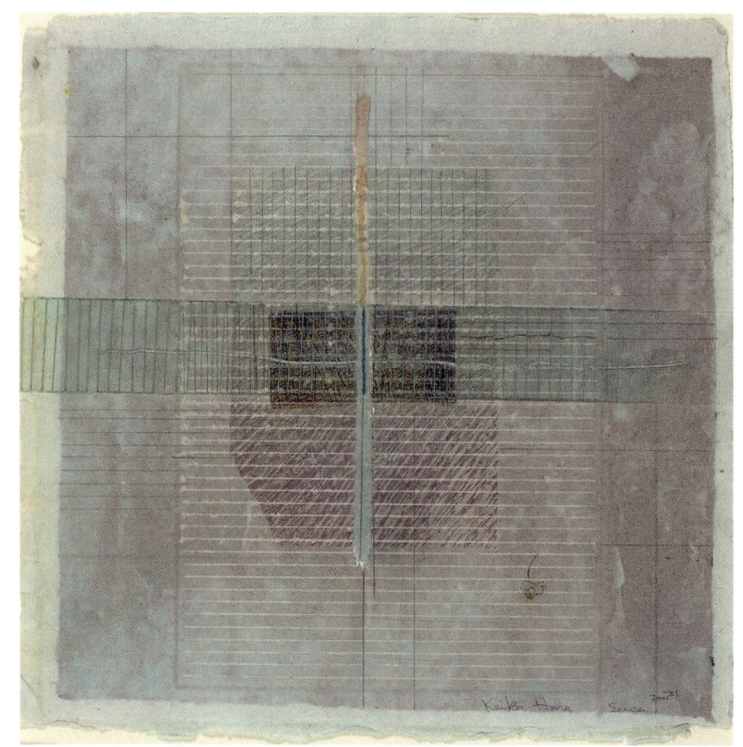

Omoi, Series 1 | 1981
Collage composed of watercolor, gouache, colored pencil, and
silver metallic paint, with printed paper, Japanese paper,
and string on handmade colored paper with embossment
11.75 x 11.25 inches
Collection of the Art Institute of Chicago, purchased
with funds provided by Margaret Fisher, 1982.1496

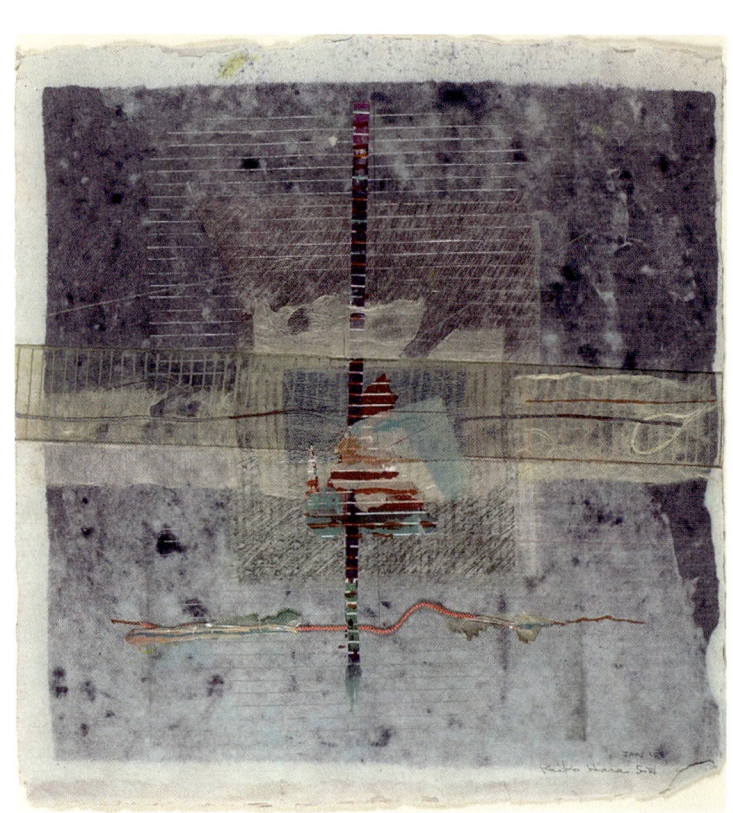

Omoi, Series 2 | 1981
Collage composed of watercolor, gouache, colored pencil, and
silver metallic paint, with printed paper, Japanese paper,
and string on handmade colored paper with embossment
11.75 x 11.25 inches
Collection of the Art Institute of Chicago, purchased
with funds provided by Margaret Fisher, 1982.1497

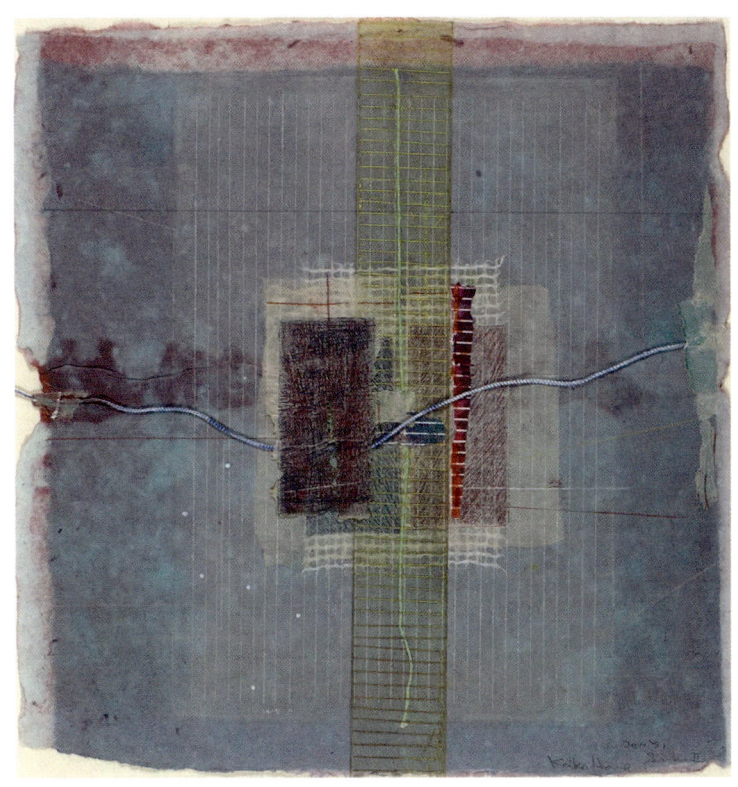

Omoi, Series 3 | 1981
Collage composed of watercolor, gouache, colored pencil, and silver metallic paint, with printed paper, Japanese paper, and string on handmade colored paper with embossment
11.75 x 11.25 inches
Collection of the Art Institute of Chicago, purchased with funds provided by Margaret Fisher, 1982.1498

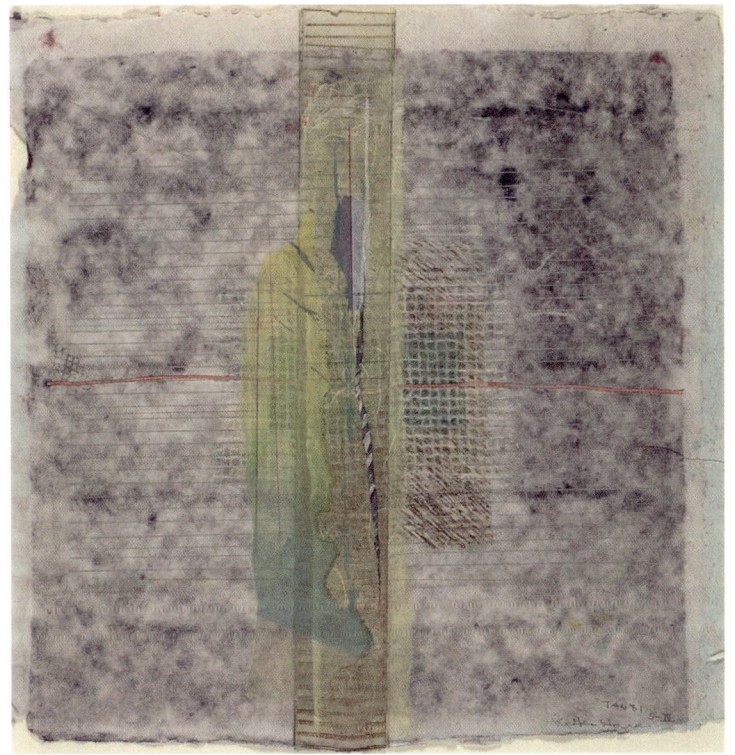

Omoi, Series 4 | 1981
Collage composed of watercolor, gouache, colored pencil, and silver metallic paint, with printed paper, Japanese paper, and string on handmade colored paper with embossment
11.75 x 11.25 inches
Collection of the Art Institute of Chicago, purchased with funds provided by Margaret Fisher, 1982.1499

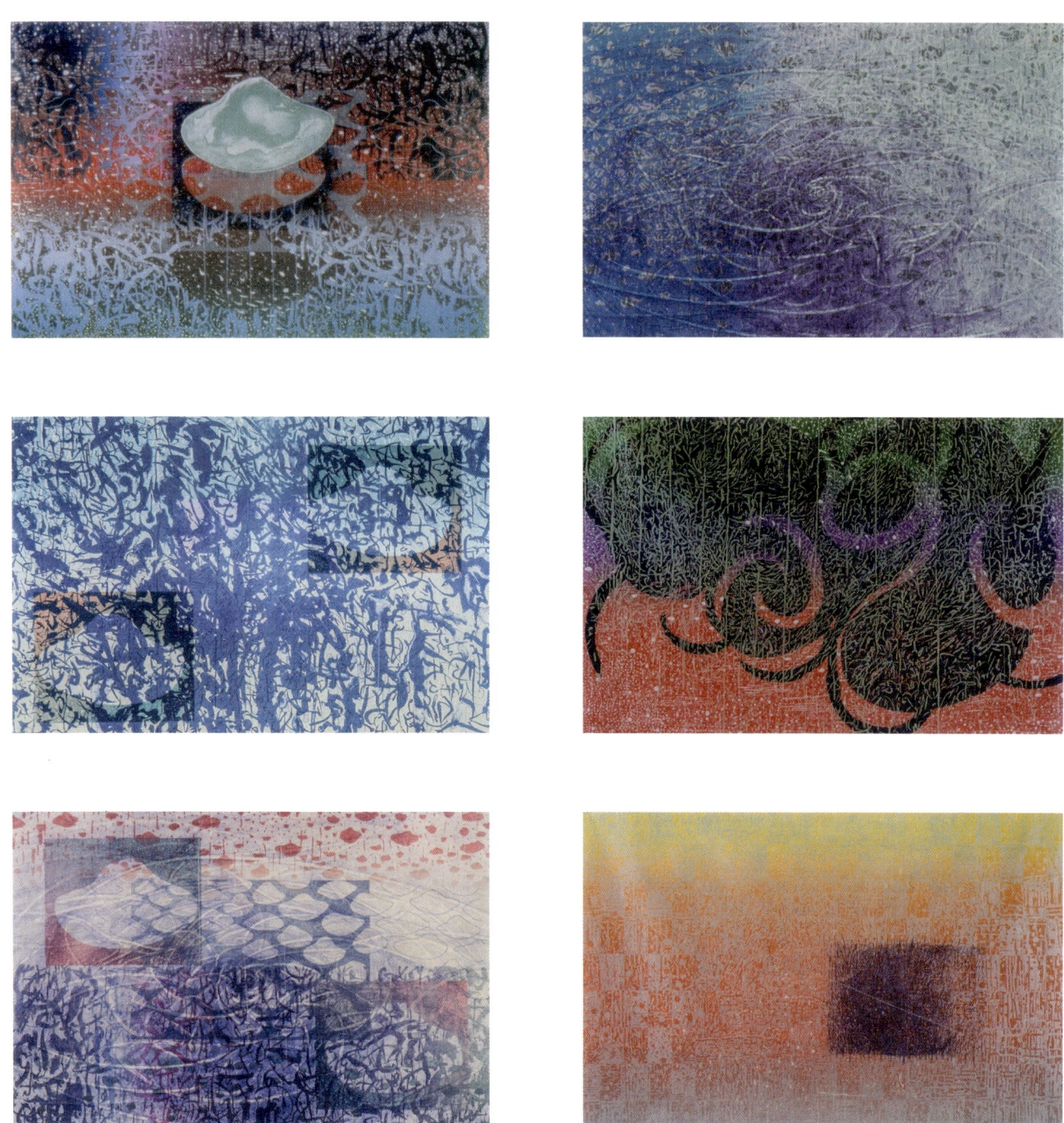

Topophilia 1 | 1981
Lithographs on handmade gampi paper with collage and machine stitching | Edition 20 (set of 12)
Published by Perimeter Press | 24 x 36 inches each

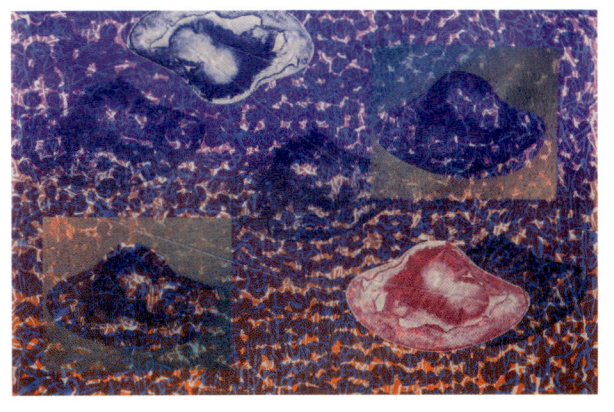
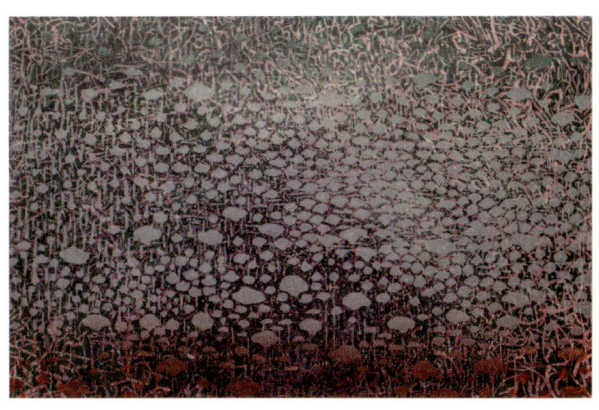

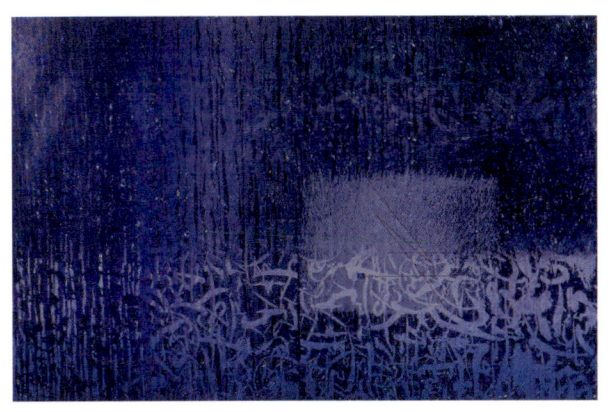
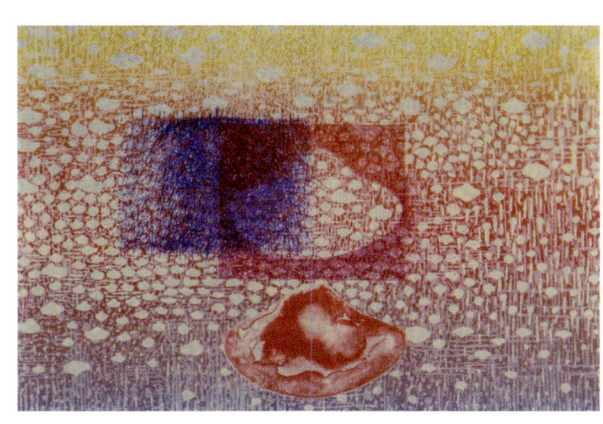

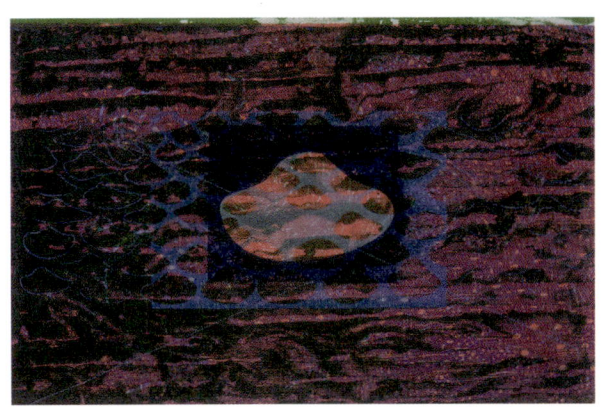
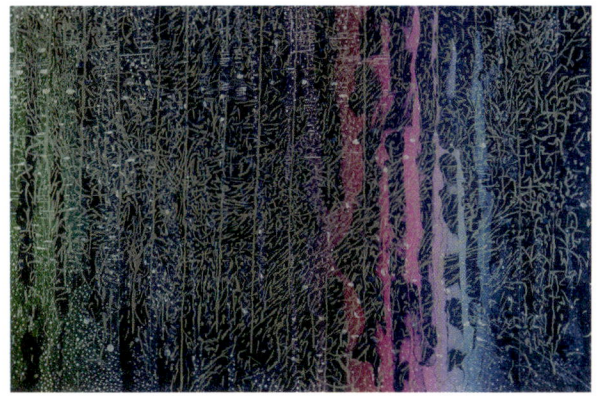

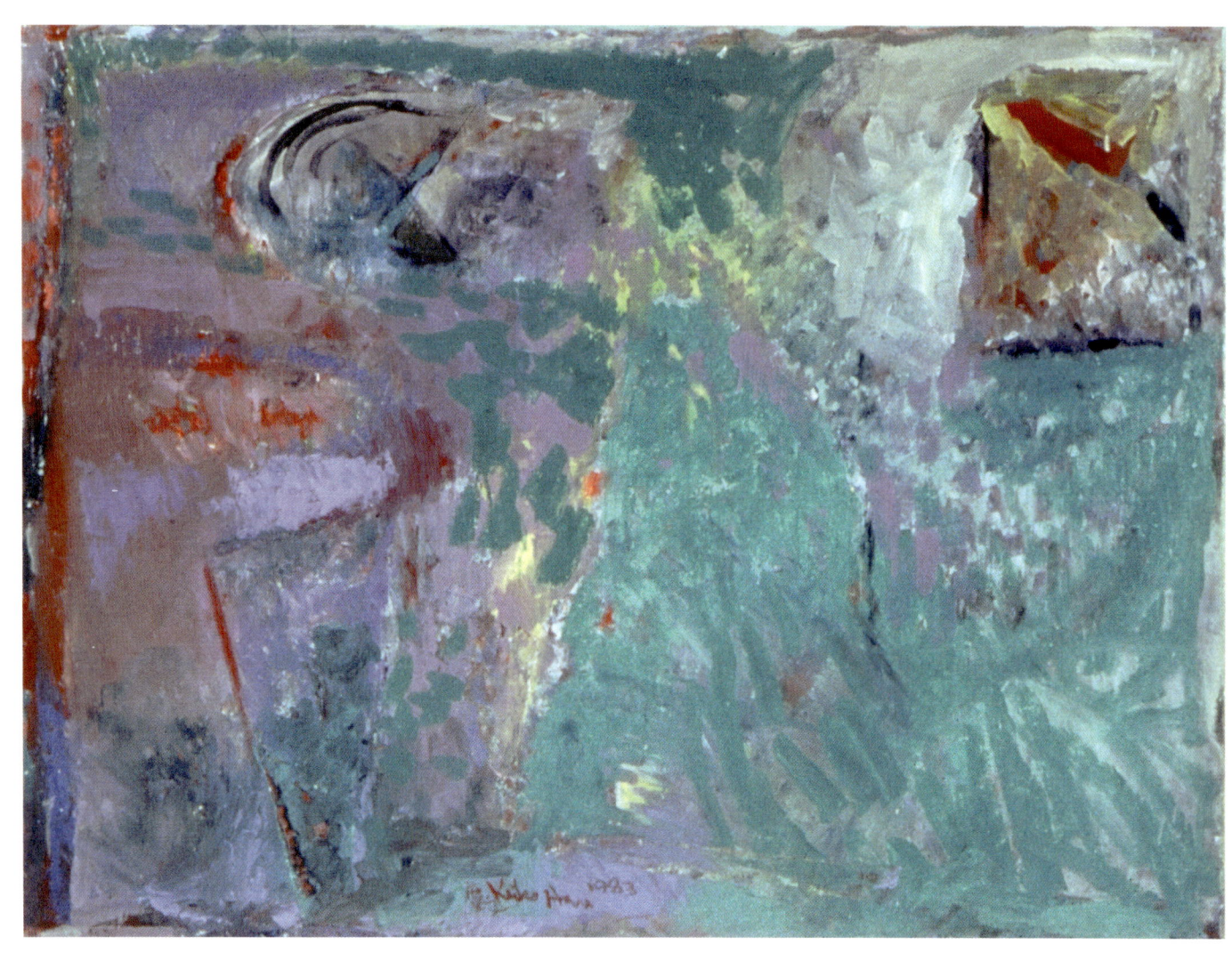

Verse · Green | 1983
Oil on linen
36 × 48 inches

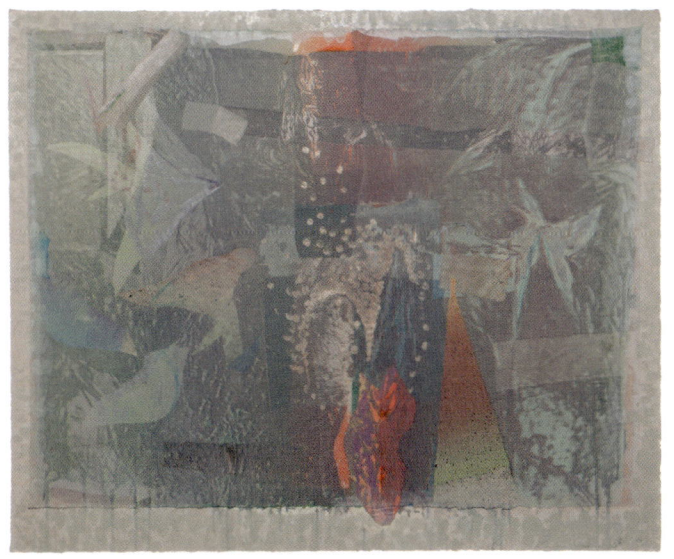

Verse 7.4.A-1 | 1984
Lithograph, monoprint with chine-collé
Printed with Yasutoshi Ishibashi in Tokyo, Japan
29.5 × 33.5 inches

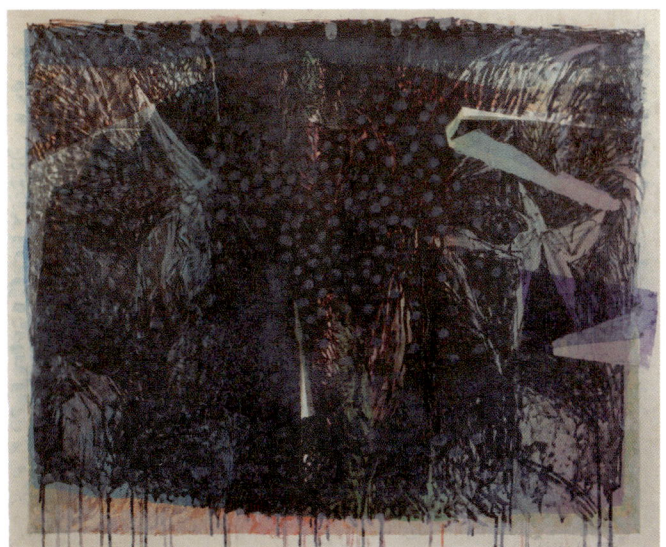

Verse 7.4.A-2 | 1984
Lithograph, monoprint with chine-collé
Printed with Yasutoshi Ishibashi in Tokyo, Japan
29.5 × 33.5 inches

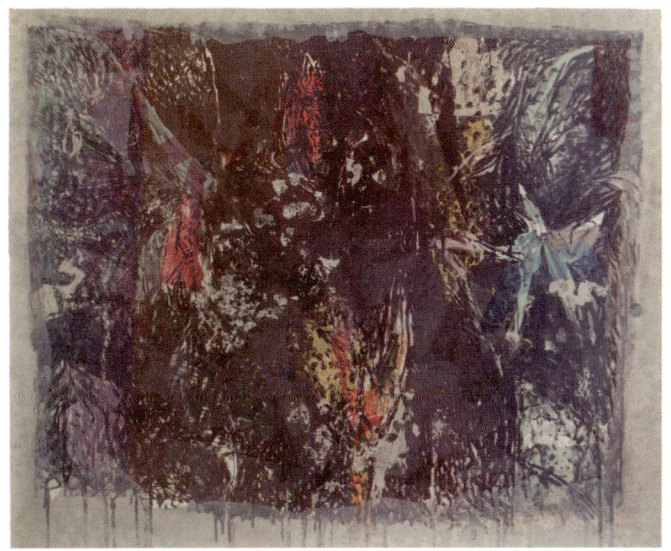

Verse 7.4.A-3 | 1984
Lithograph, monoprint with chine-collé
Printed with Yasutoshi Ishibashi in Tokyo, Japan
29.5 × 33.5 inches

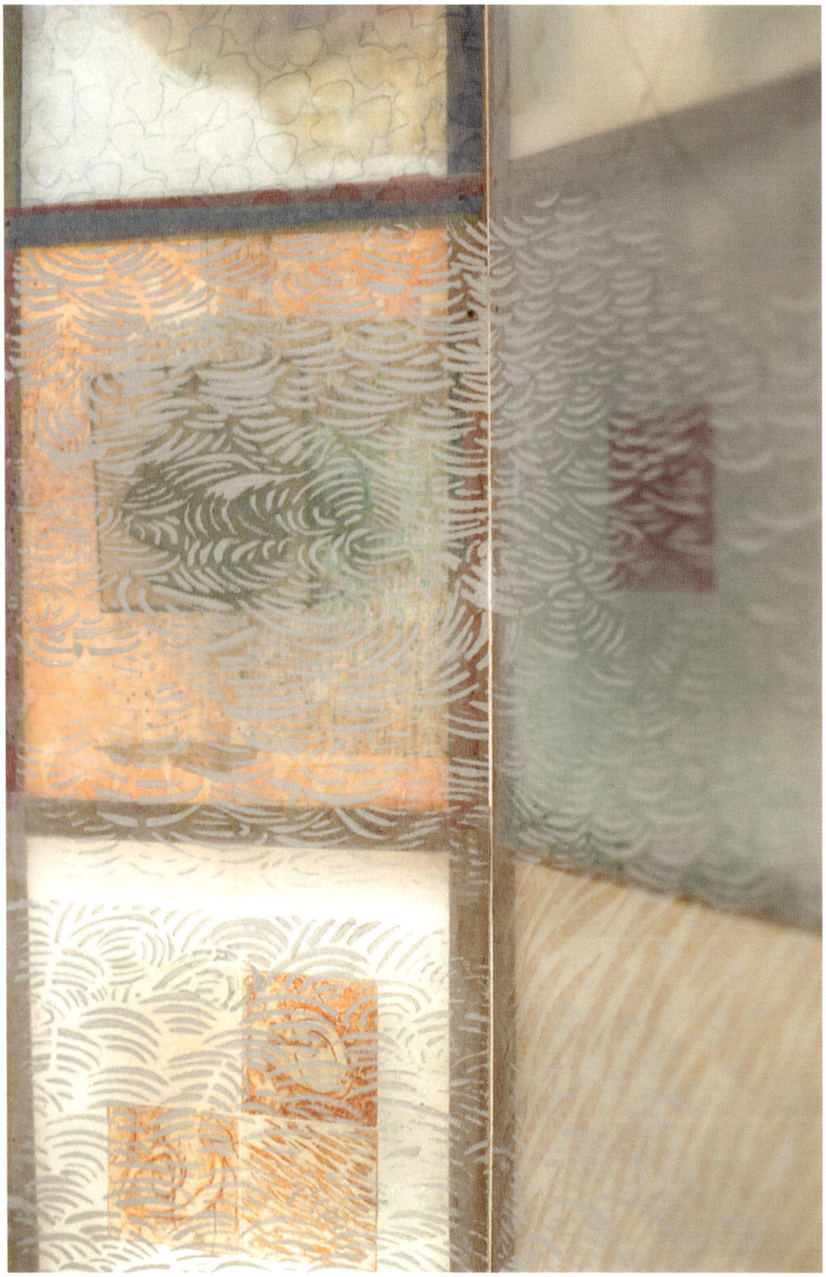

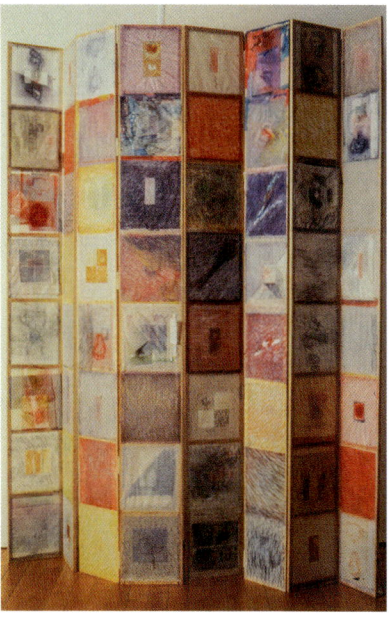

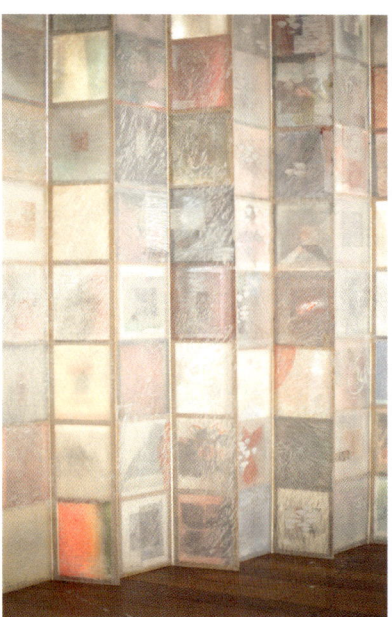

Verse · 8.2.8 | 1983
Monoprints with intaglio, stencil, and chine-collé printed on
translucent washi paper, mounted on wood structure
57 × 58 inches

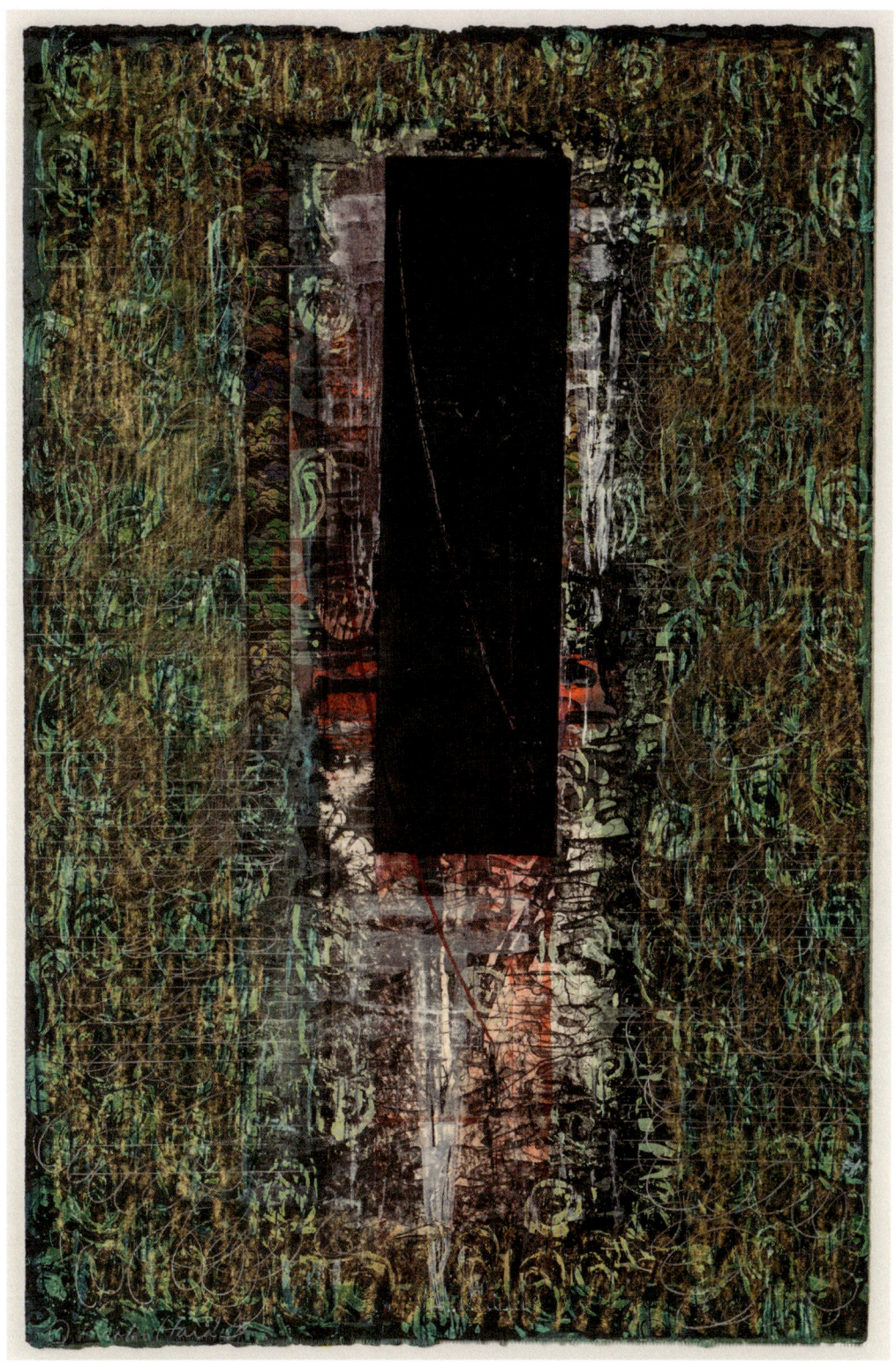

Topophilia 2 | 1989
Mixed-media monoprint with intaglio, lithography, and chine-collé
Published by Perimeter Press
22.5 × 15 inches | Private collection

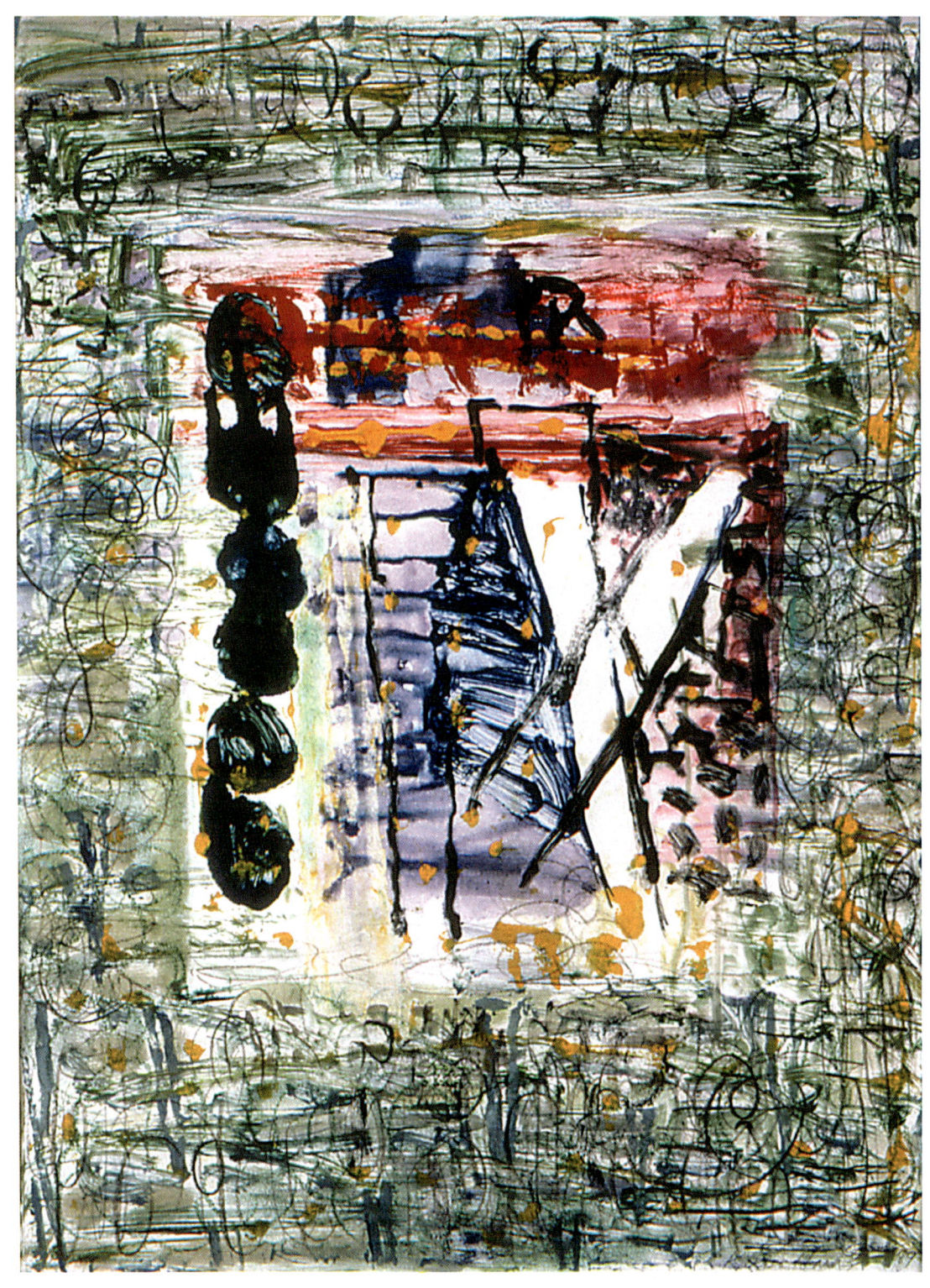

Topophilia 2 · Red Wood 1 | 1989
Monotype
21.5 × 16 inches | Private collection

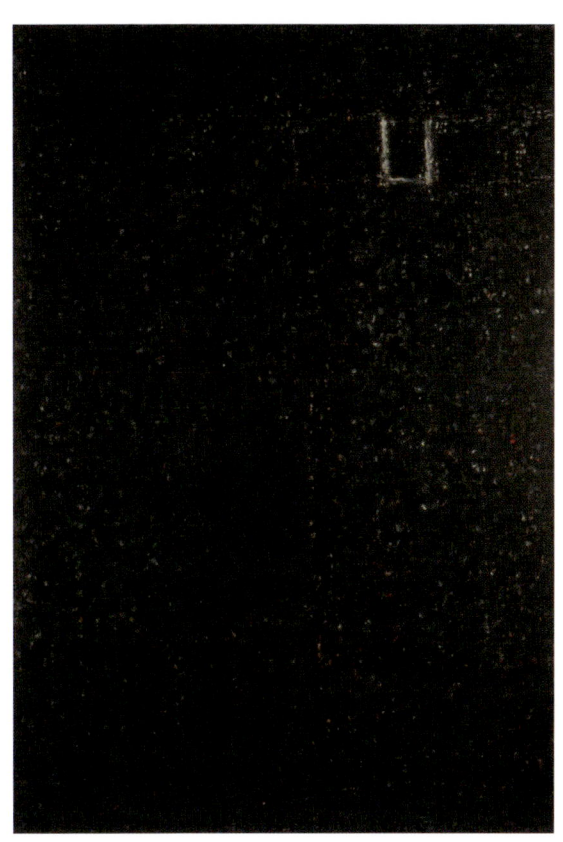

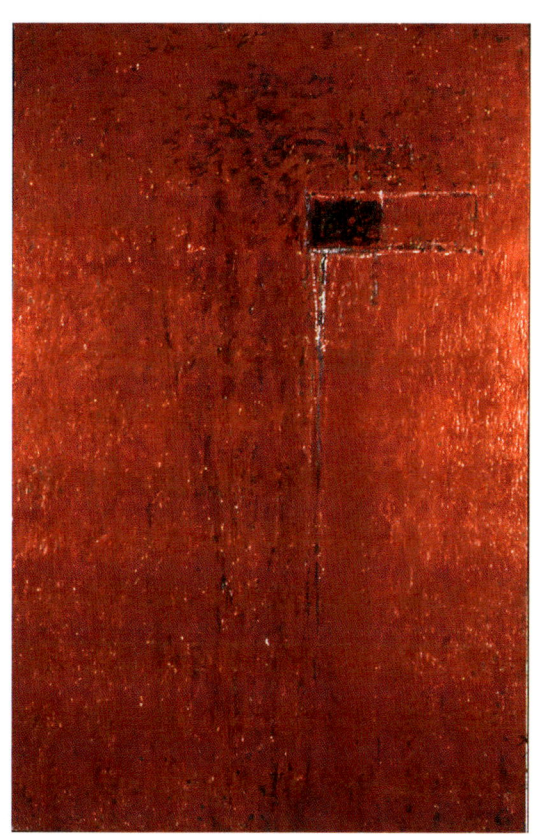

Topophilia 2 · Black | 1990
Oil on linen
62 × 54 inches

Topophilia 2 · Red | 1990
Oil on linen
62 × 54 inches

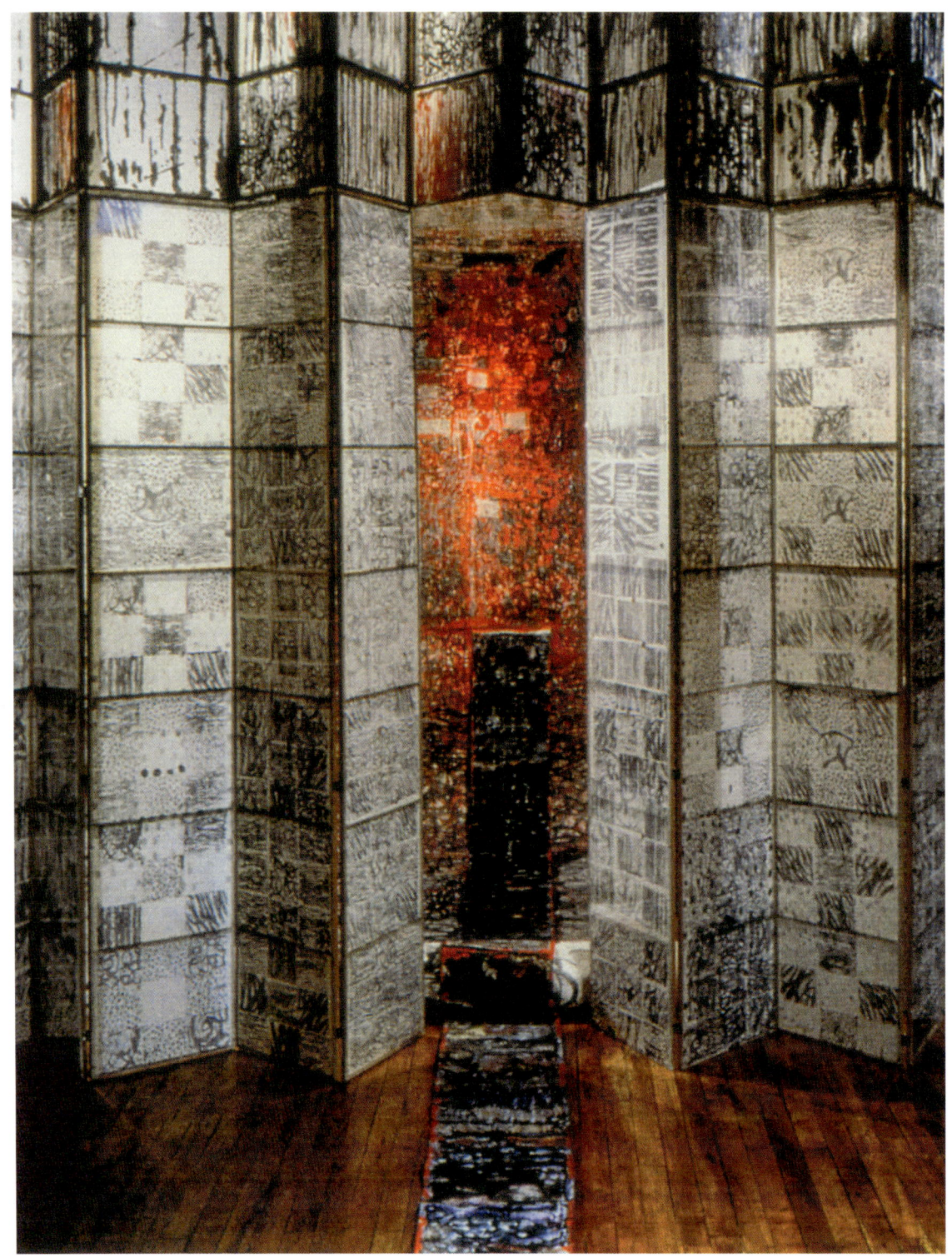

Topophilia 3 · Quilt Work | 1992
Mixed-media installation; woodblock and serigraphy on washi paper and painting with collage on linen
144 × 240 × 108 inches
Installation at the Art Gym, Marylhurst University

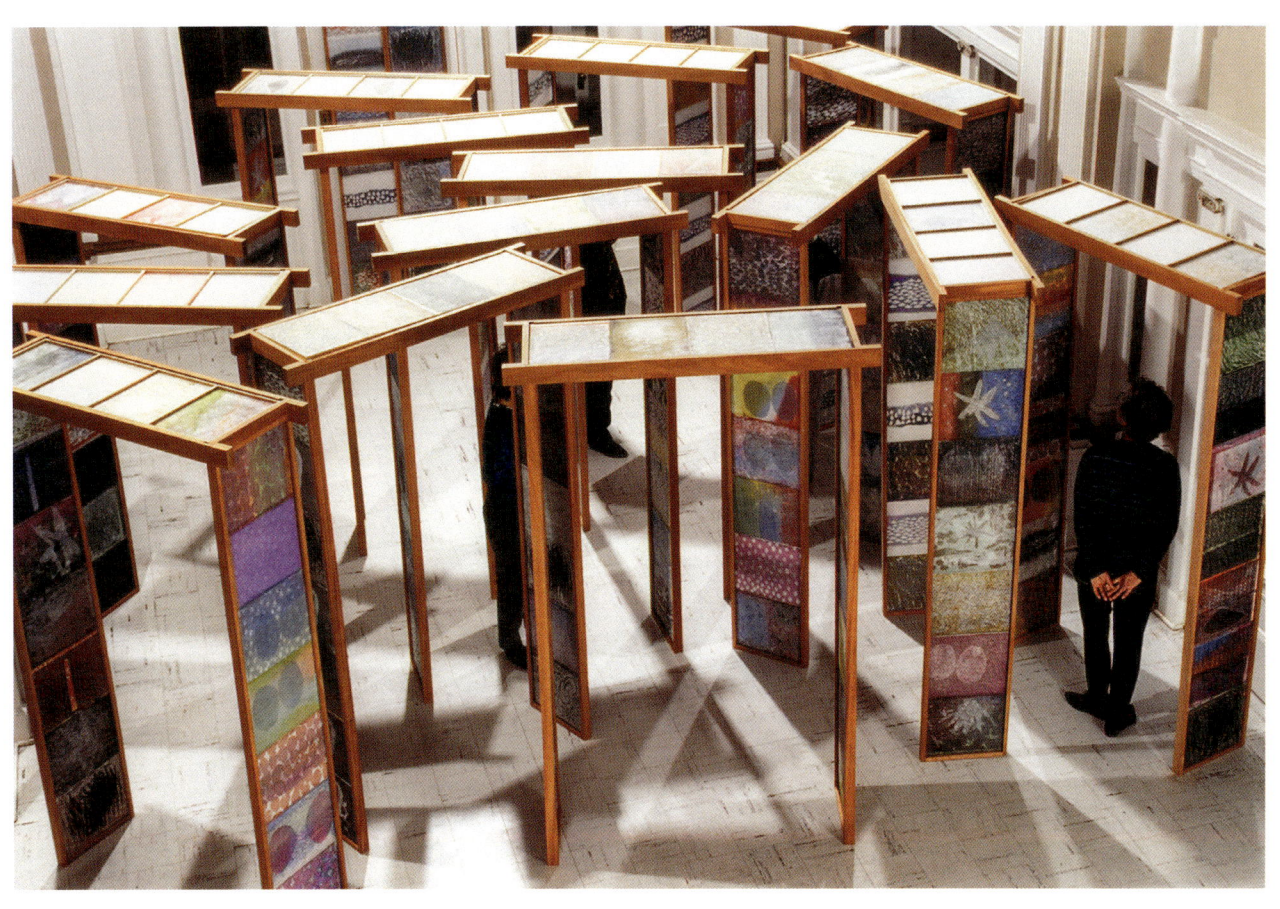

Topophilia 5 · 100 Gates | 1994
Multi-media installation with monoprints mounted on wood structure
84 × 48 × 15 inches each
Installation at Tacoma Art Museum

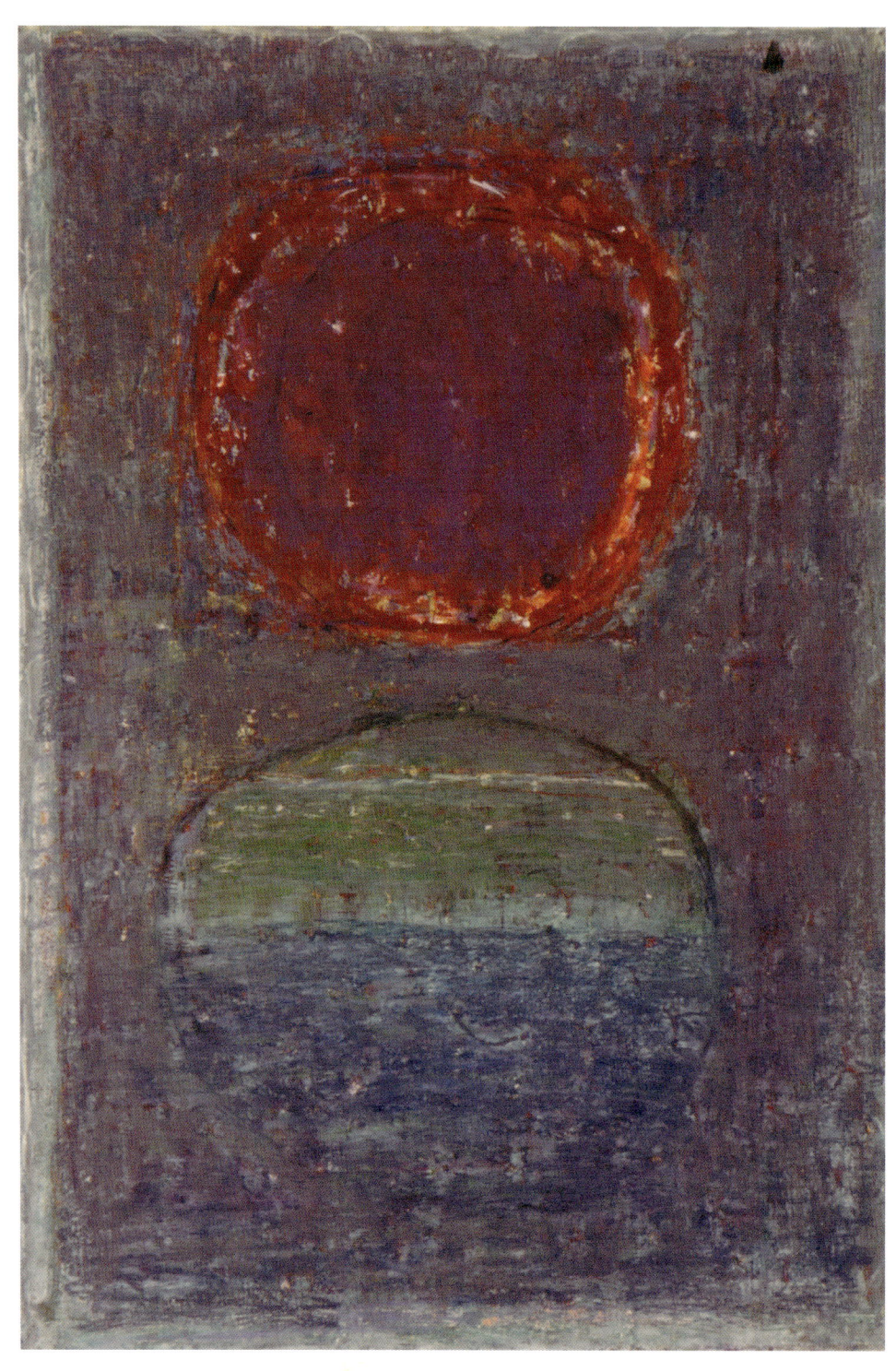

Verse 3·912 · Red and Green in Grey | 1993
Work on paper
30 × 20.25 inches

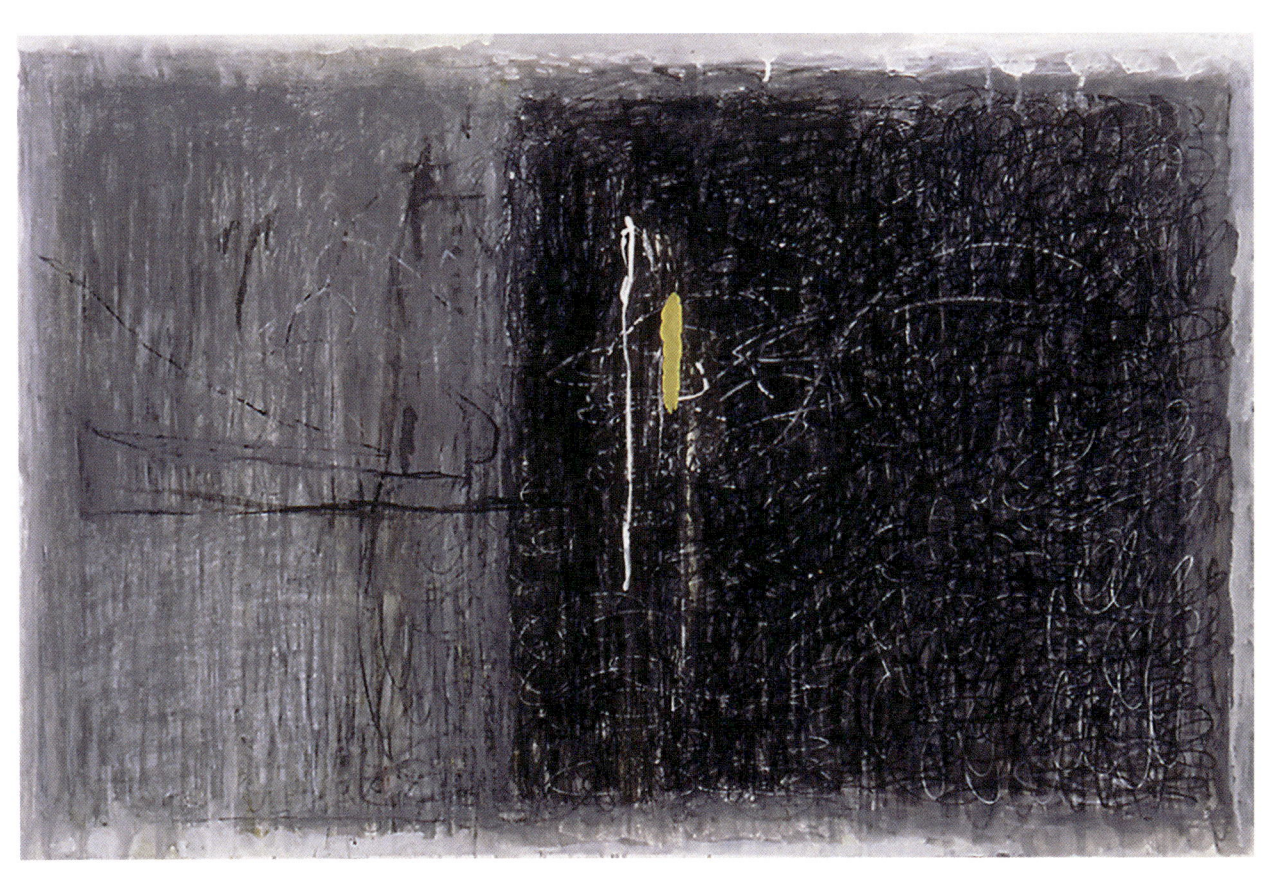

Verse · Sumida River | 1996
Work on paper
32 × 40 inches

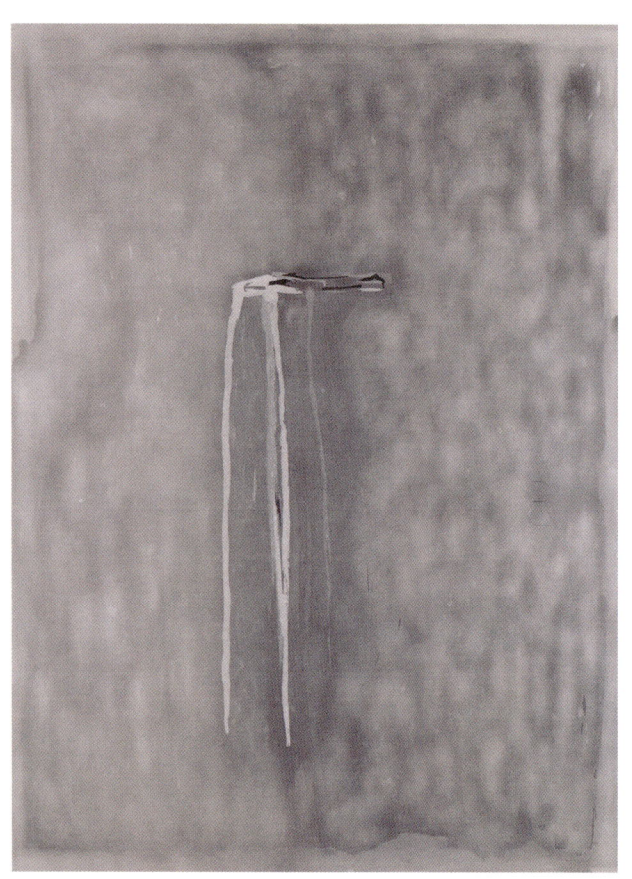

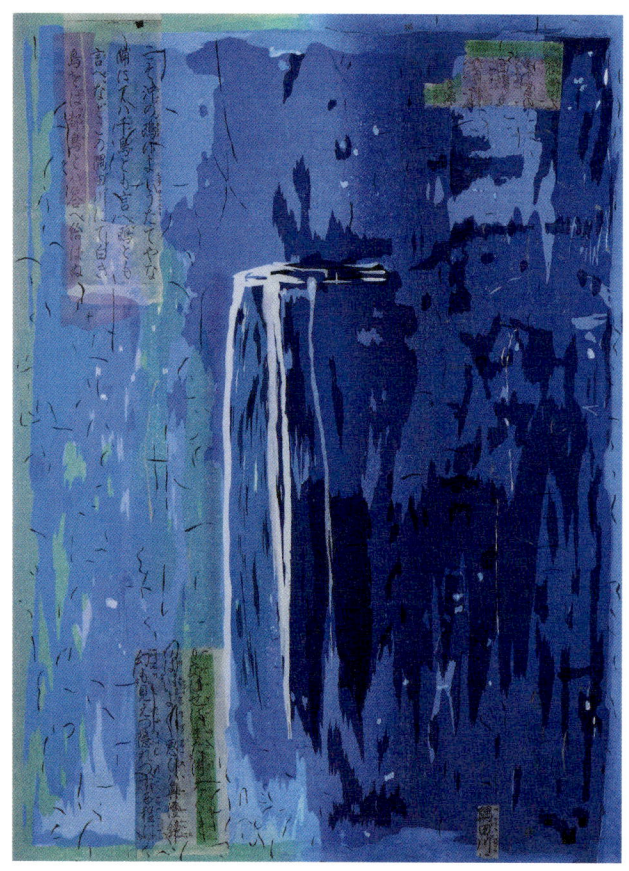

Topophilia 7 · Grey | 1996
Ukiyo-e woodblock print with stencil and collage | Edition 20
Printed with Tadashi Toda in Kyoto, Japan
32 x 24 inches
Collection of the Portland Art Museum

Topophilia 7 · Blue | 1996
Ukiyo-e woodblock print with stencil and collage | Edition 20
Printed with Tadashi Toda in Kyoto, Japan
32 x 24 inches
Collection of the Portland Art Museum

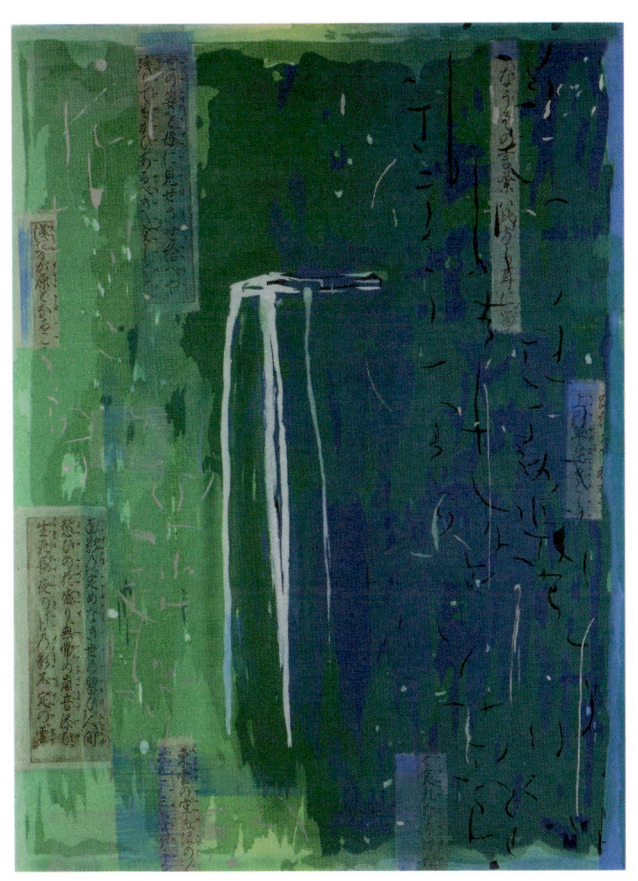

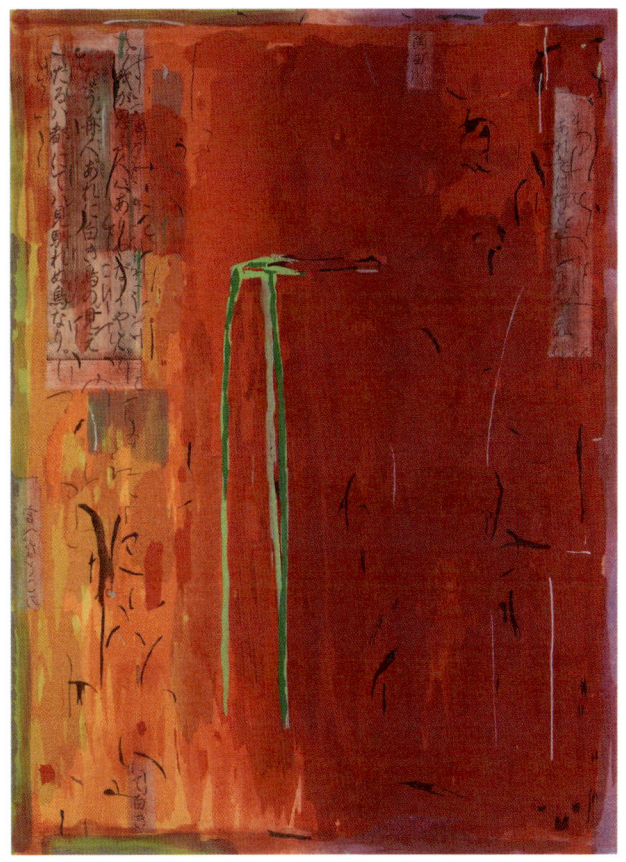

Topophilia 7 · Green | 1996
Ukiyo-e woodblock print with stencil and collage | Edition 20
Printed with Tadashi Toda in Kyoto, Japan
32 x 24 inches
Collection of the Portland Art Museum

Topophilia 7 · Red | 1996
Ukiyo-e woodblock print with stencil and collage | Edition 20
Printed with Tadashi Toda in Kyoto, Japan
32 x 24 inches
Collection of the Portland Art Museum

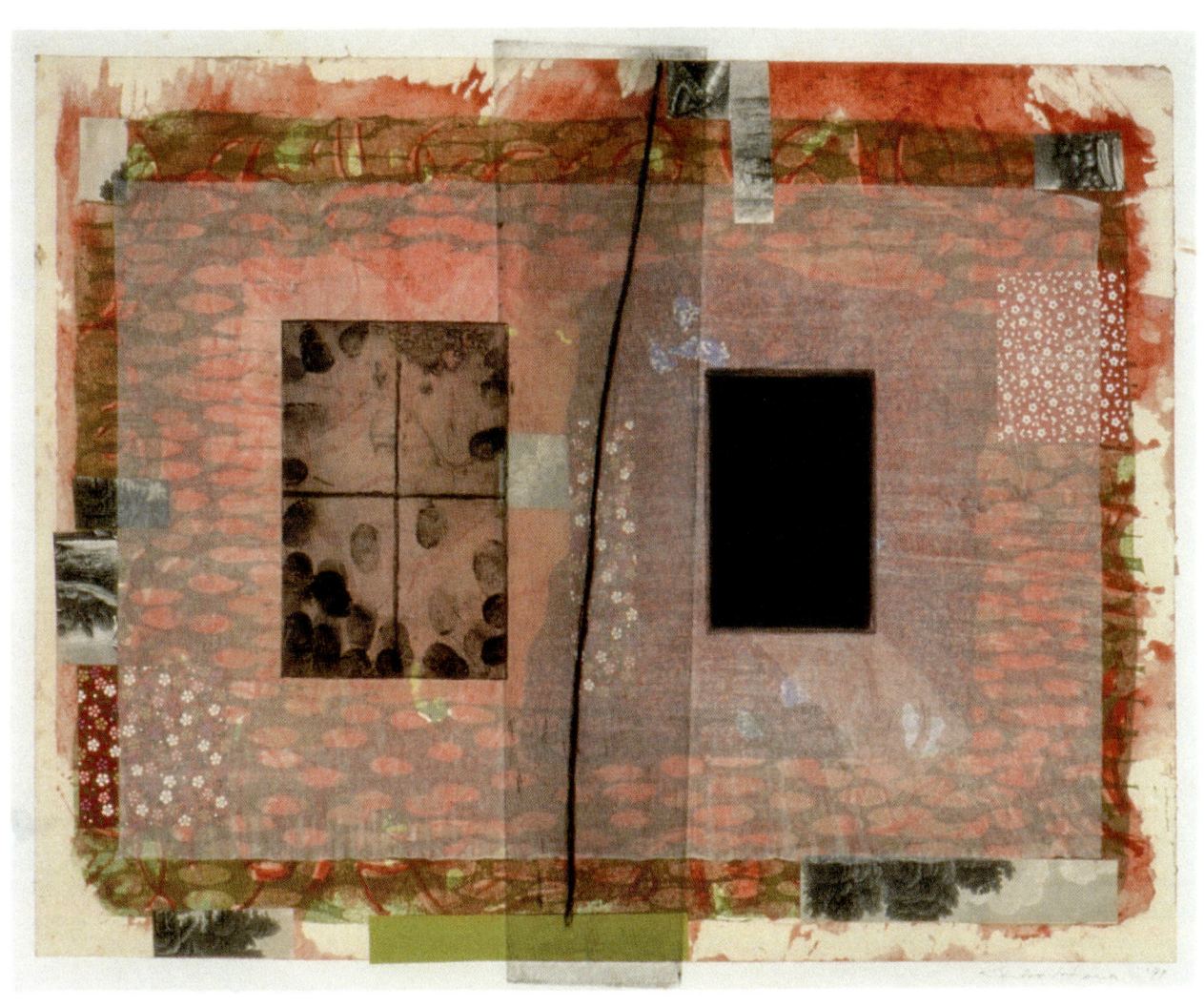

Verse · Semaru | 1997
Mixed-media monoprint using intaglio, stencil, and collage
20 × 16 inches
Private collection

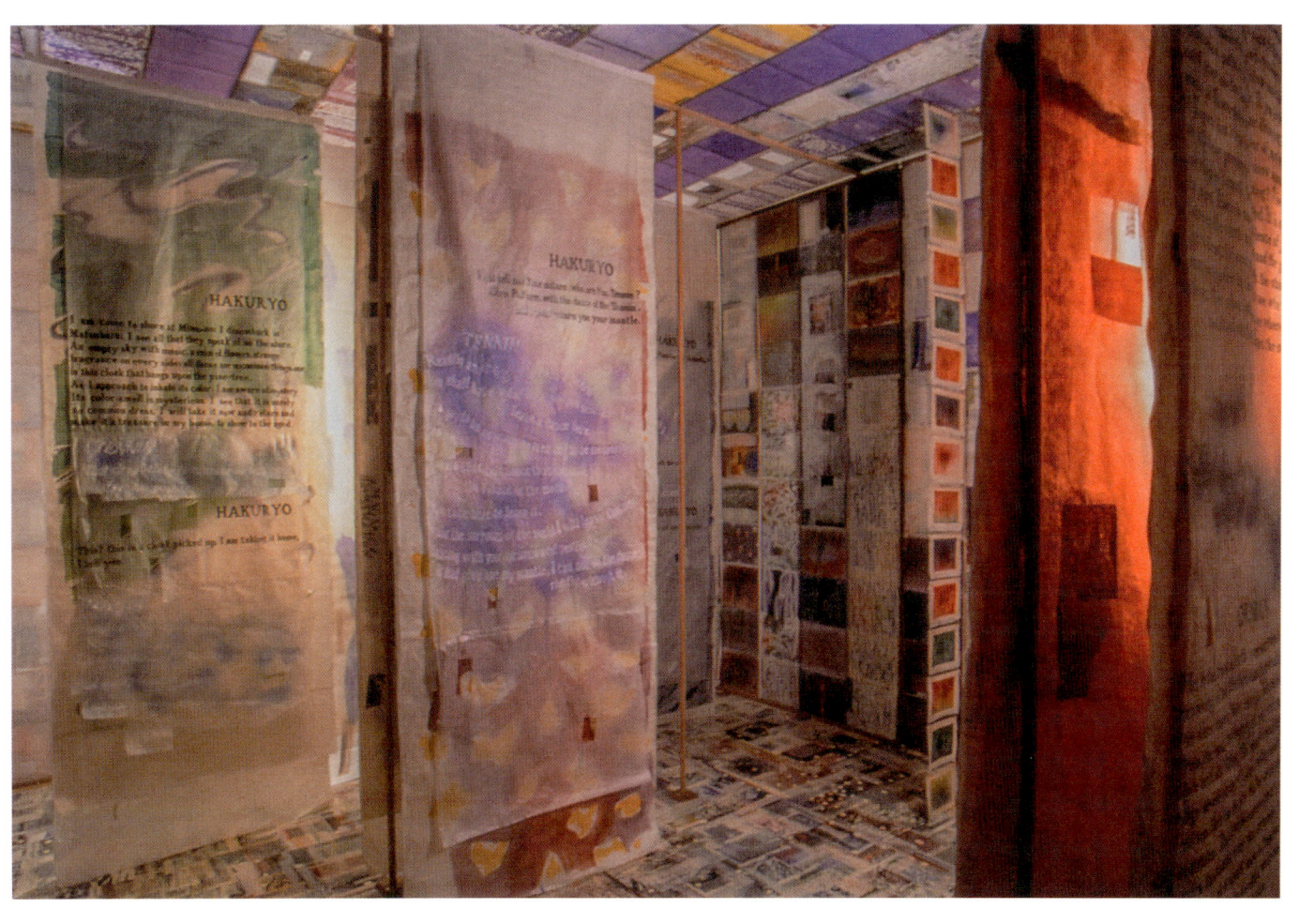

Topophilia · Hagoromo | 1998
Mixed-media installation with typography, stencil, woodblock, collage, silk, and wood
264 × 132 inches

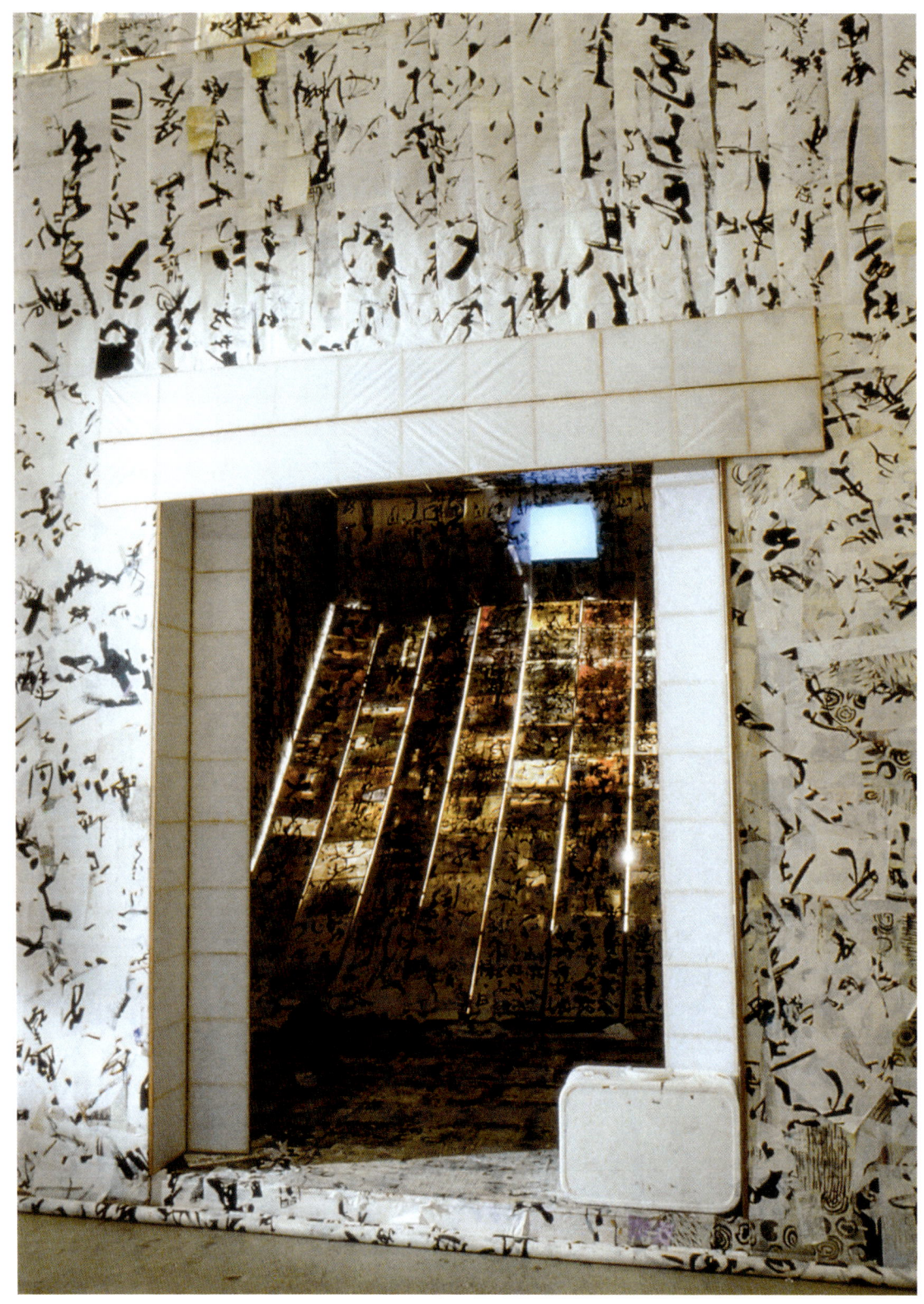

Topophilia · Departing | 1998
Multi-media installation with video and audio
120 × 190 × 264 inches | Installation at the Art Gym, Marylhurst University

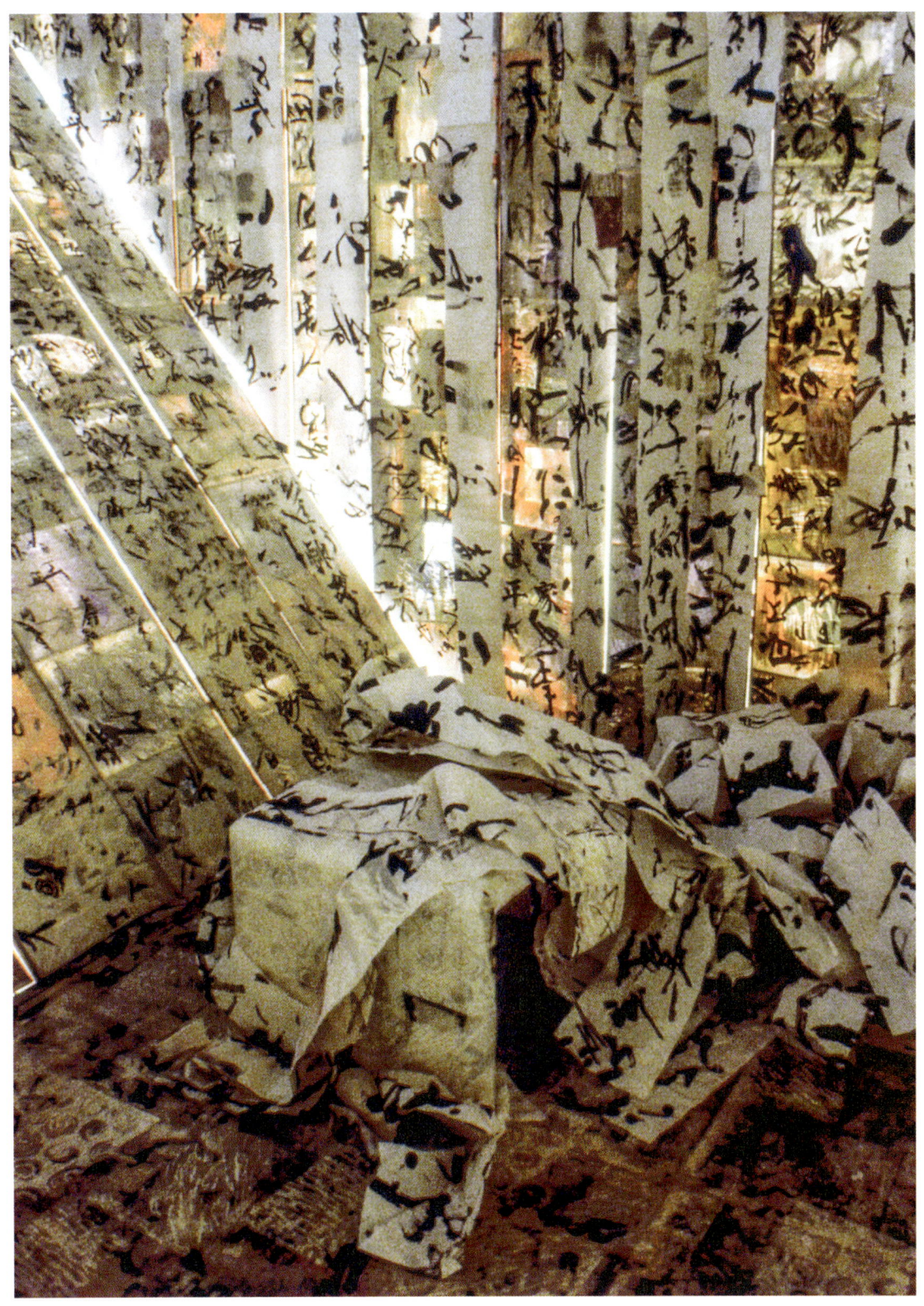

Topophilia · Departing (interior) | 1998
Multi-media installation with video and audio
120 × 190 × 264 inches | Installation at the Art Gym, Marylhurst University

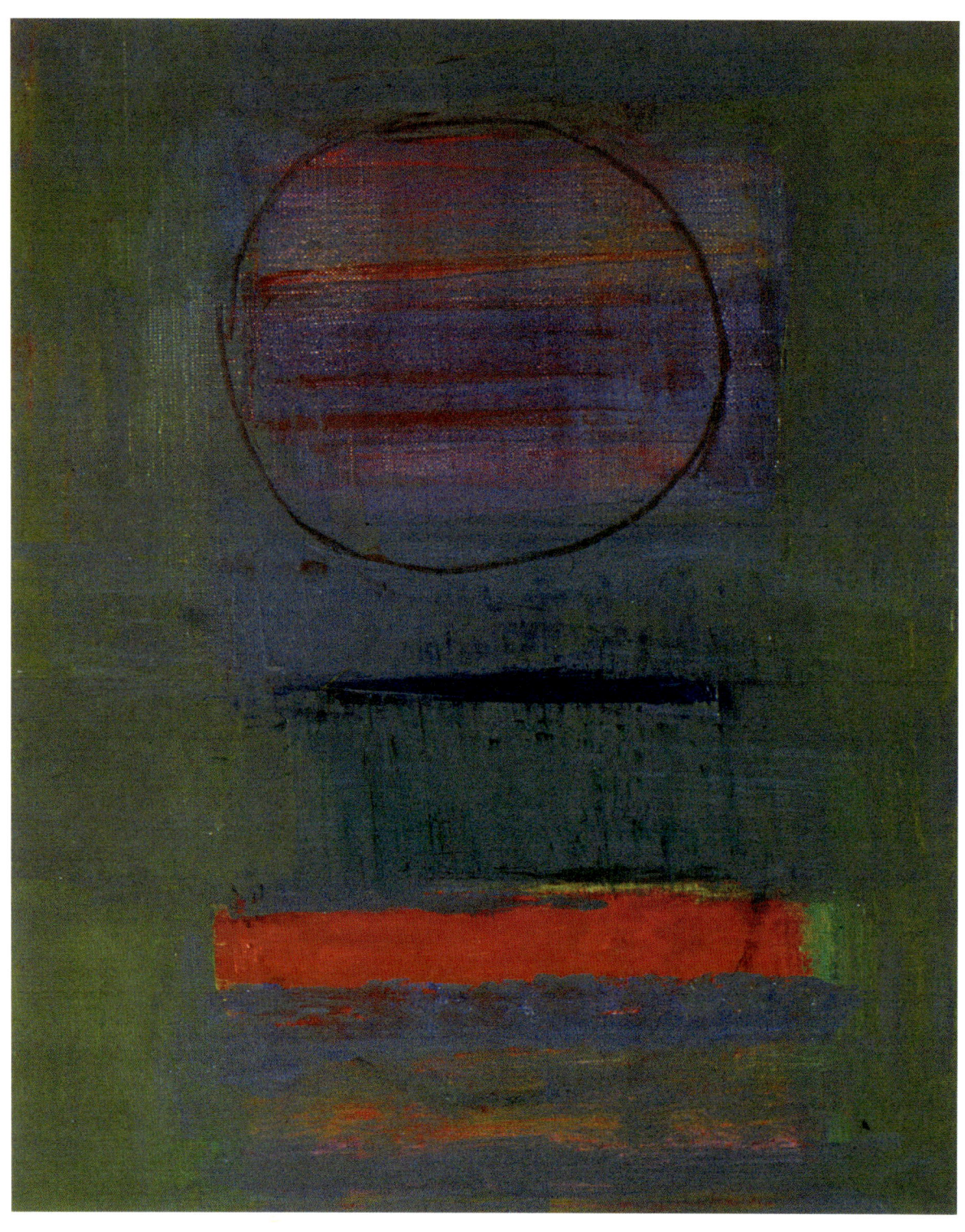

Verse · Maru 2 | 1998
Oil on linen
20 × 16 inches

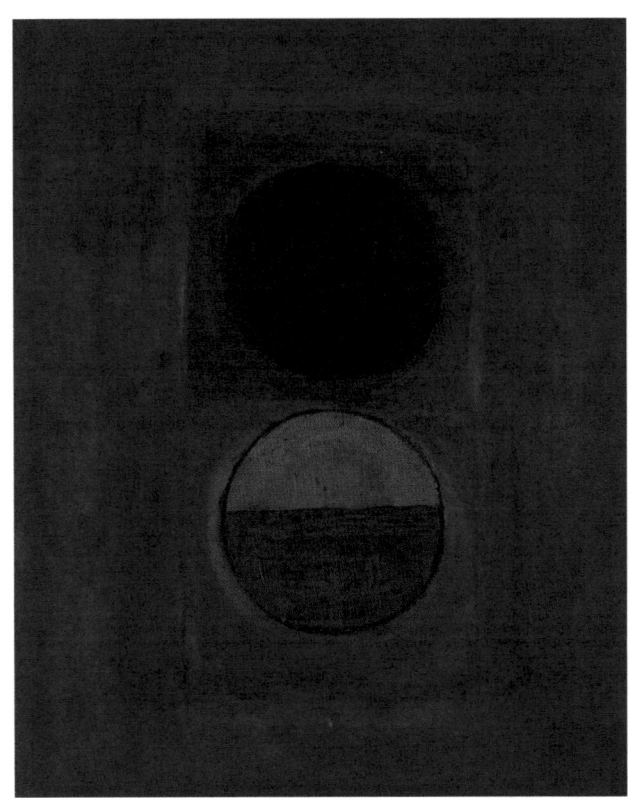

Verse · Maru 4 | 1998
Oil on linen
20 × 16 inches

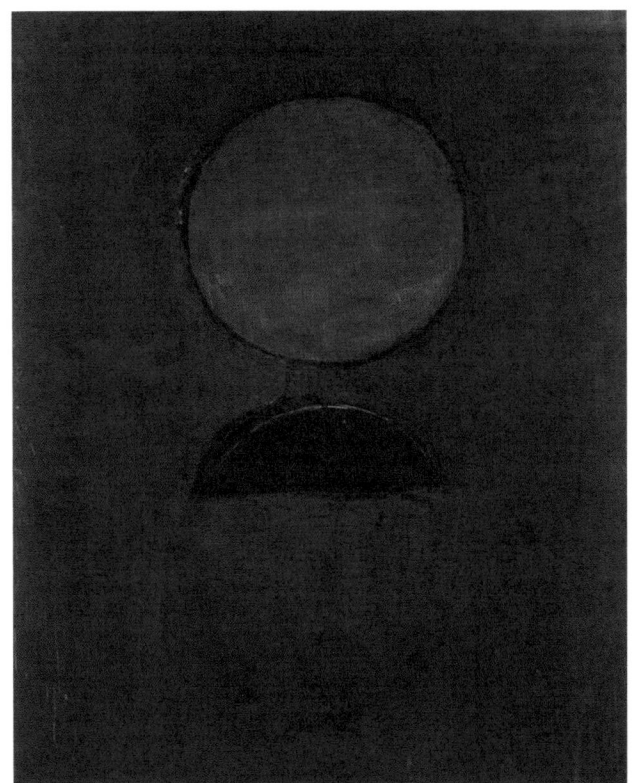

Verse · Maru 7 | 1998
Oil on linen
20 × 16 inches

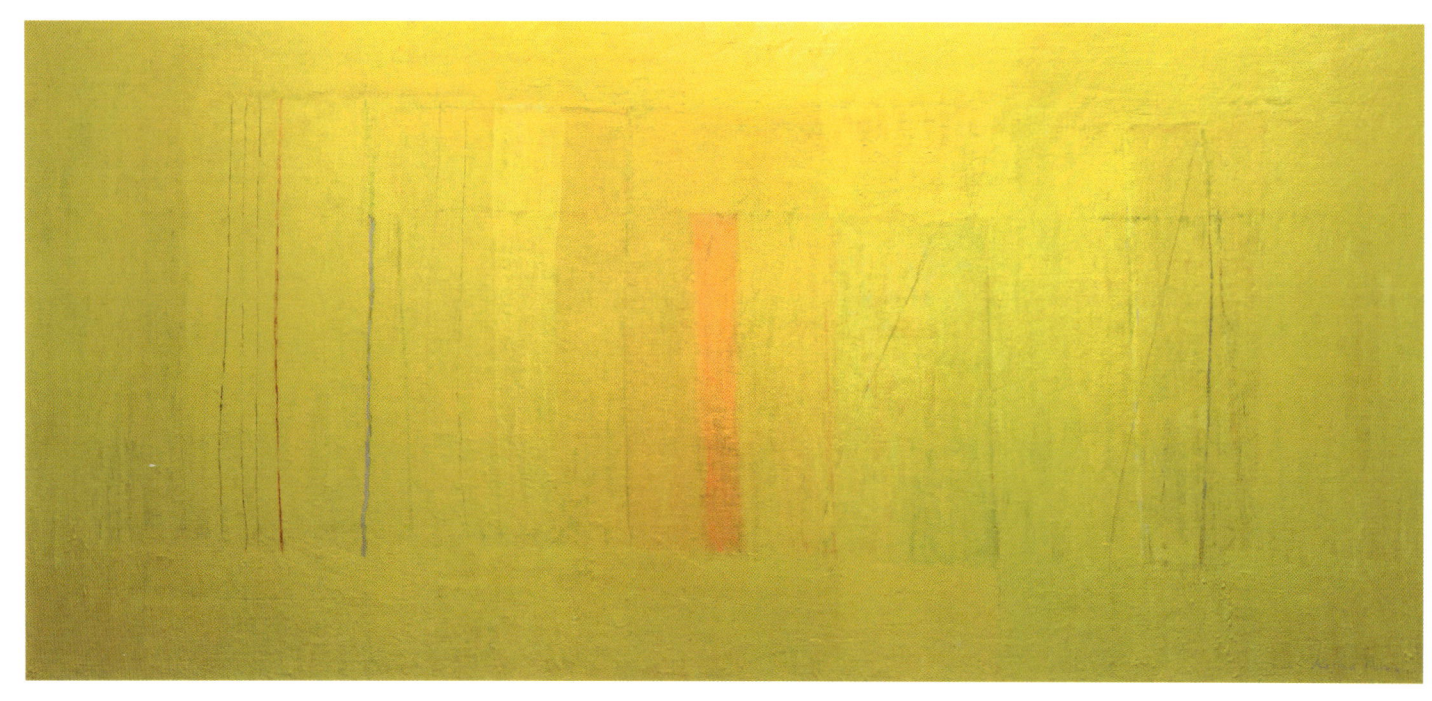

Topophilia · Semaru Yellow | 1999
Oil on linen
42 x 92 inches | Collection of the Sheehan Gallery, Whitman College, Walla Walla
Photo: Tara Graves

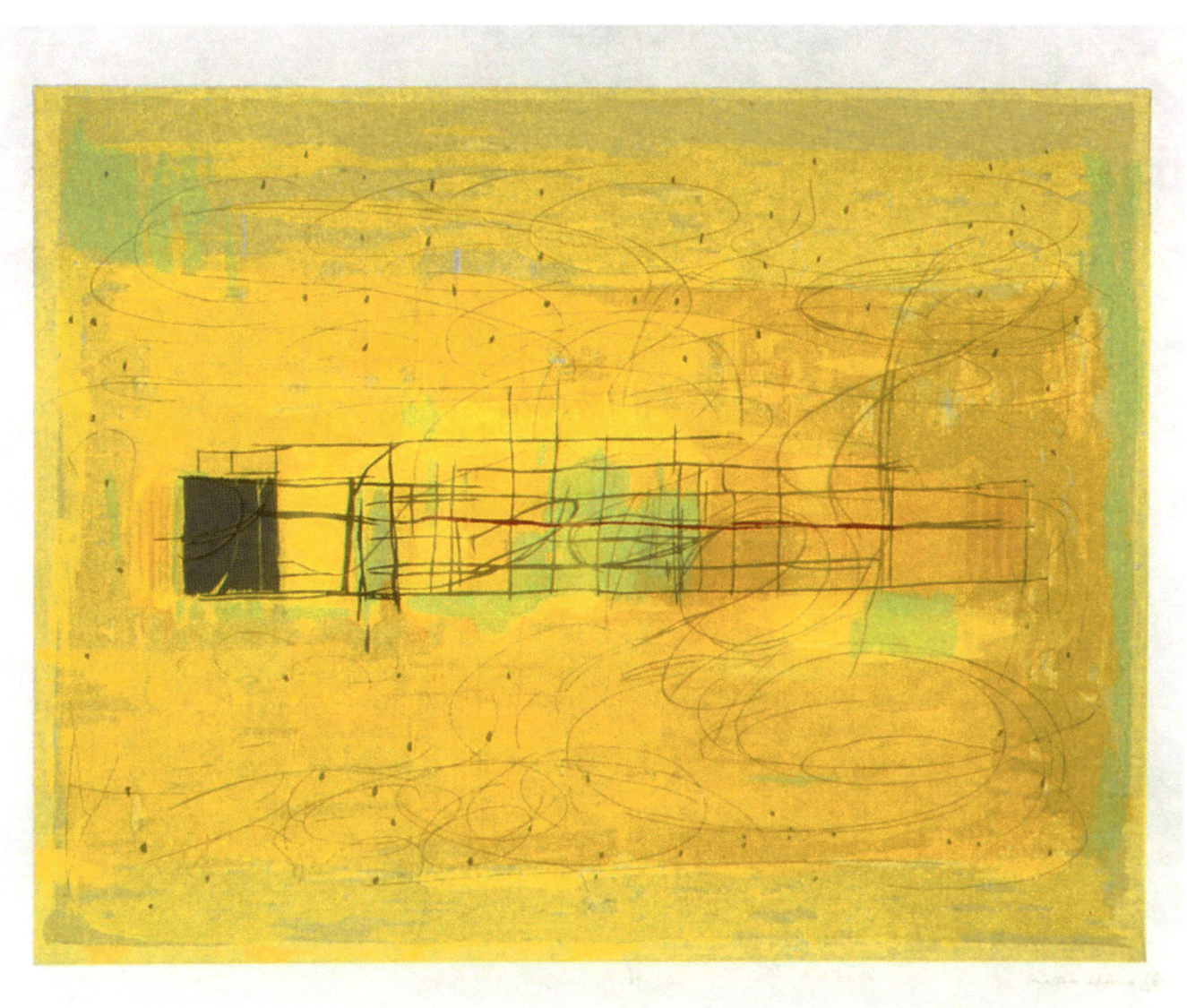

Verse · Wind | 1999
Ukiyo-e woodblock and stencil print
Edition 20 | Printed with Tadashi Toda in Kyoto, Japan
20 × 15 inches

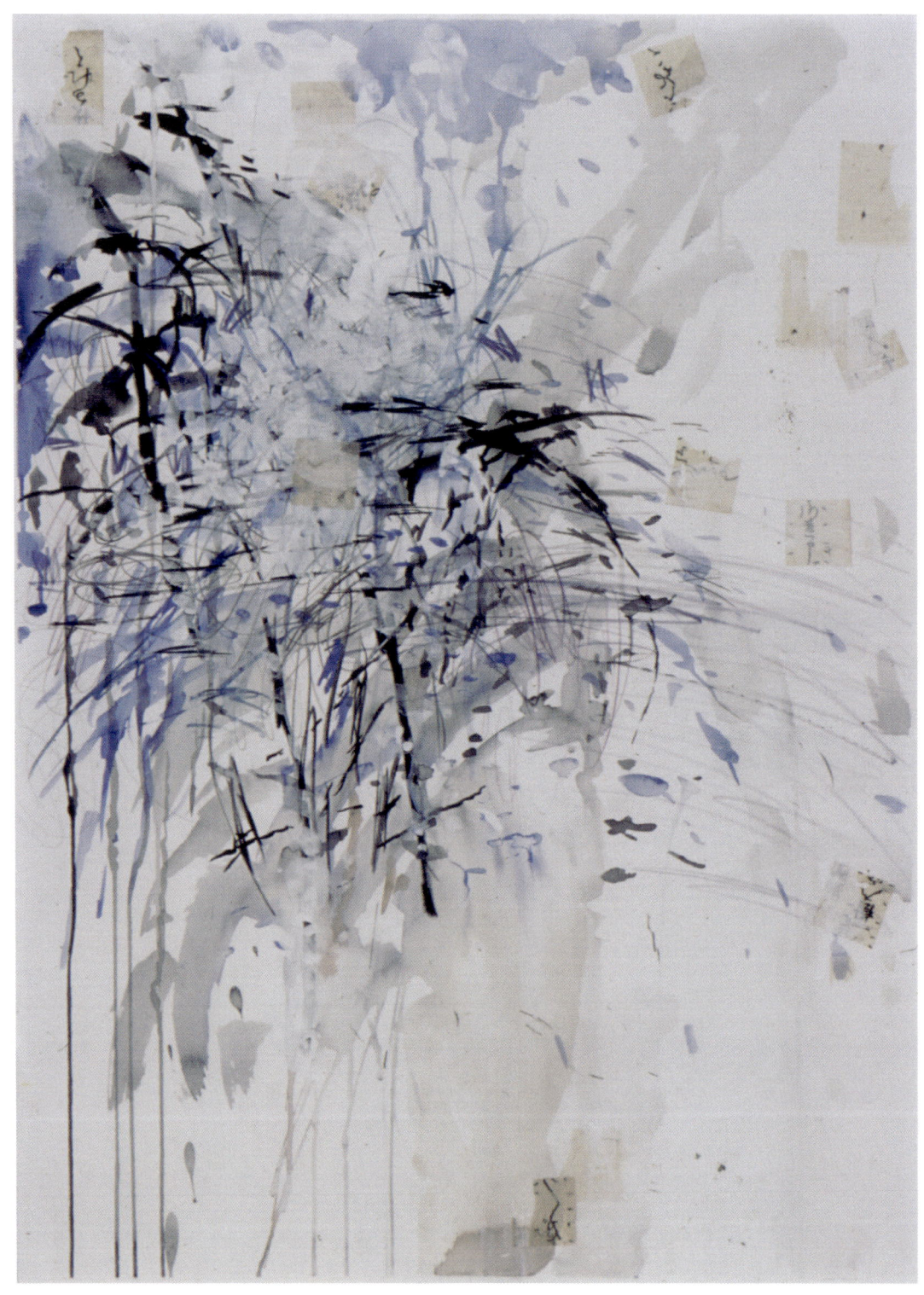

Verse · Kumo | 2001
Work on paper
30 × 22 inches
Collection of the Racine Art Museum

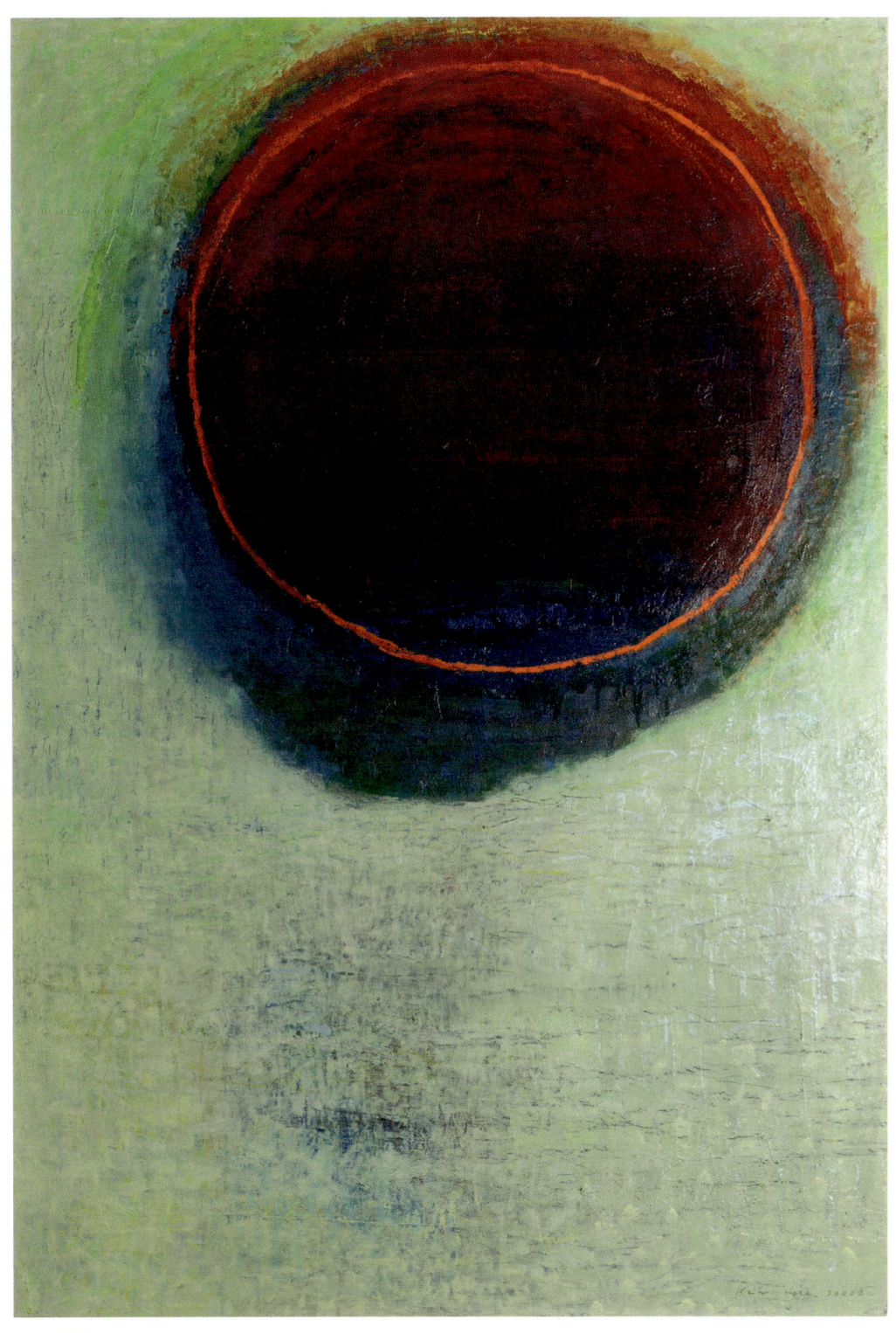

Verse · Maru | 2002
Oil on linen
60.5 x 42 inches
Collection of the Northwest Museum of Arts and Culture, Spokane

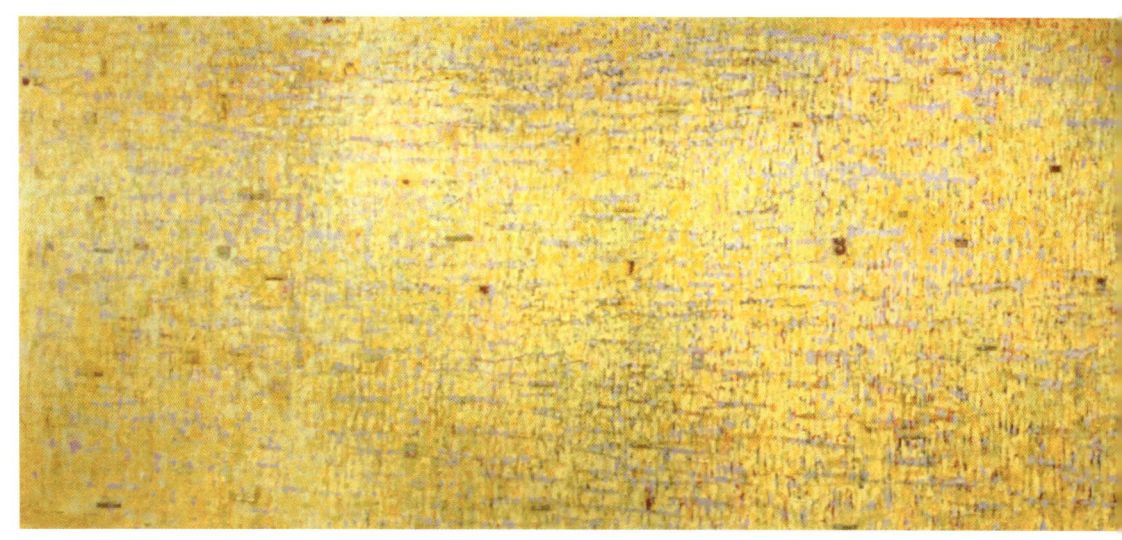

Verse · Imbuing in Yellow | 2002
Oil, sumi ink, drawing media, and collage on linen
74 × 336 inches

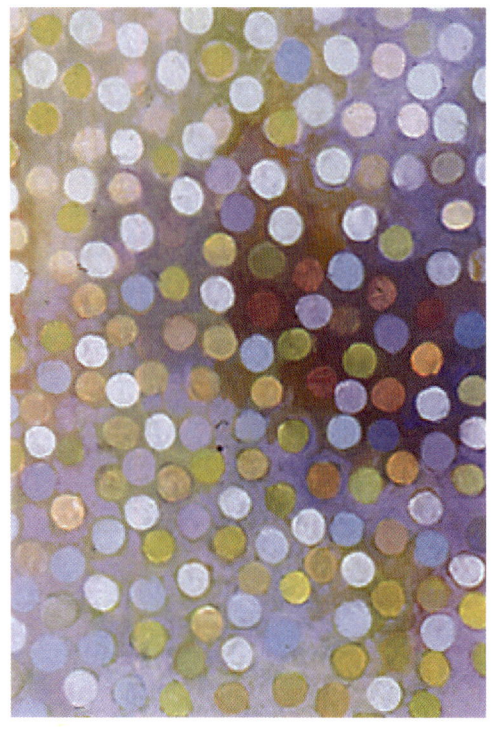 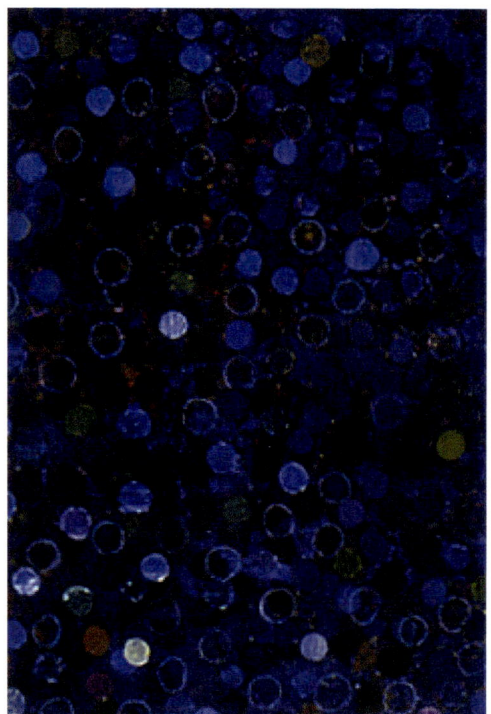

Verse 1.1.1.1 | 2002
Oil on linen
30 × 80 inches
Private collection

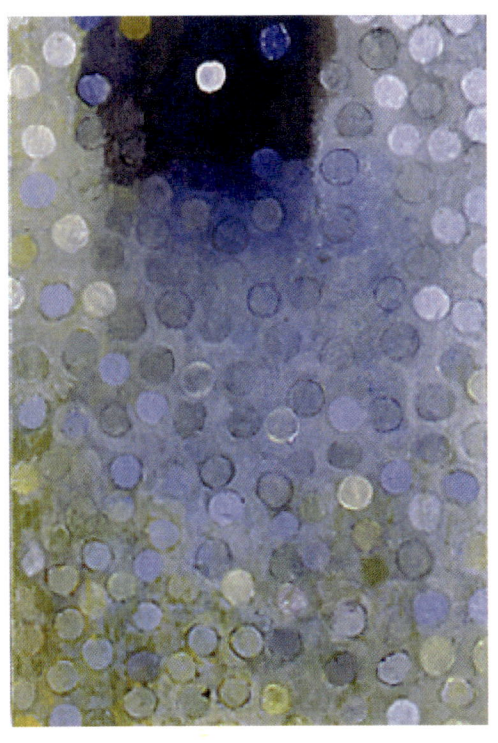
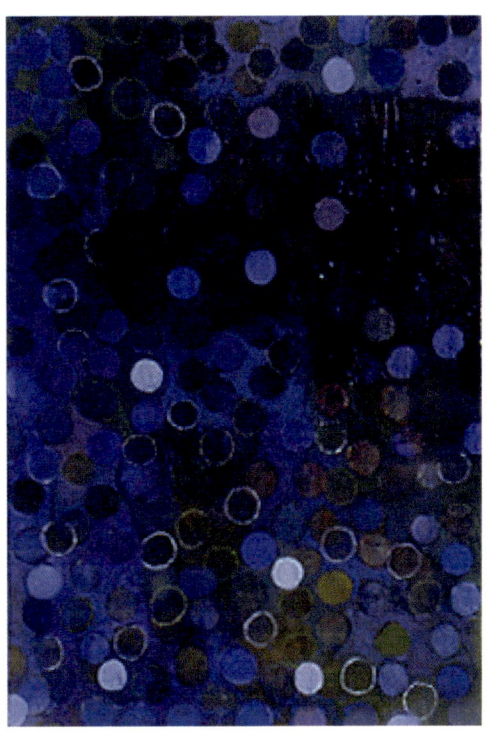

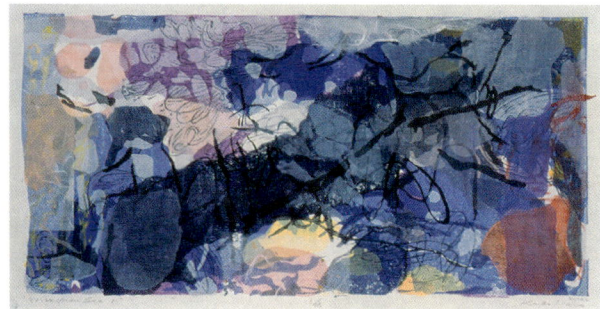
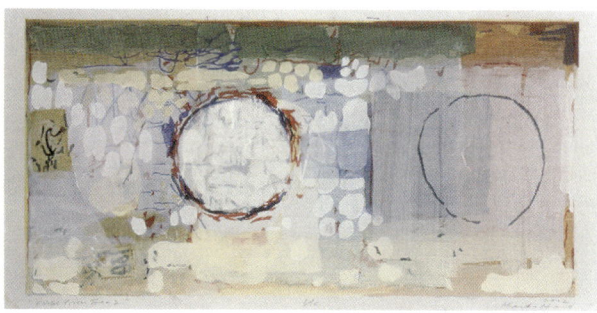
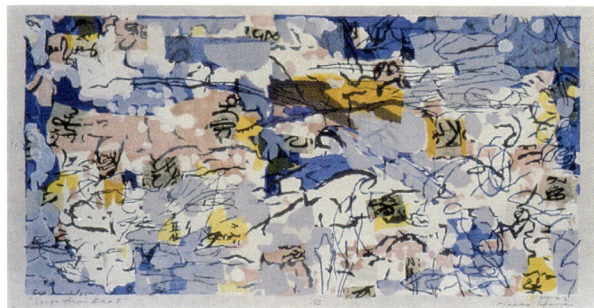
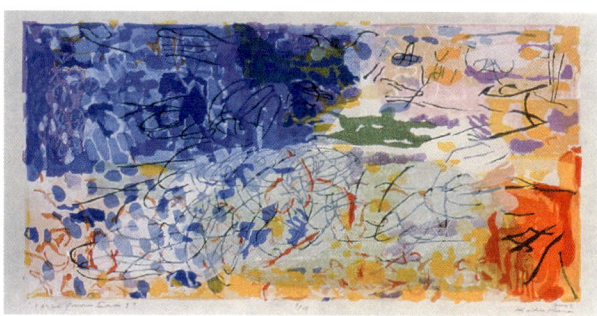
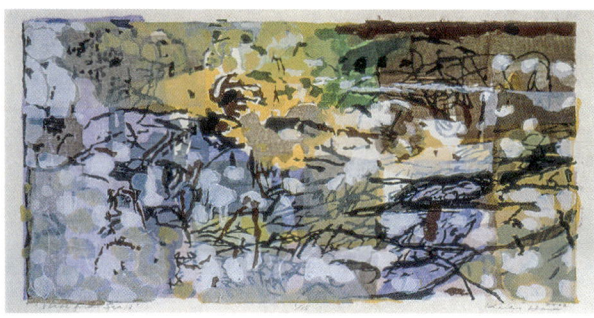
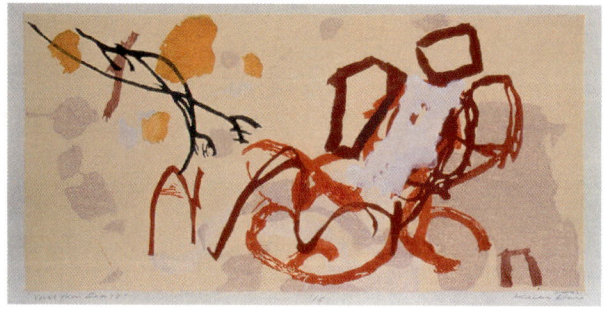

Verse from Sea | 2002
Mokuhanga woodblock, stencil, and collage print | Edition 15 (set of 12)
10 x 20 inches each
Collection of Harborview Medical Center, Seattle

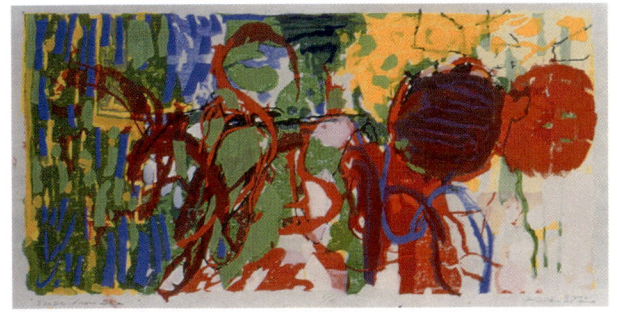 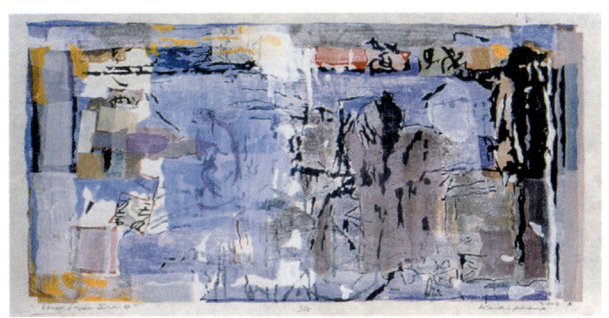

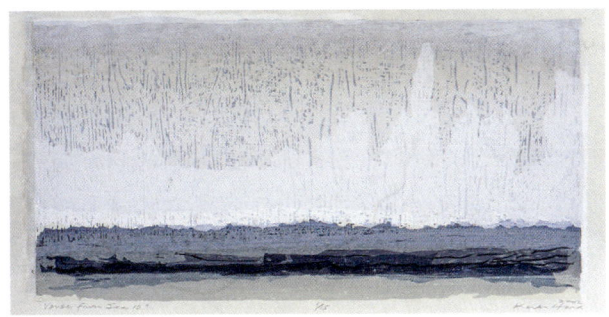 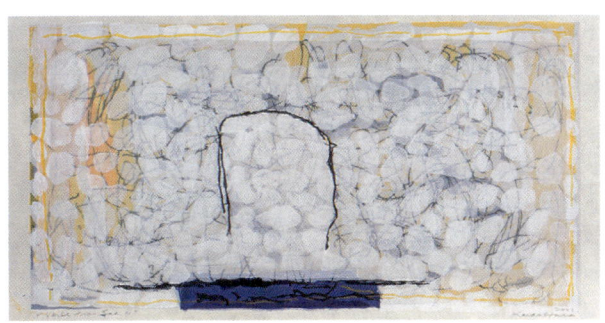

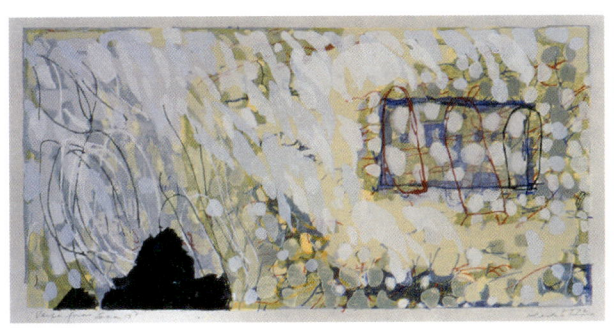 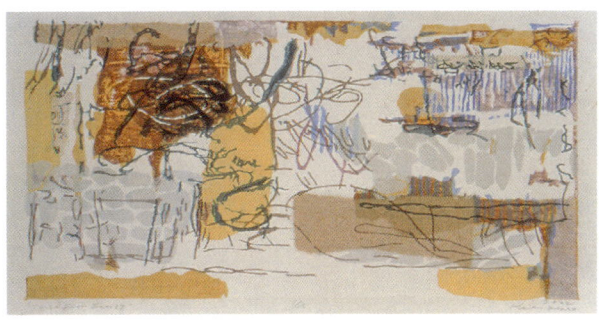

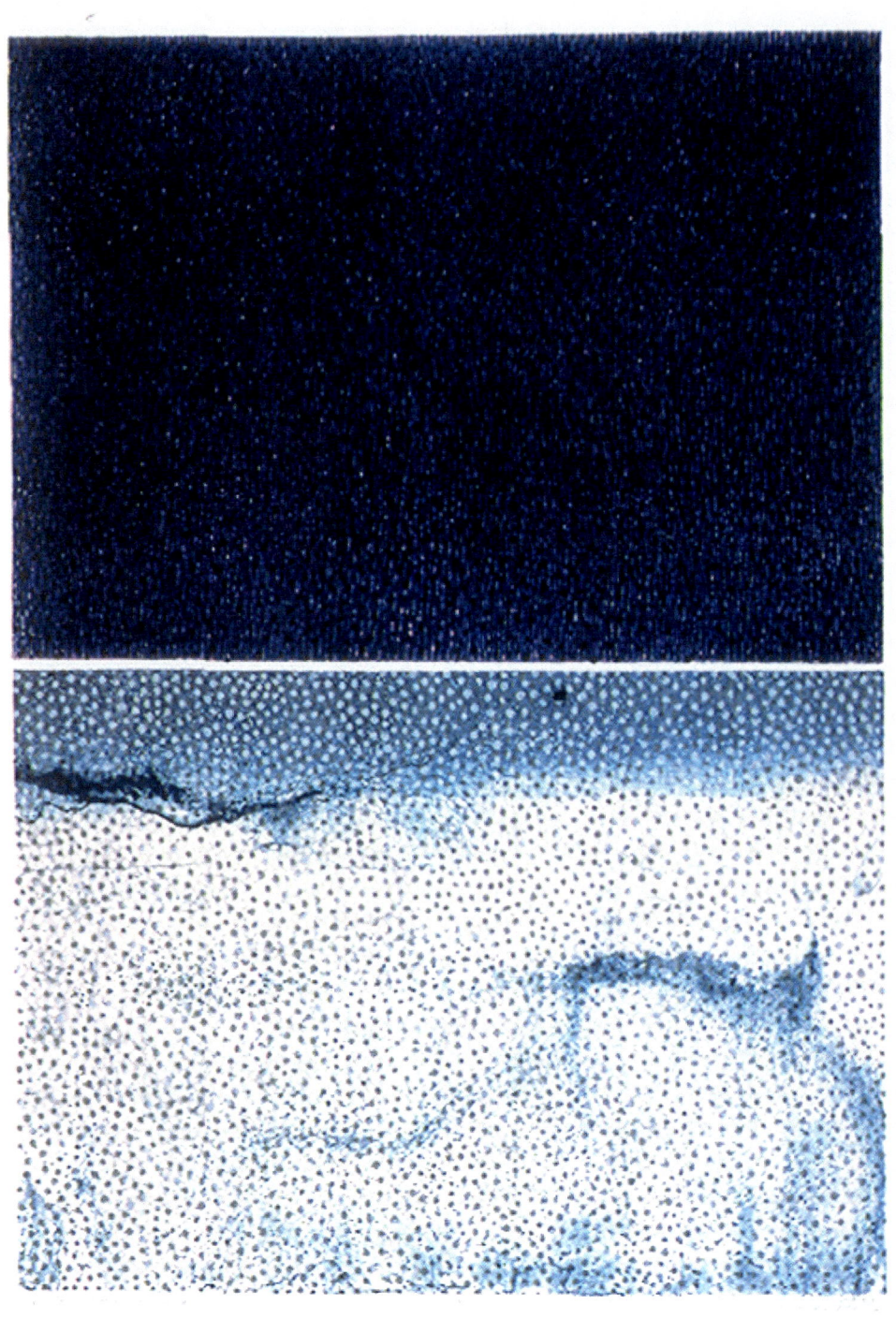

Verse · Imbuing in Blue | 2003
Lithography with chine-collé | Edition 25
Printed with Craig Cornwall at Trilobite Workshop | 28 x 20 inches

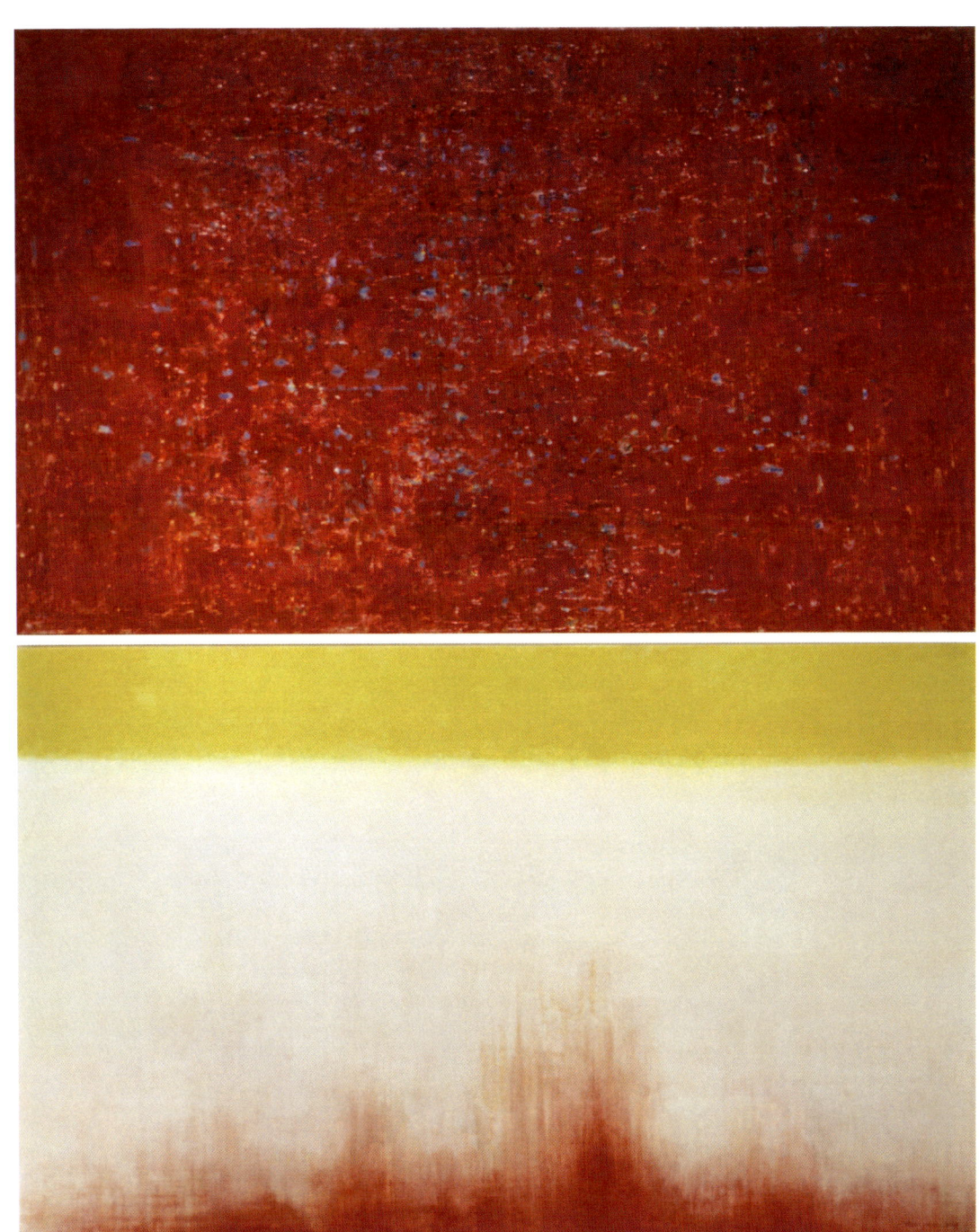

Verse · Imbuing in Red | 2004
Oil on linen over panel
49 × 78 inches

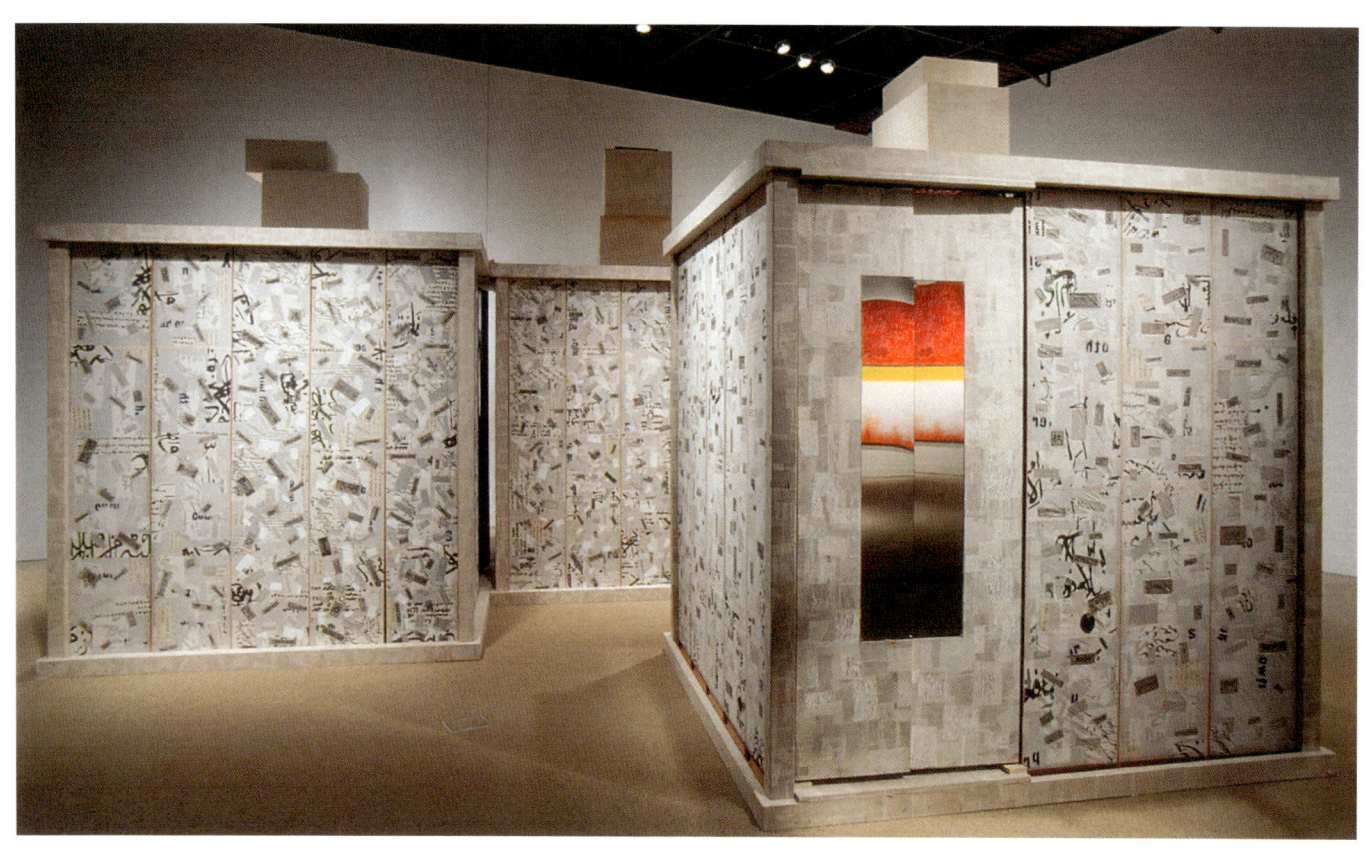

Topophilia · Imbuing Seasons | 2004
Multi-media installation with printed images, projections, and sound
89 × 92 × 89 inches each of 4 rooms
Installation at the Northwest Museum of Arts and Culture, Spokane

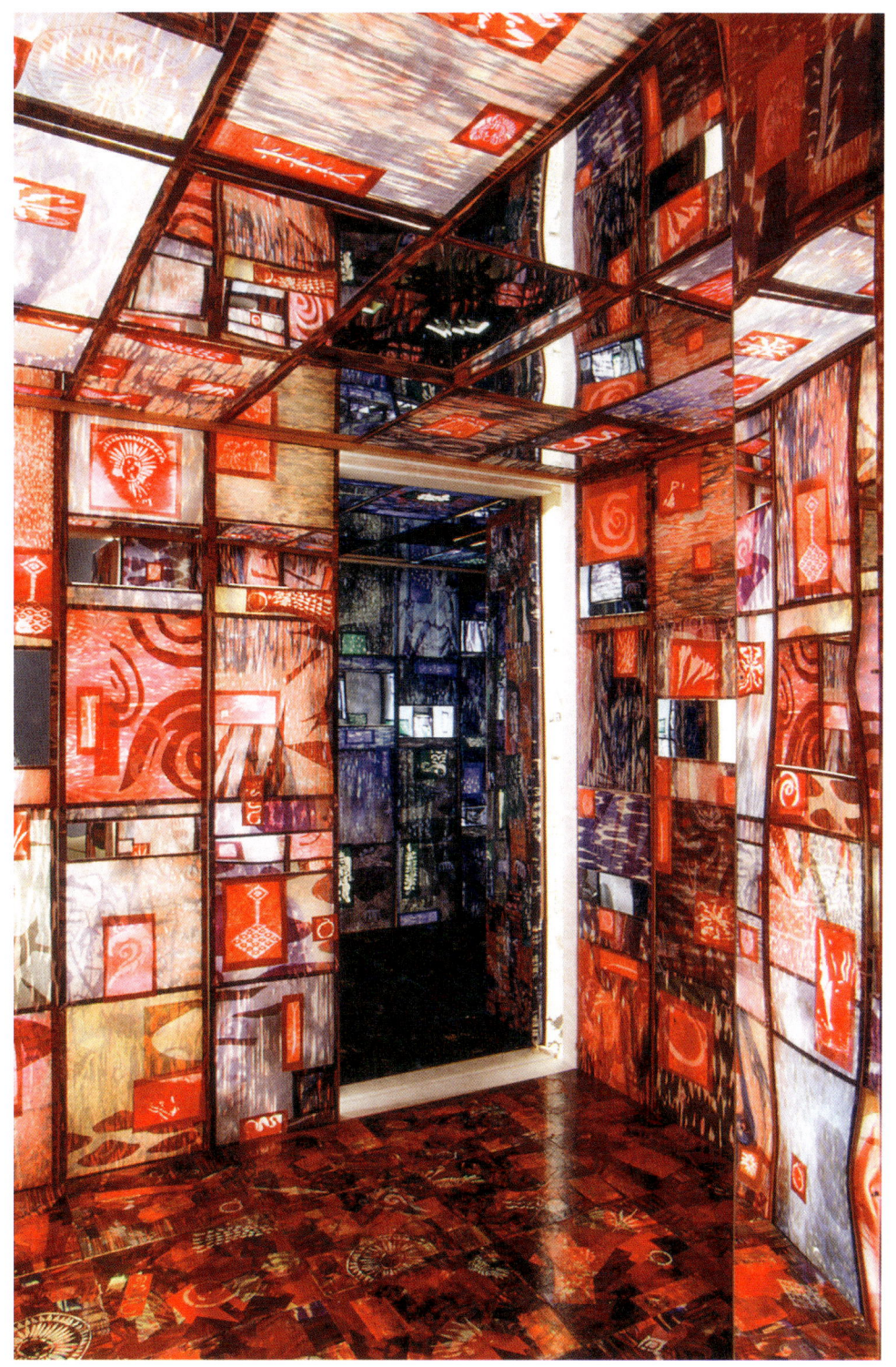

Topophilia · Imbuing Seasons (interior) | 2004
Multi-media installation with printed images, projections, and sound
89 × 92 × 89 inches each of 4 rooms
Installation at the Northwest Museum of Arts and Culture, Spokane

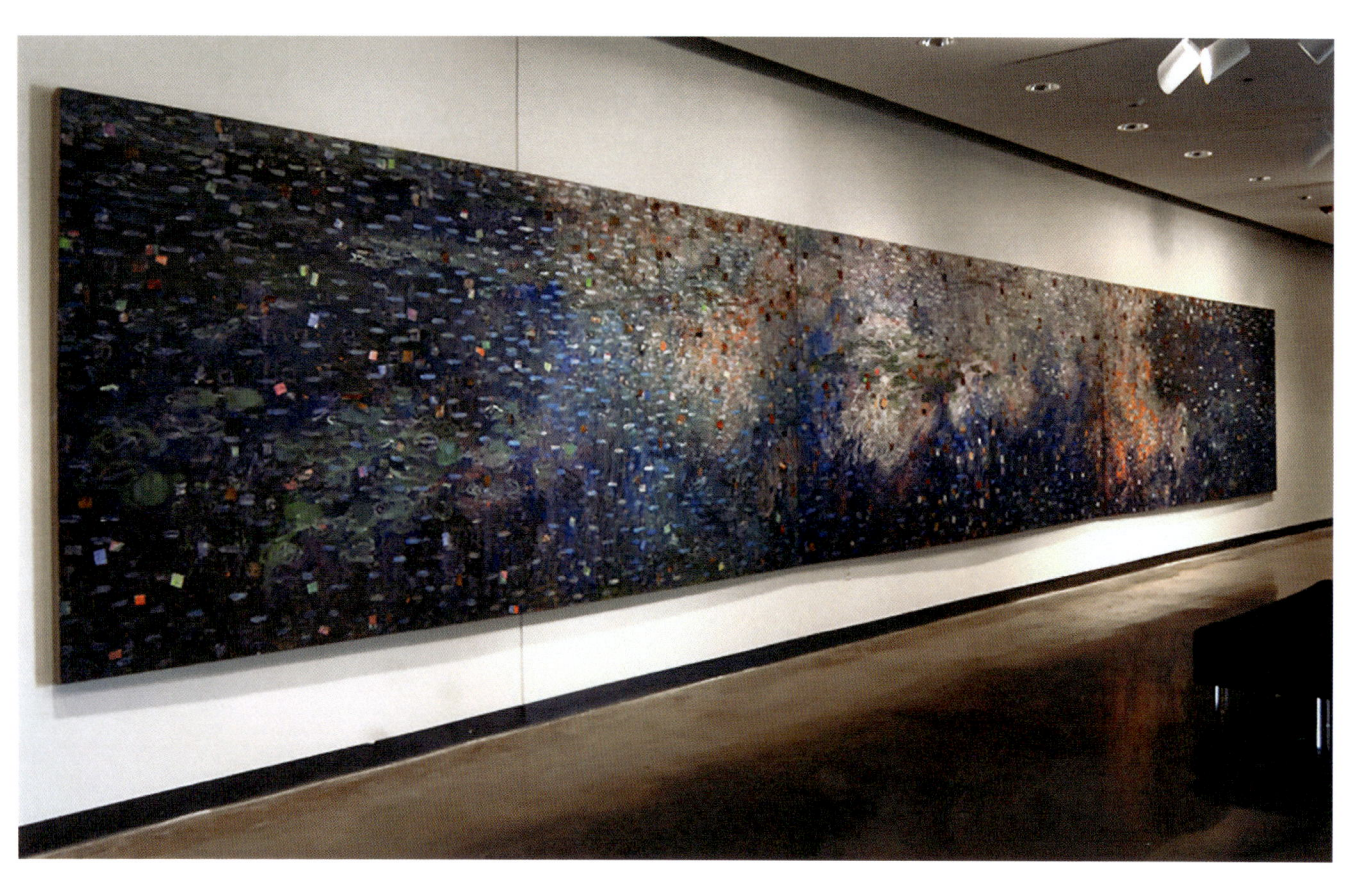

Topophilia · Imbuing in Monet | 2005
Oil and collage on linen
72 × 504 inches
Private collection

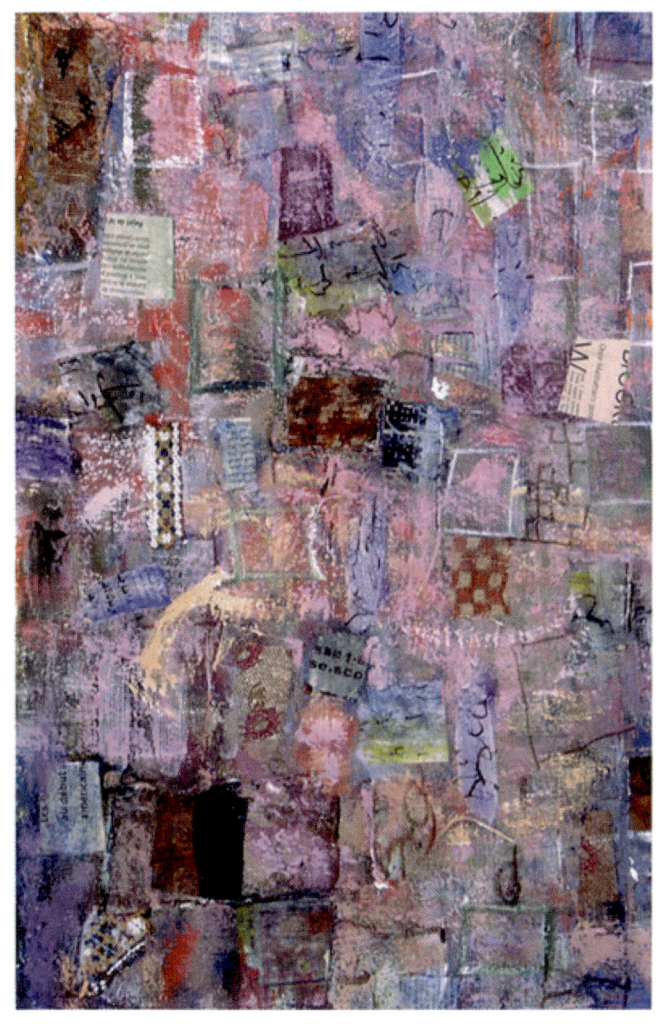

Topophilia · Imbuing in Monet (detail) | 2005
Oil and collage on linen
72 × 504 inches
Private collection

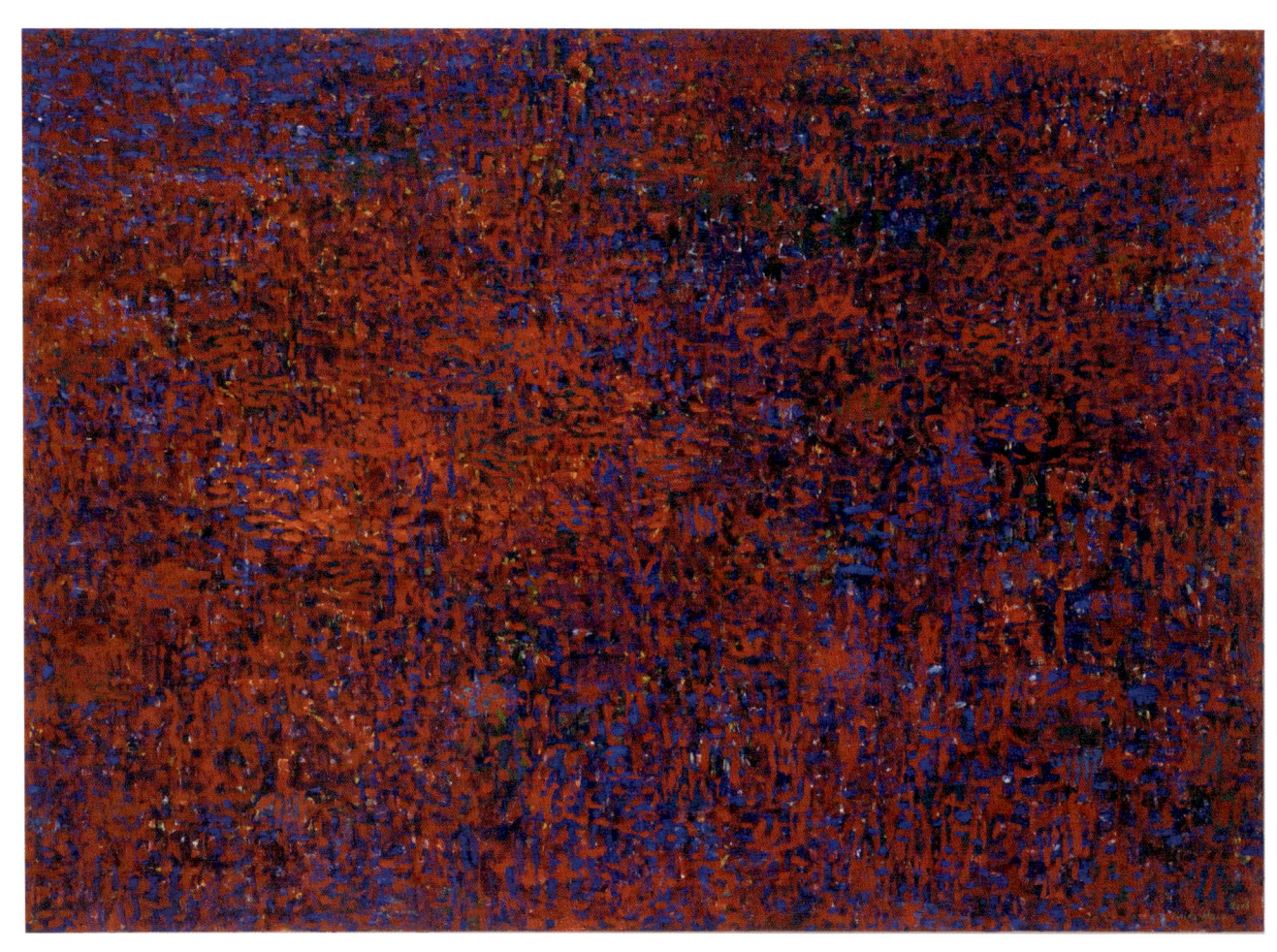

Space M · Red and Blue | 2006
Oil on linen
52 × 74 inches
Private collection

Space M · White | 2006
Graphite and gouache on paper
47 × 31.5 inches

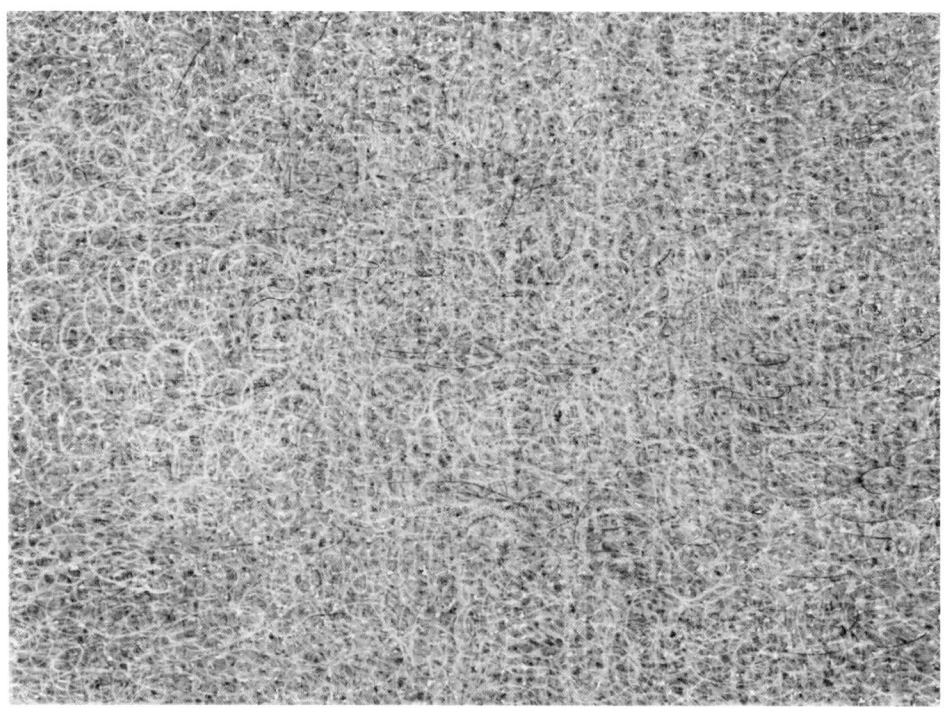

Verse · Space M-I | 2006
Lithograph and stencil print | Edition 25
Printed with Craig Cornwall at Trilobite Workshop | 22 × 30 inches
Collection of the National Gallery of Art, Washington, DC

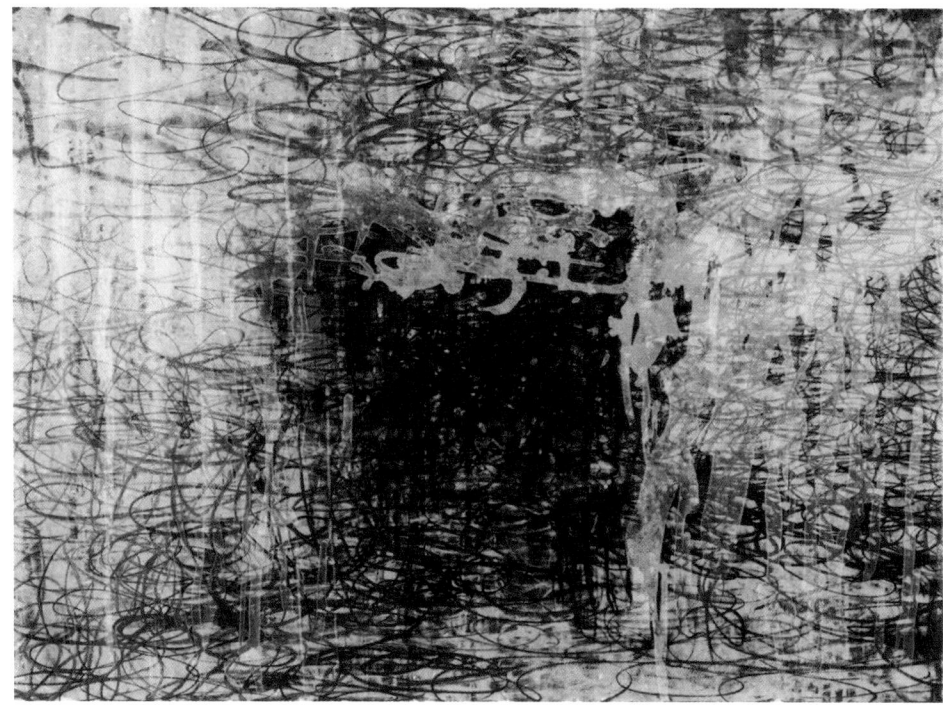

Verse · Space M-II | 2006
Lithograph and stencil print | Edition 25
Printed with Craig Cornwall at Trilobite Workshop | 22 × 30 inches
Collection of the National Gallery of Art, Washington, DC

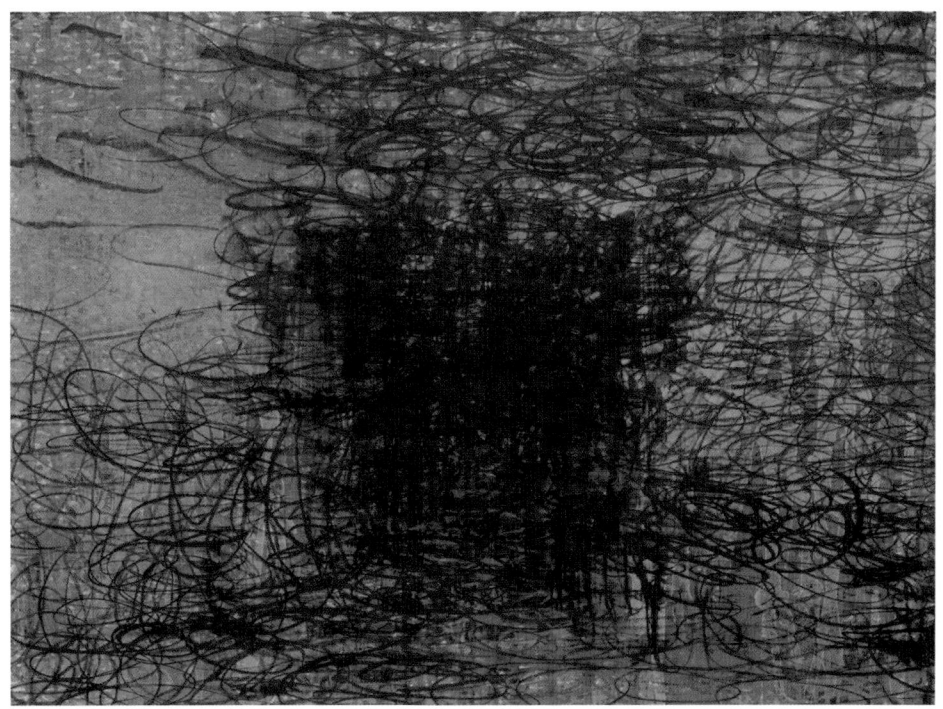

Verse · Space M-III | 2006
Lithograph and stencil print | Edition 25
Printed with Craig Cornwall at Trilobite Workshop | 22 × 30 inches
Collection of the National Gallery of Art, Washington, DC

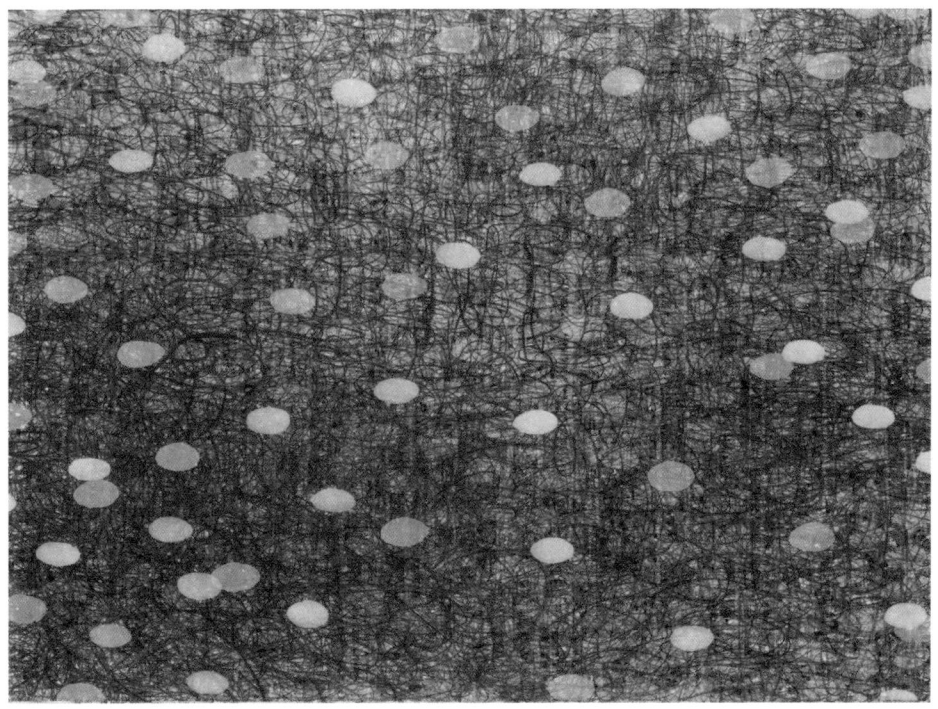

Verse · Space M-IV | 2006
Lithograph and stencil print | Edition 25
Printed with Craig Cornwall at Trilobite Workshop | 22 × 30 inches
Collection of the National Gallery of Art, Washington, DC

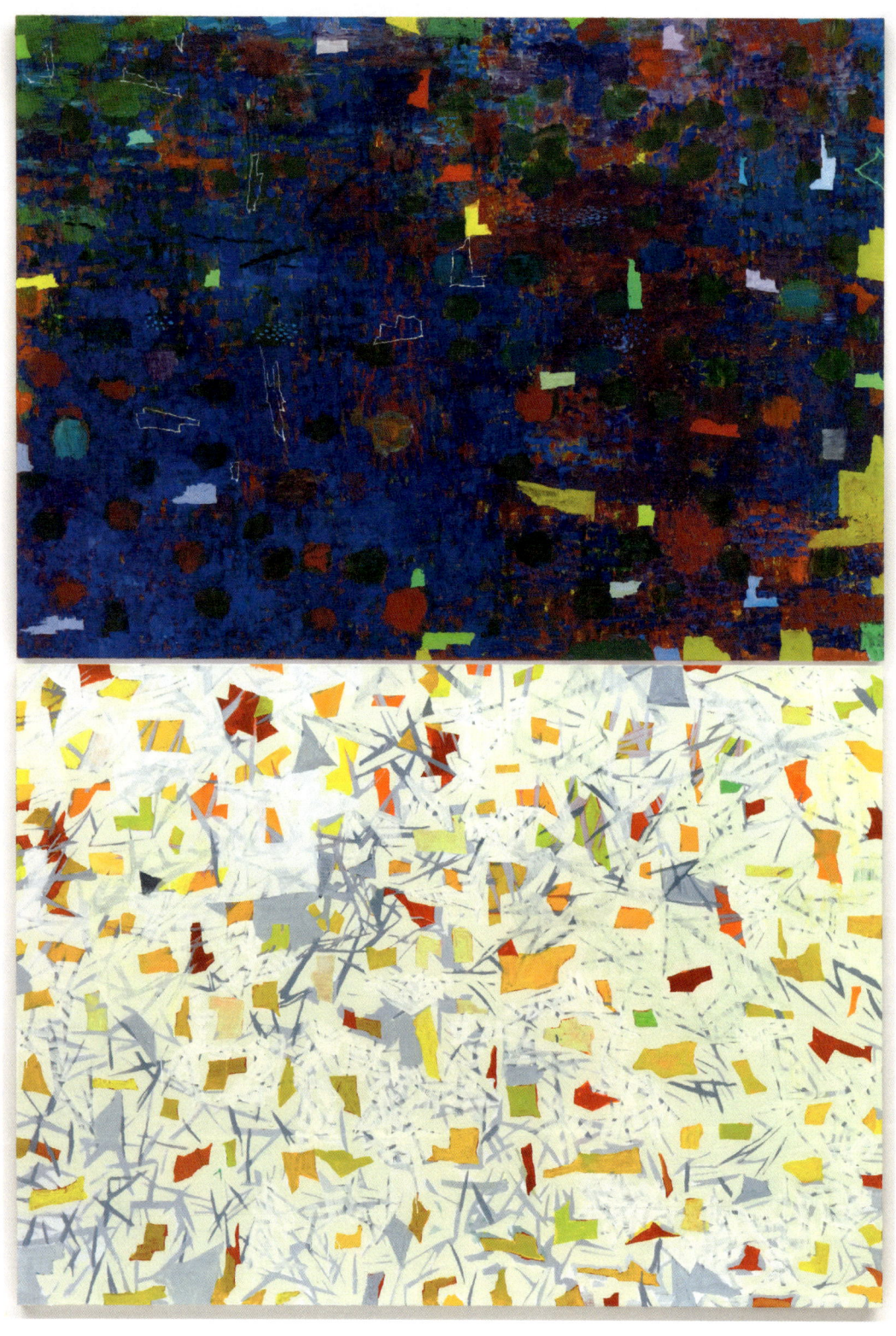

Verse · Imbuing in Space M | 2007
Oil on linen over panel
109 × 76 inches

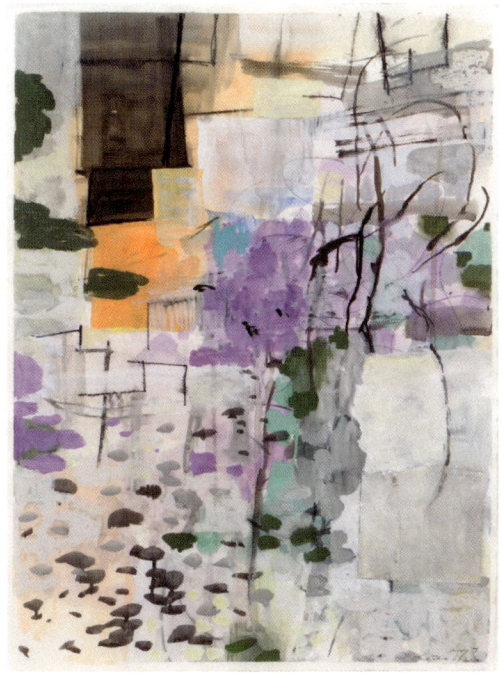

Verse · Space M b | 2007
Work on paper
22 × 15 inches
Private collection

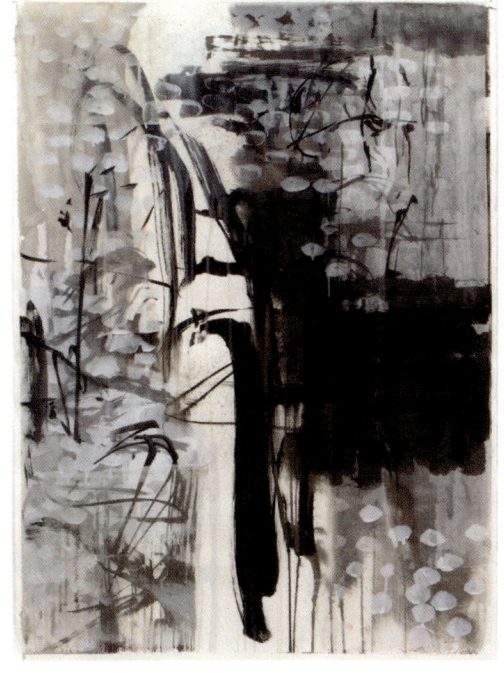

Verse · Space M c | 2007
Work on paper
22 × 15 inches
Private collection

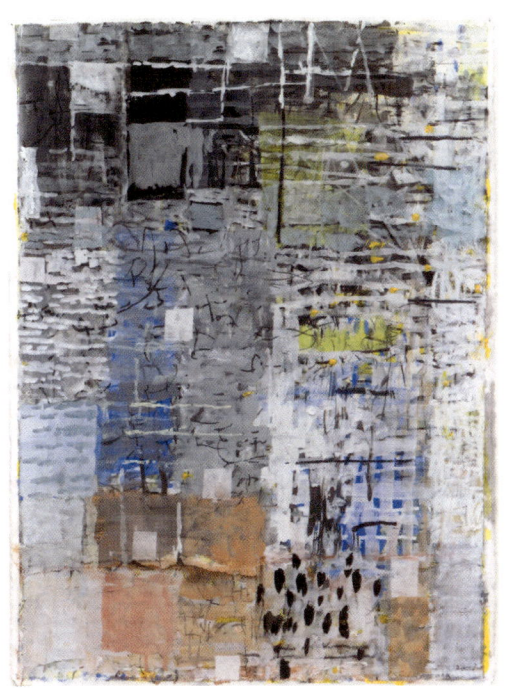

Verse · Space M d | 2007
Work on paper
22 × 15 inches
Private collection

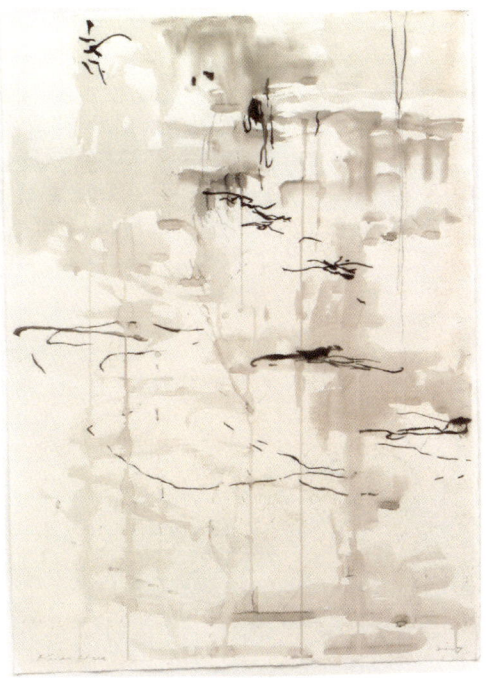

Verse · Space M e | 2007
Work on paper
22 × 15 inches
Private collection

  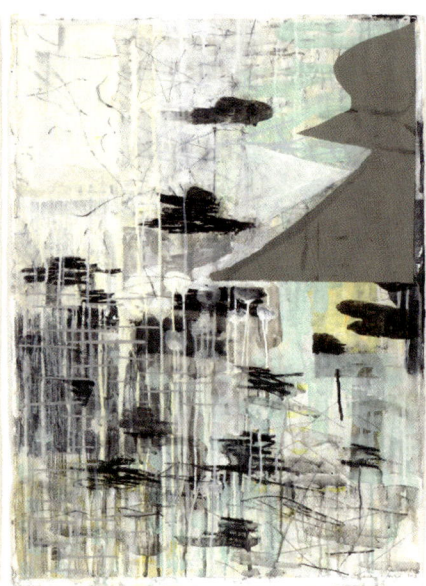

Space · Sukumu | 2010
Work on paper
42 × 91 inches

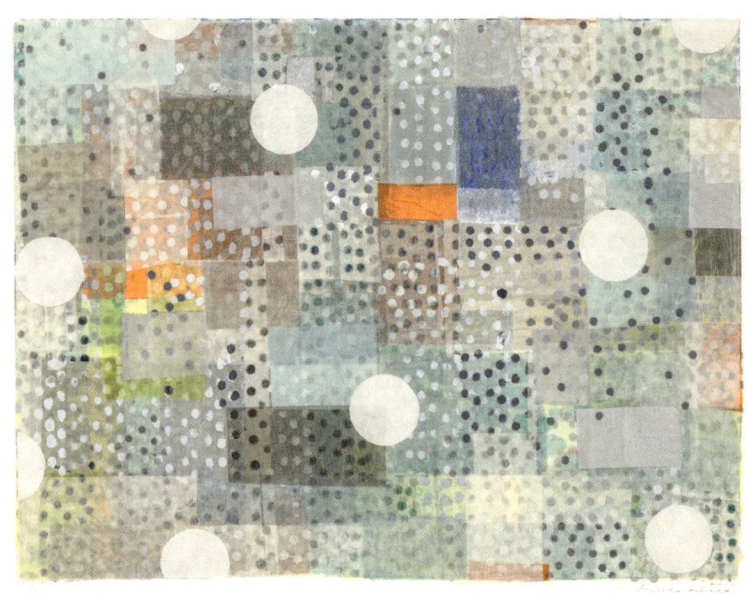

Space · Uraraka | 2010
Monotype with collage | Printed with Kathy Kuehn in New York
15 × 28 inches
Collection of the Racine Art Museum

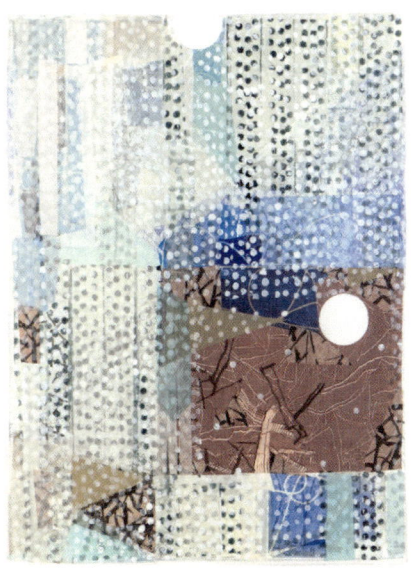
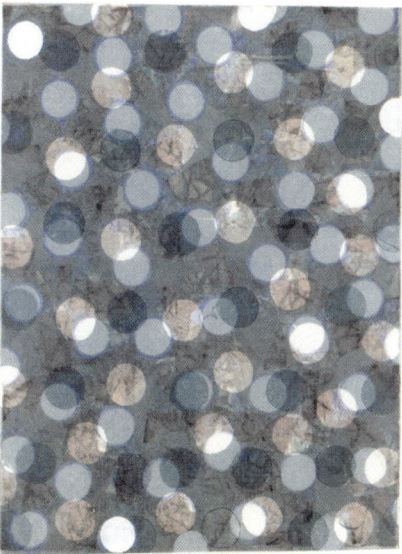
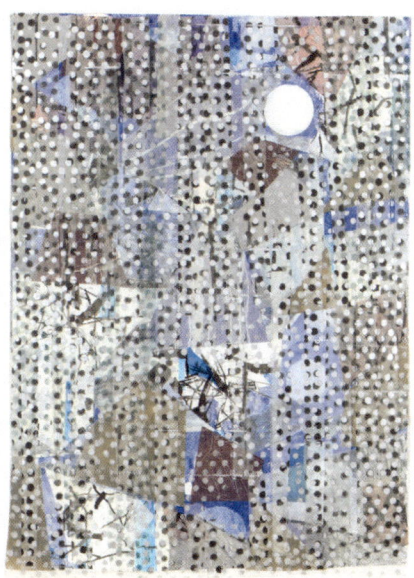

Space Sukumu · Sky 17 | 2010
Triptych monotype with collage and hand work | Printed with Kathy Kuehn in New York
20 × 46 inches
Private collection

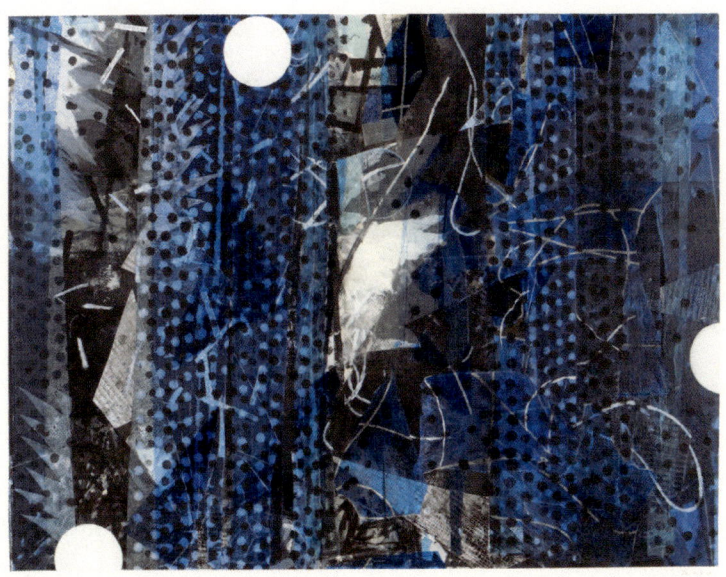

Space · Sumuko · Sky 1 | 2010
Monotype with collage | Printed with Kathy Kuehn in New York
15 × 28 inches
Collection of the Racine Art Museum

Space · Kirameku in White and Blue | 2011
Oil on linen | 84 x 216 inches
Collection of the Jordan Schnitzer Museum of Art WSU, Pullman

Verse · Gray | 2011
Work on paper
15 × 11.125 inches
Private collection

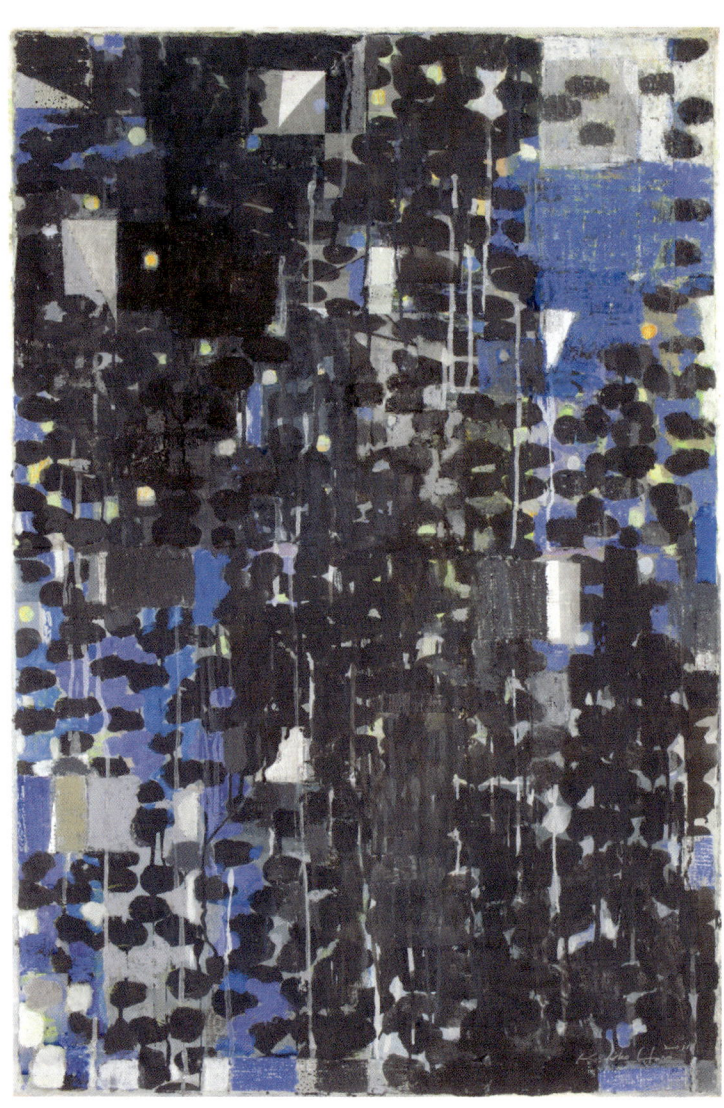

Space · Flattening | 2011
Work on paper
30 × 43.75 inches
Private collection

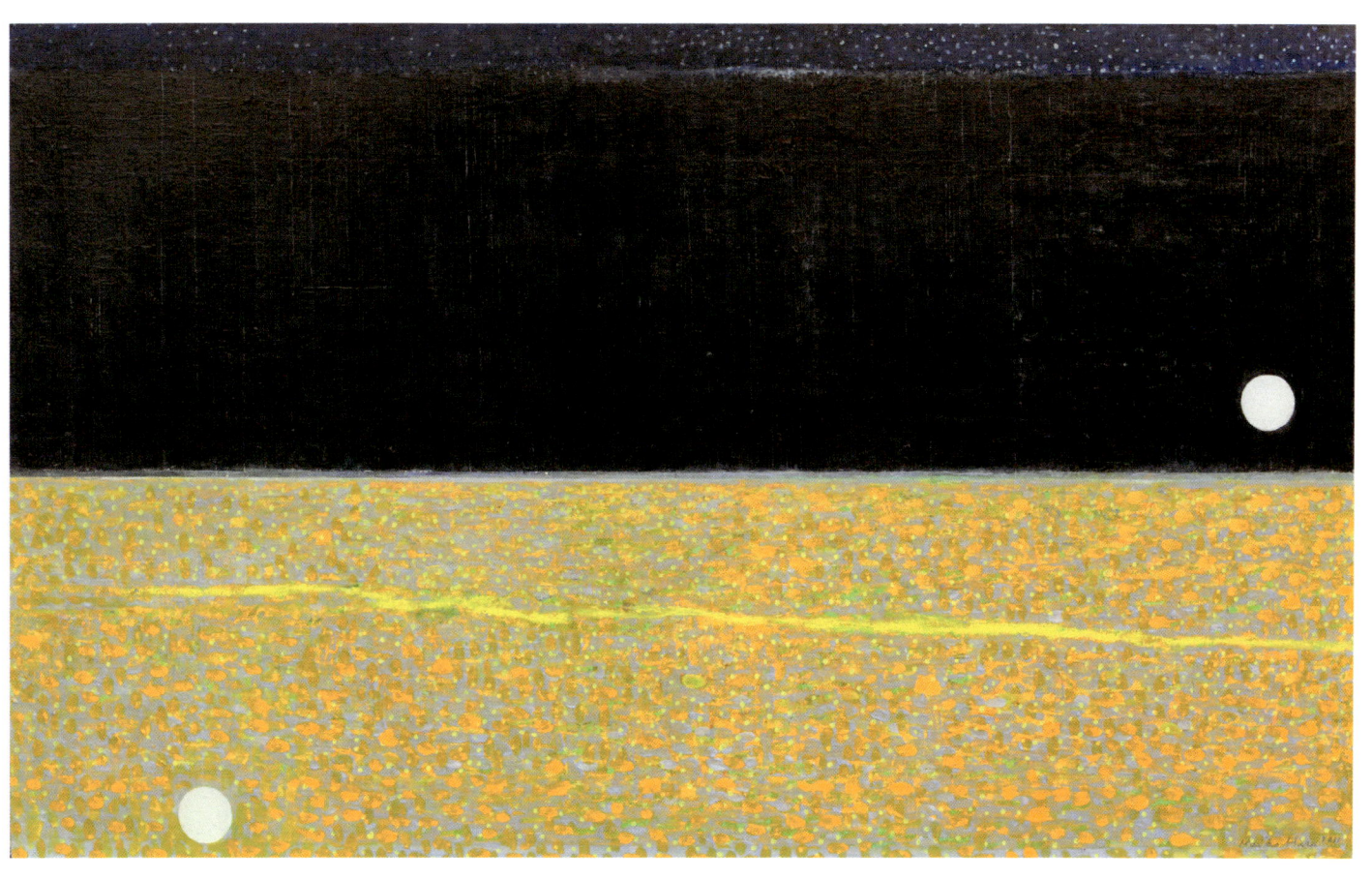

Space · 1.1 | 2011
Oil on linen
30 × 50 inches
Private collection

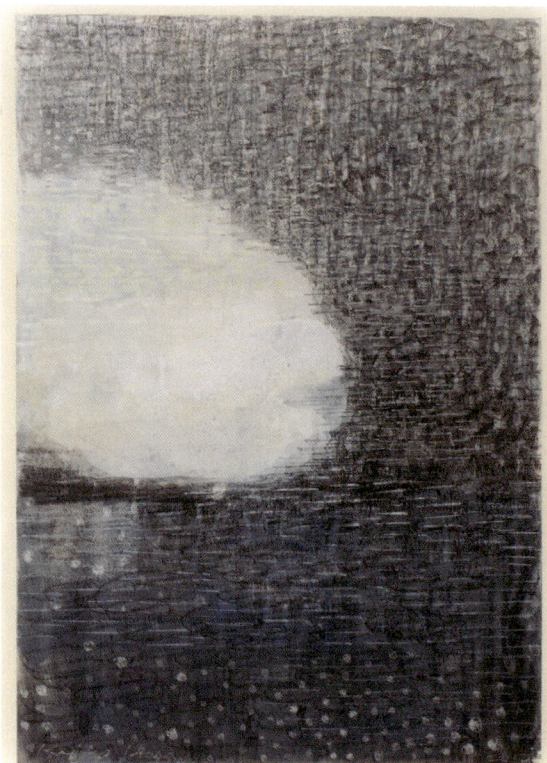

Verse · Semaru | 2012
Quadriptych; mixed-media on paper
12 × 36 inches
Private collection

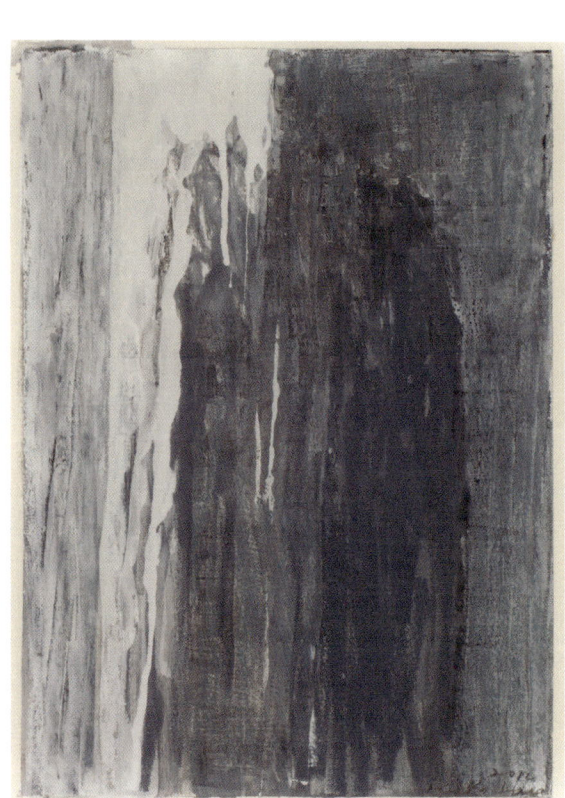
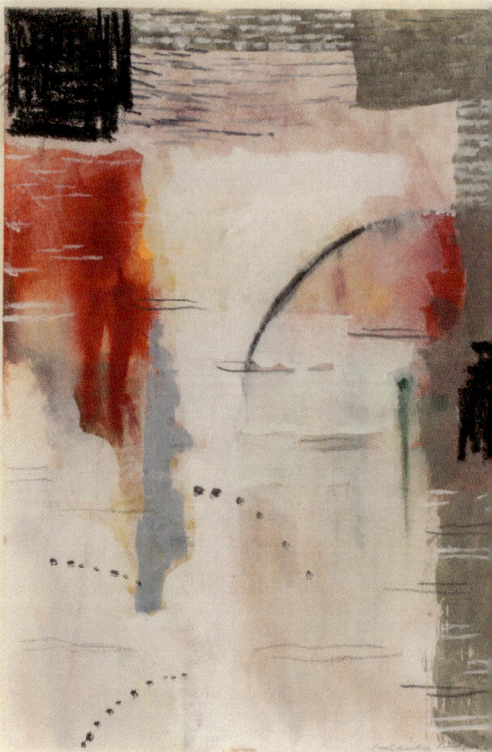

Verse · Shinto | 2012
Quadriptych; mixed-media on paper
12 × 36 inches
Private collection

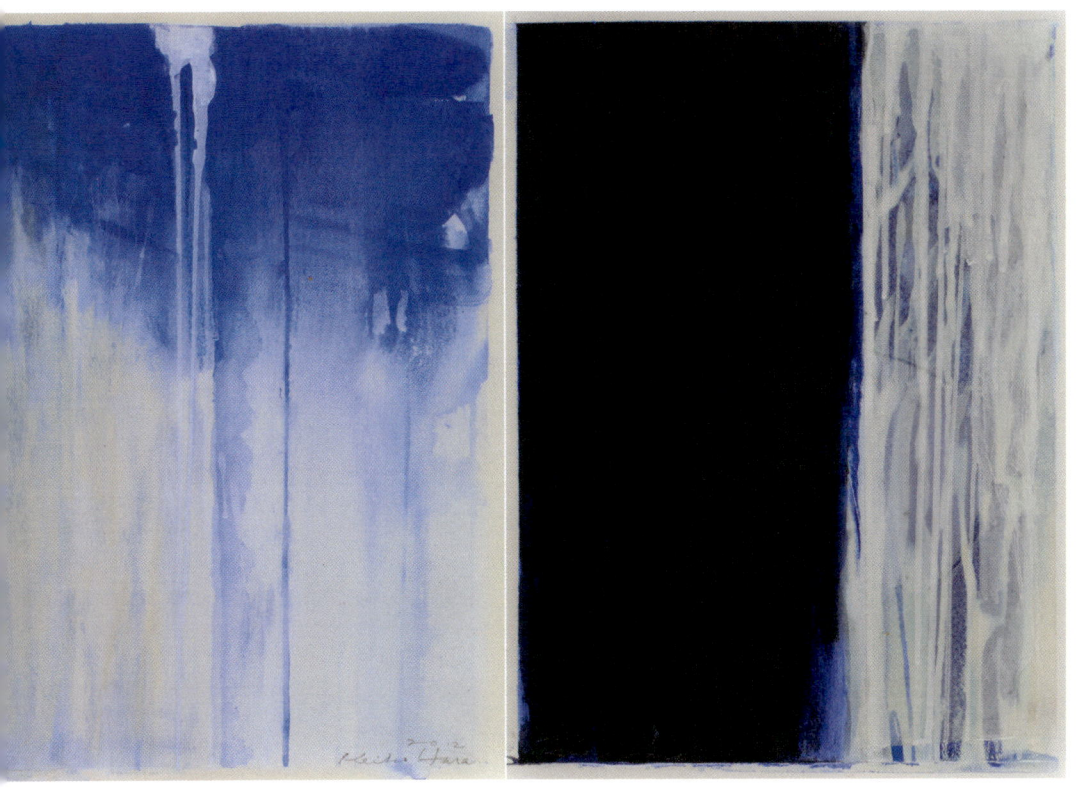

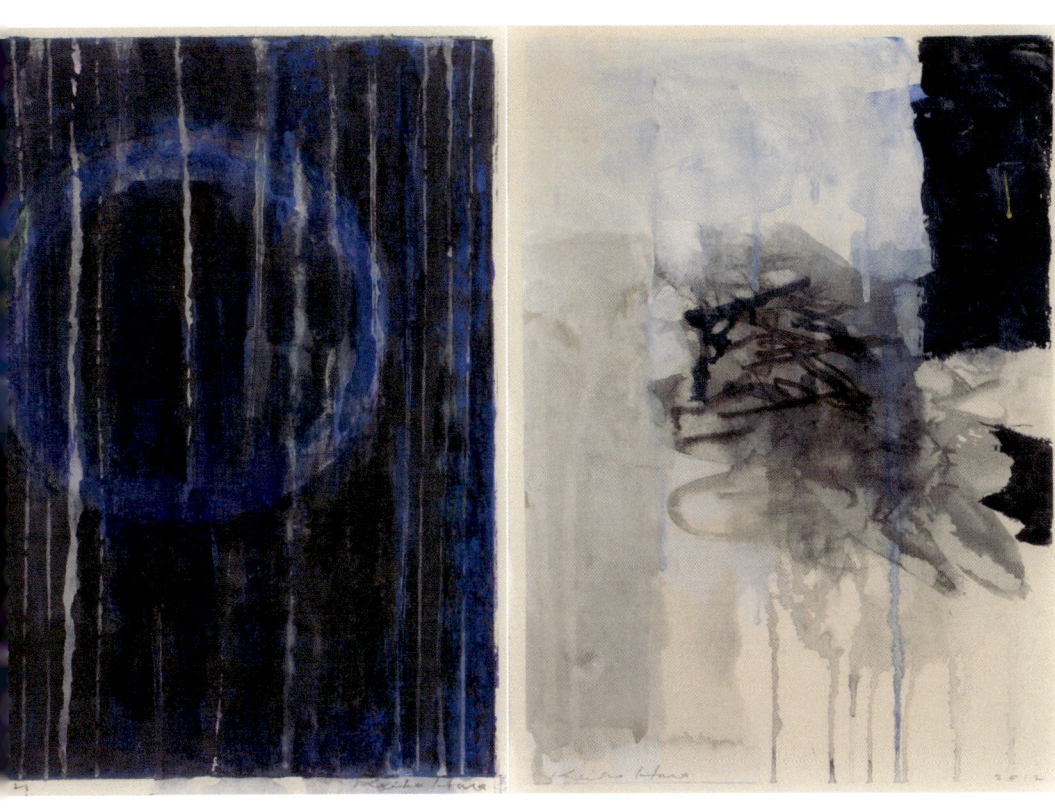

83

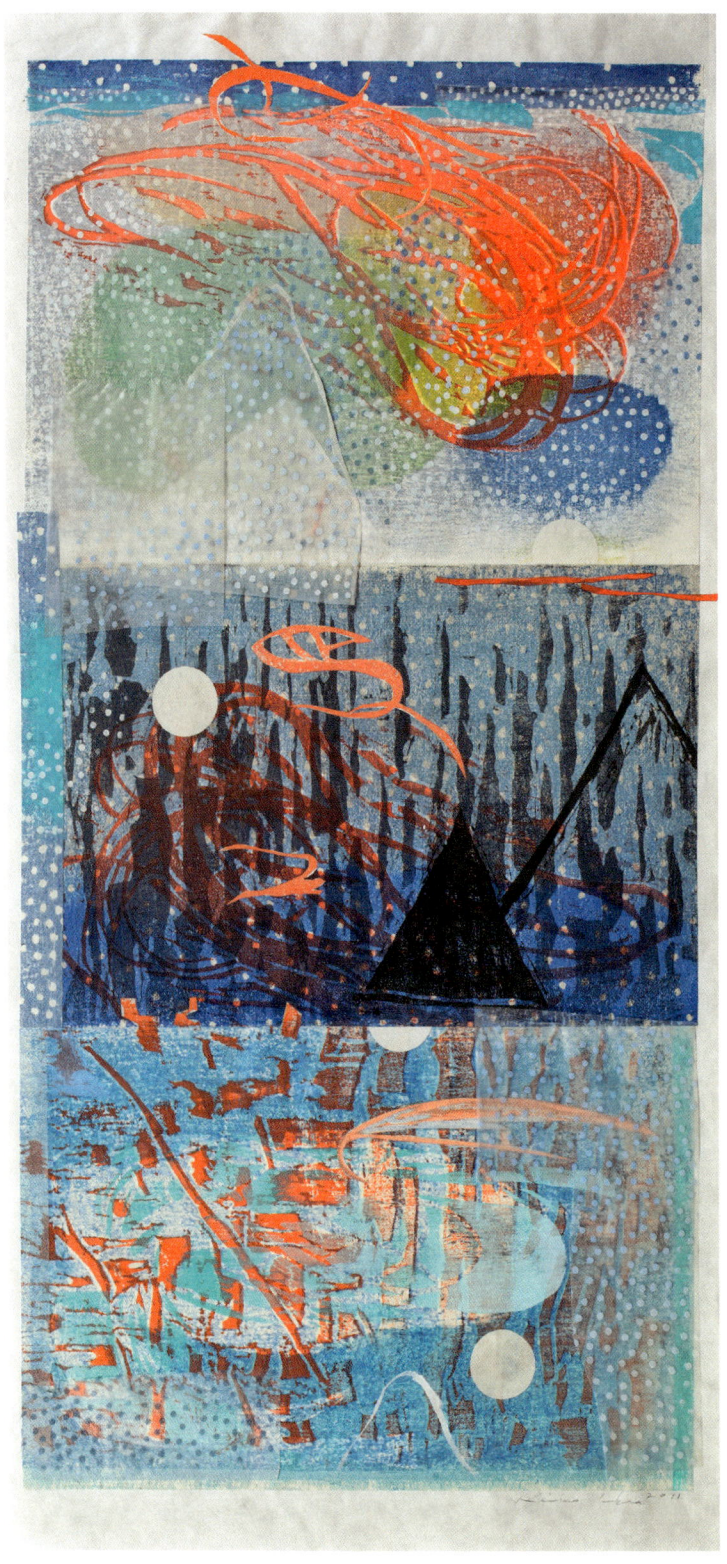

Verse · Sukumu 1.3.12 | 2012
Monoprint with mokuhanga woodblock, stencil, and collage
32 × 16 inches
Private collection

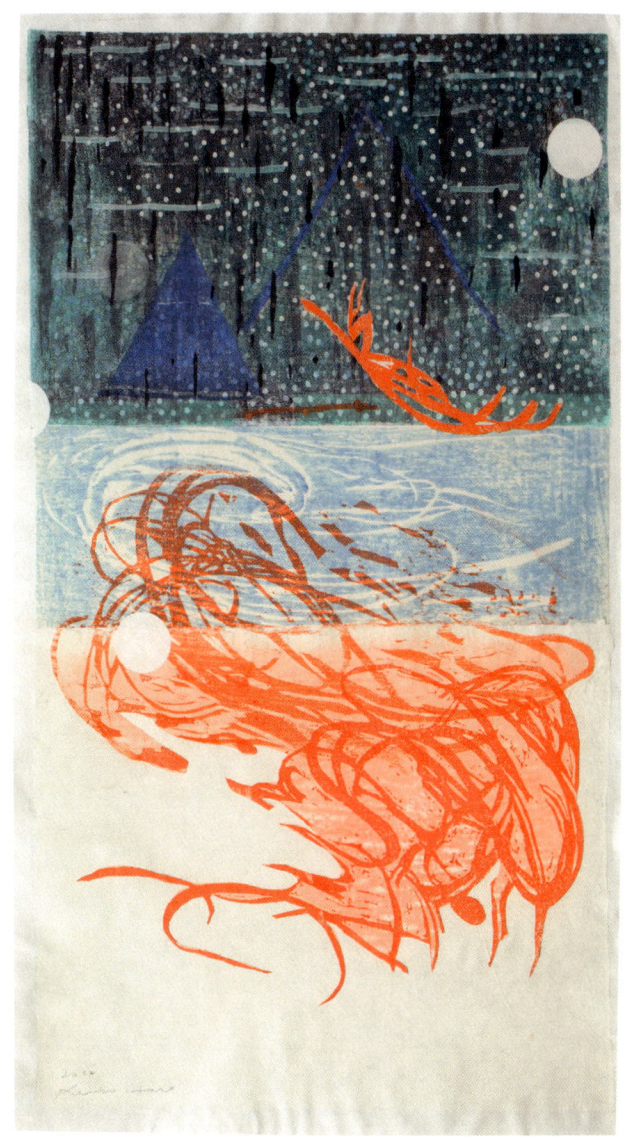

Verse · Sukumu 2.3.12 | 2012
Monoprint with mokuhanga woodblock, stencil, and collage
21.5 × 16 inches
Private collection

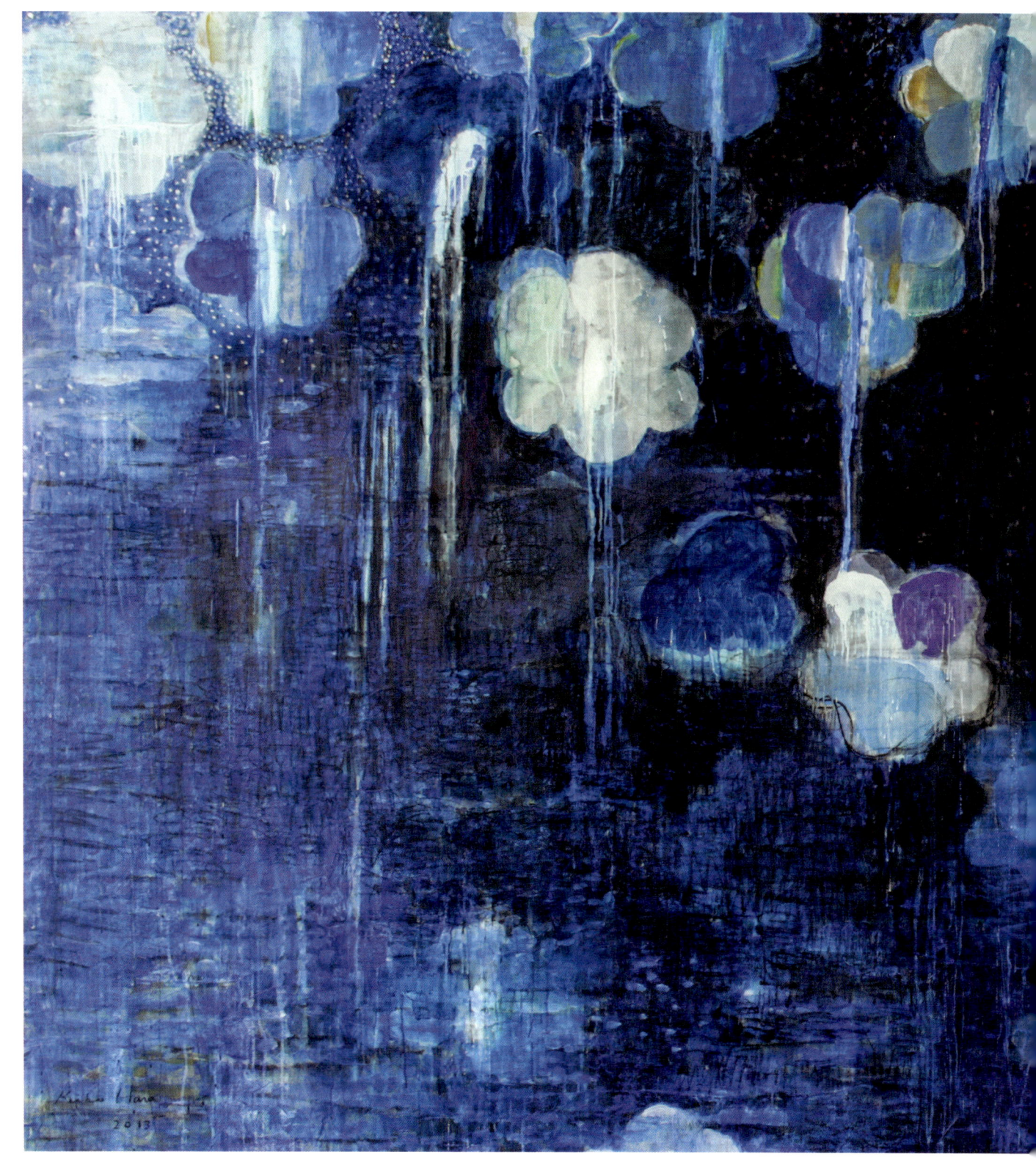

Verse · Ma and Ki | 2013
Water-based mixed-medium, oil, and collage on linen
74 × 140 inches

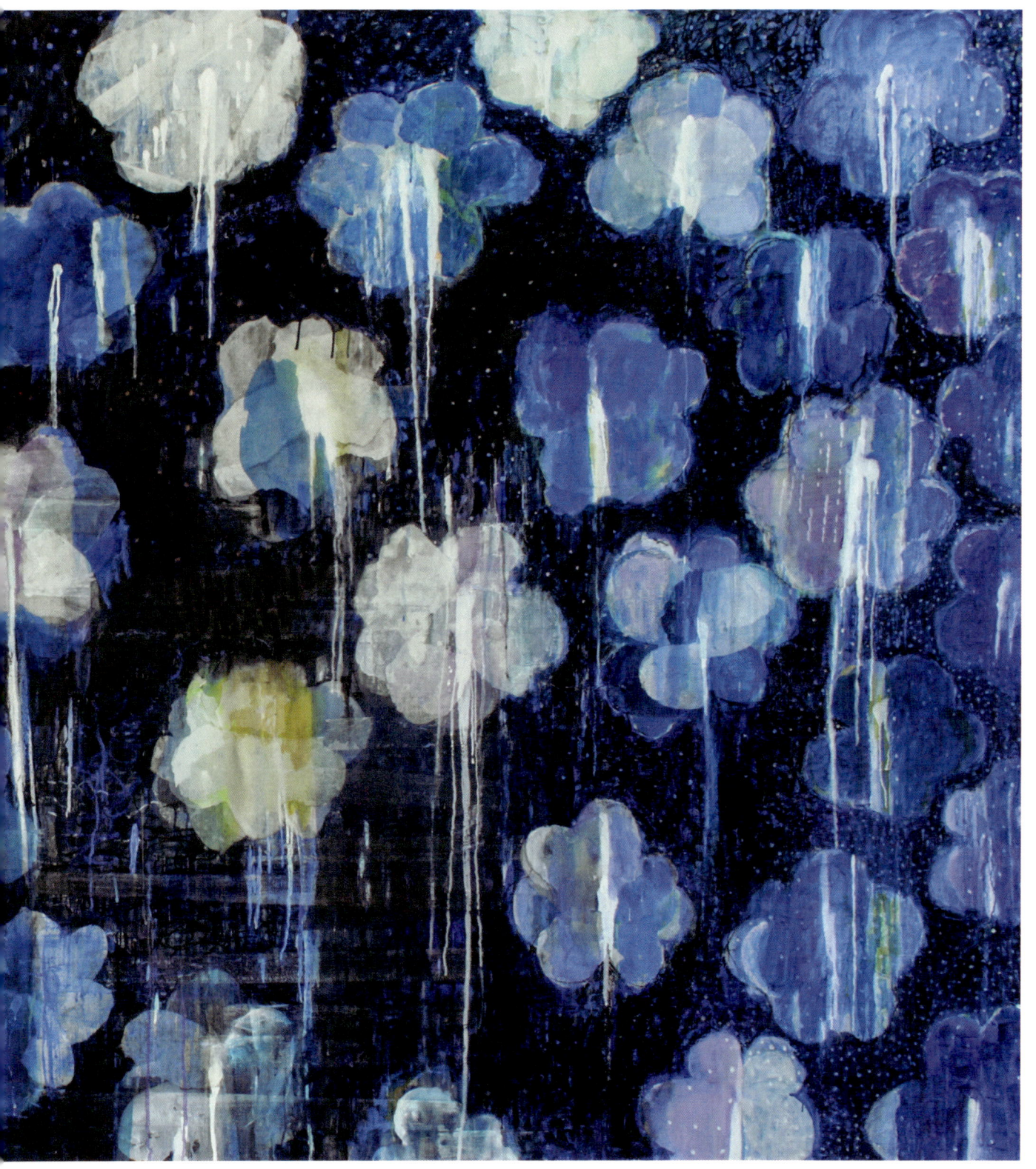

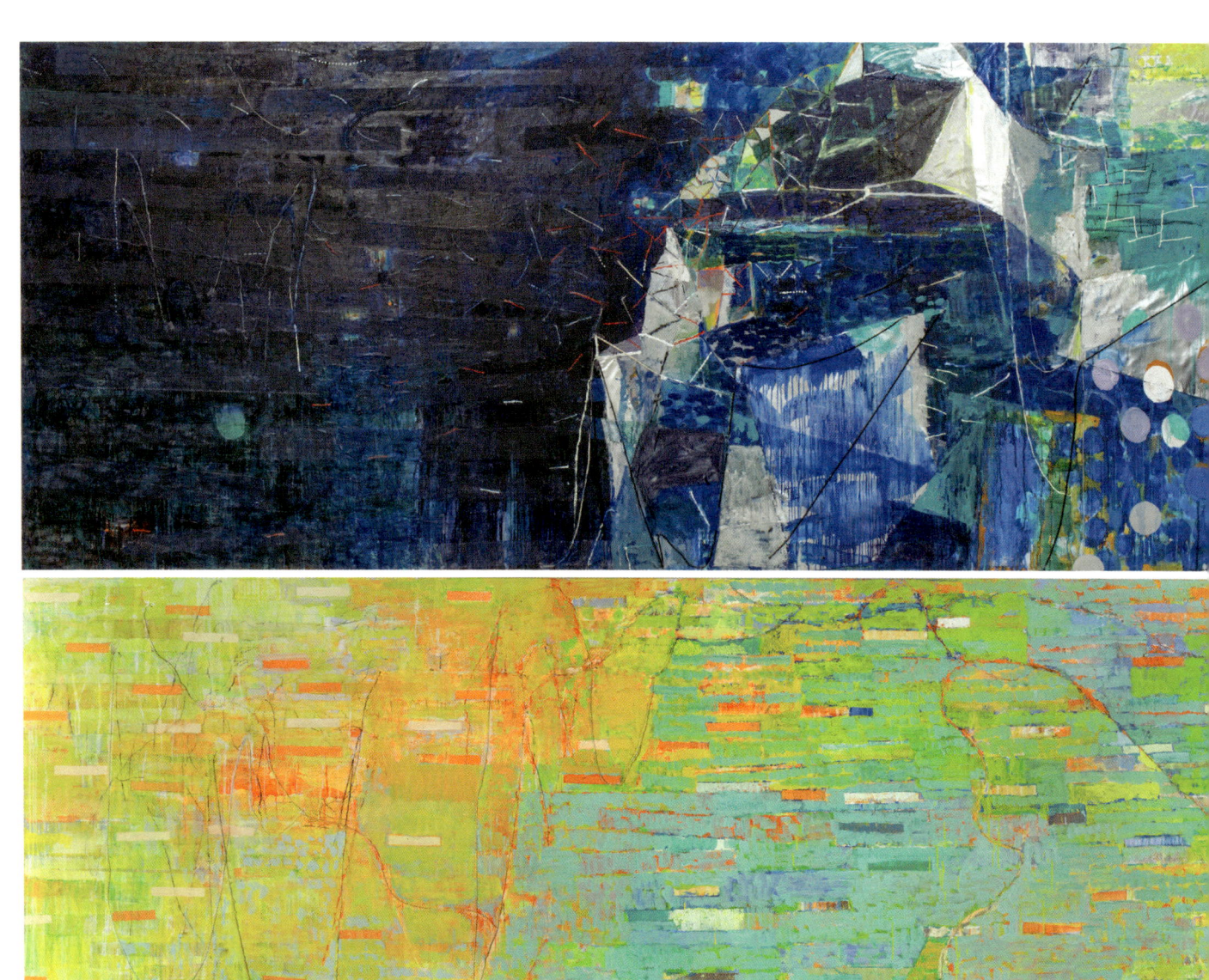

Topophilia · Ma and Ki in Memory | 2015
Oil with collage on canvas
142 × 288 inches

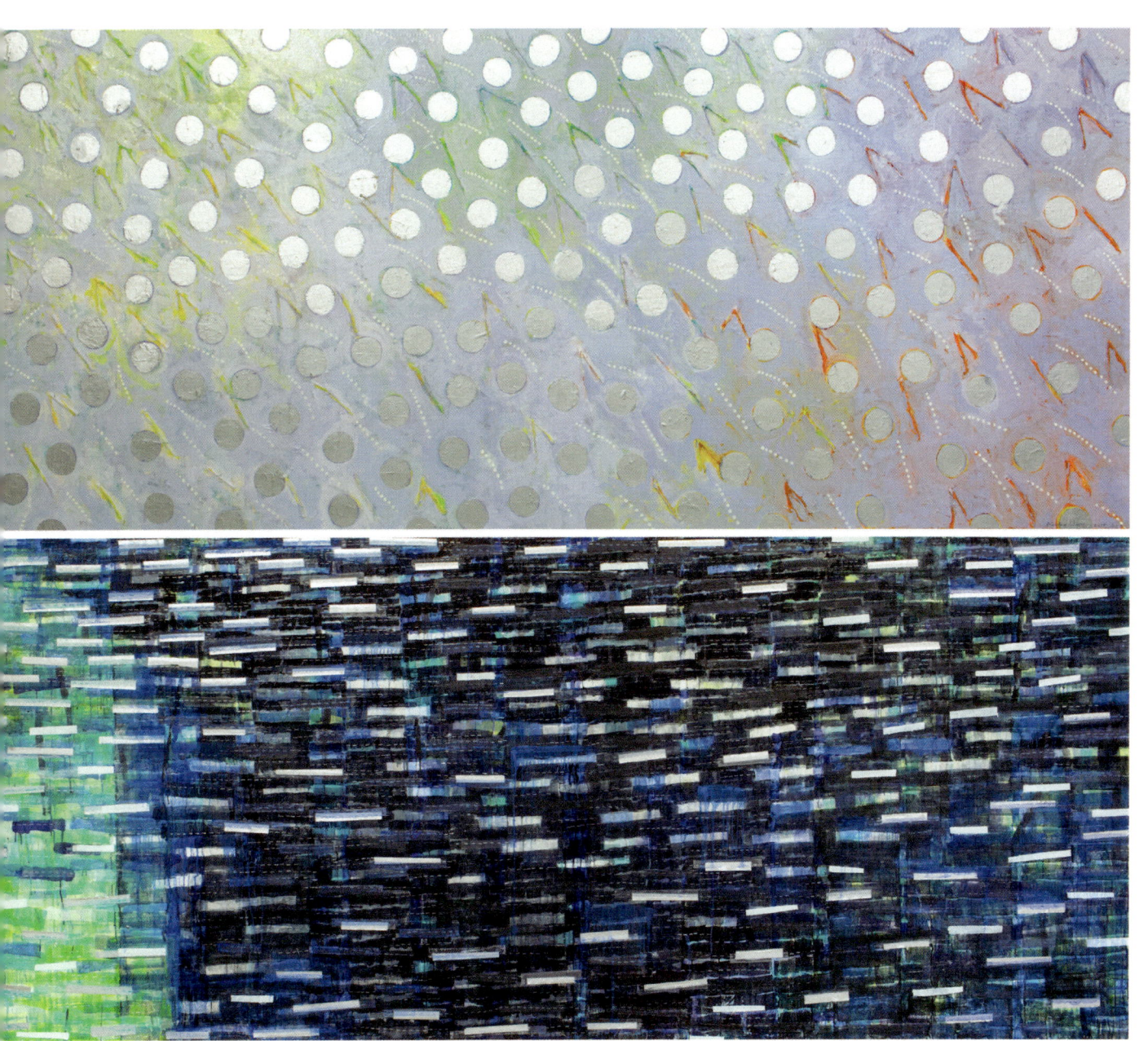

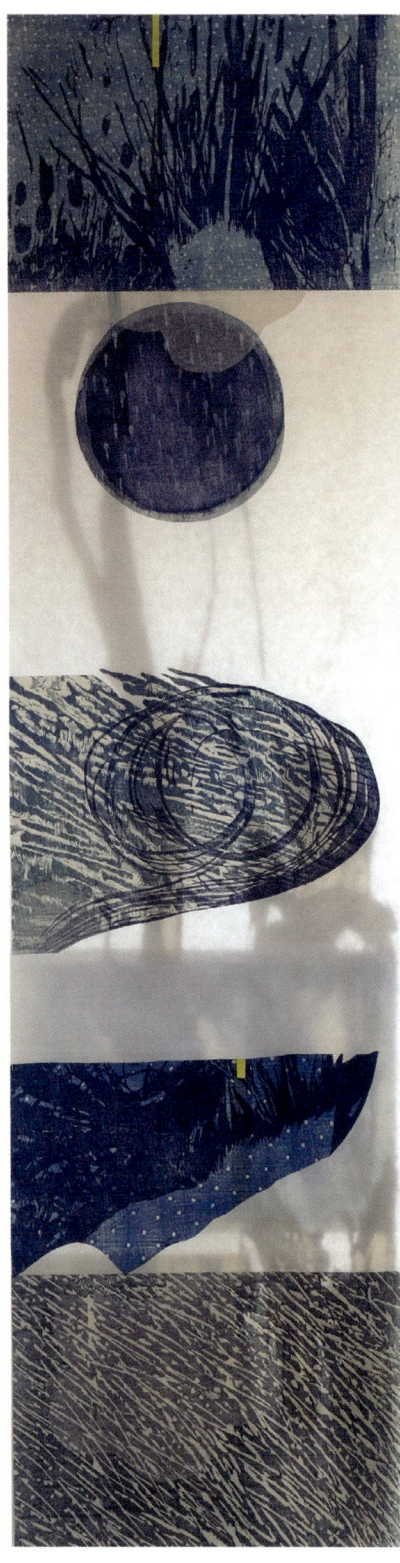

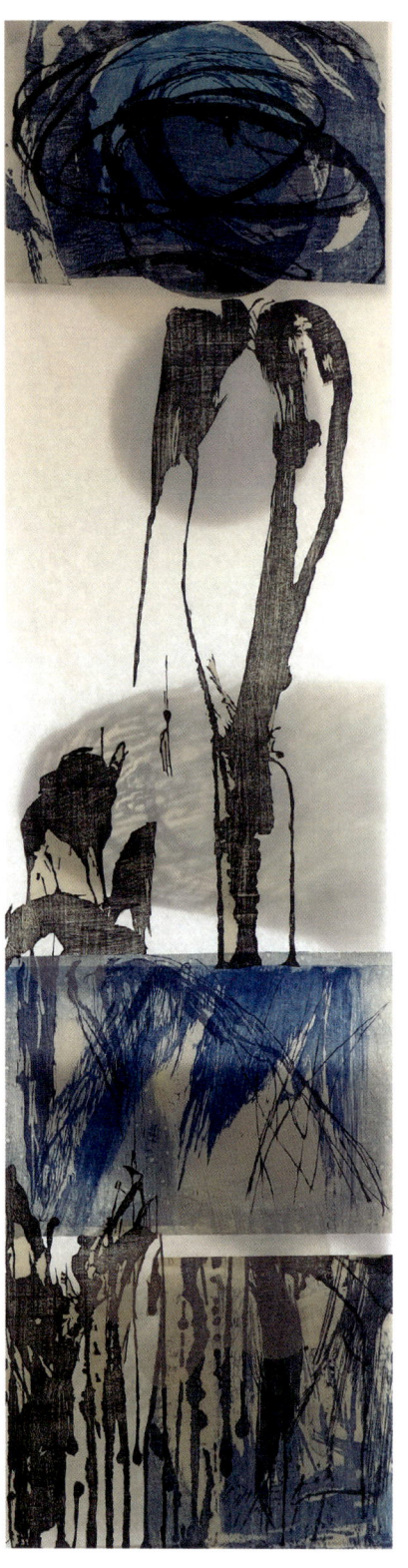

Verse · Ma and Ki · Memory (front) | 2016
Mokuhanga monoprint with collage and silk gauze
Two panels hung back-to-back | 84 × 24 inches

Verse · Ma and Ki · Memory (back) | 2016
Mokuhanga monoprint with collage and silk gauze
Two panels hung back-to-back | 84 × 24 inches

Verse R · Black and White | 2017
Mokuhanga print
13 × 11 inches
Private collection

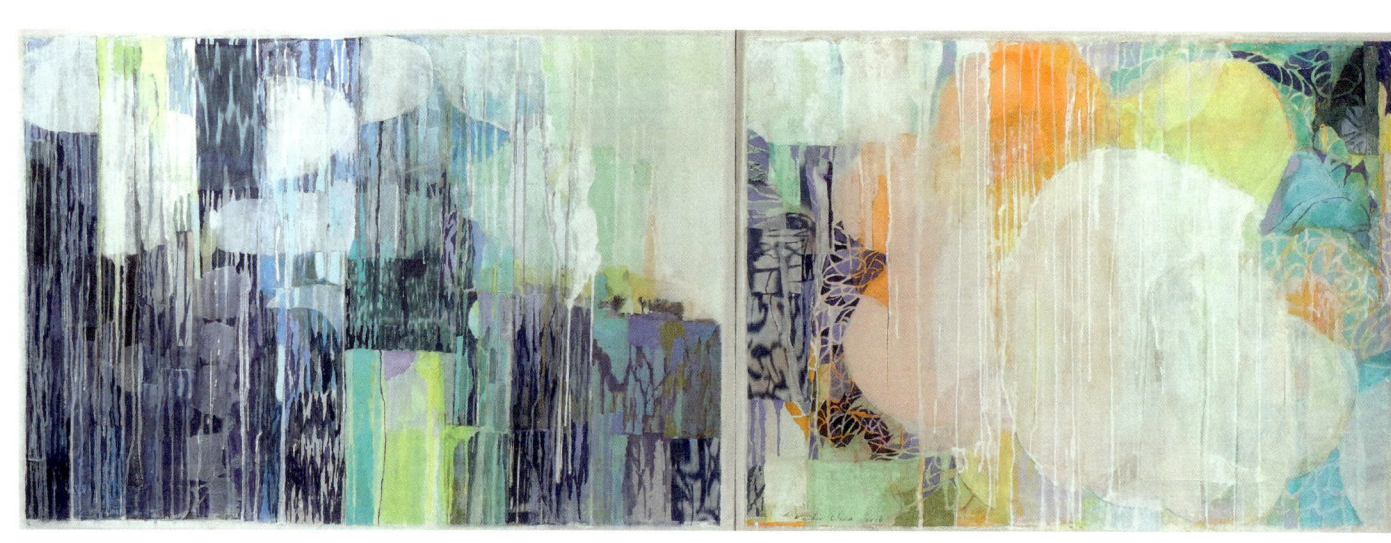

Verse · Ma and Ki I | 2016
Paper and mixed-media on board
45.5 × 75 inches
Private collection

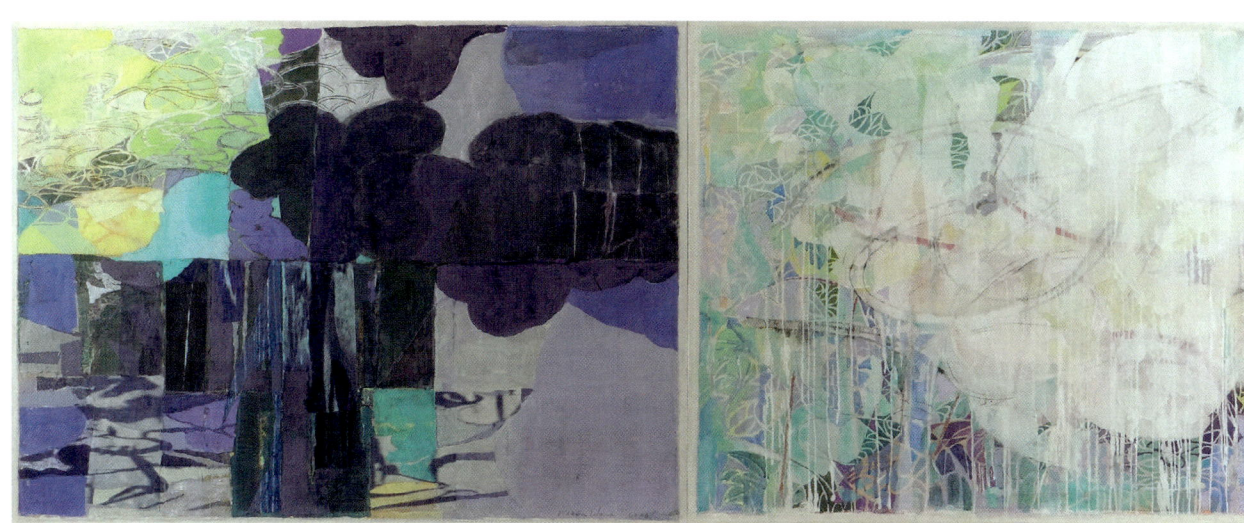

Verse · Ma and Ki II | 2016
Paper and mixed-media on board
45.5 × 75 inches
Private collection

Verse · Space · Yellow | 2016
Paper and mixed-media on board
40 × 79 × 2 inches
Private collection

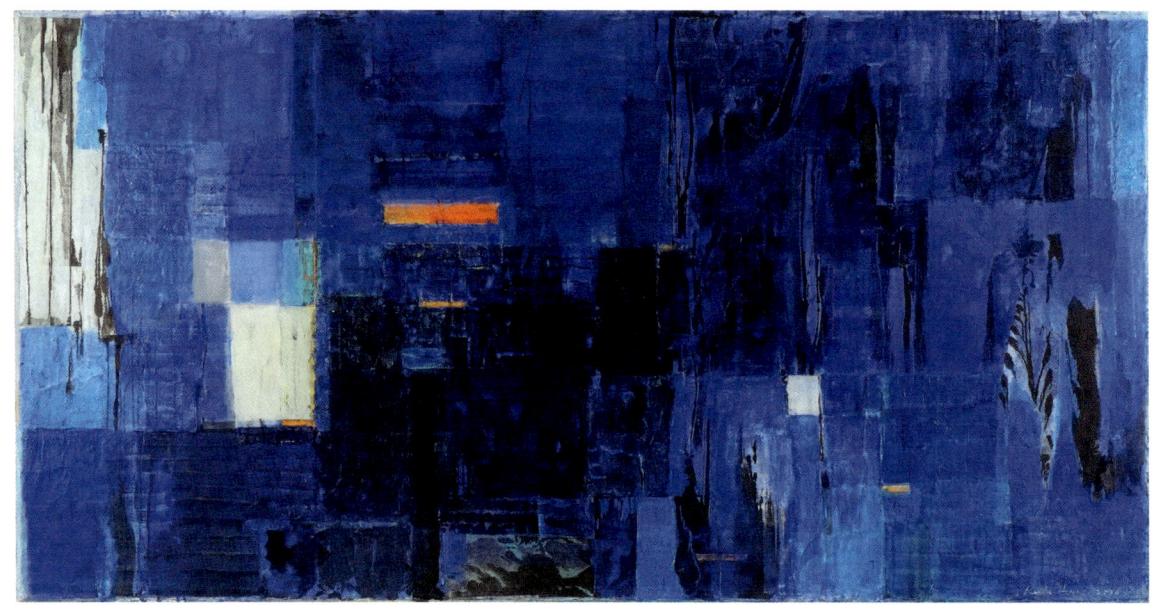

Verse · Blue with Orange | 2016
Paper and mixed-media on board
40 × 79 × 2 inches
Private collection

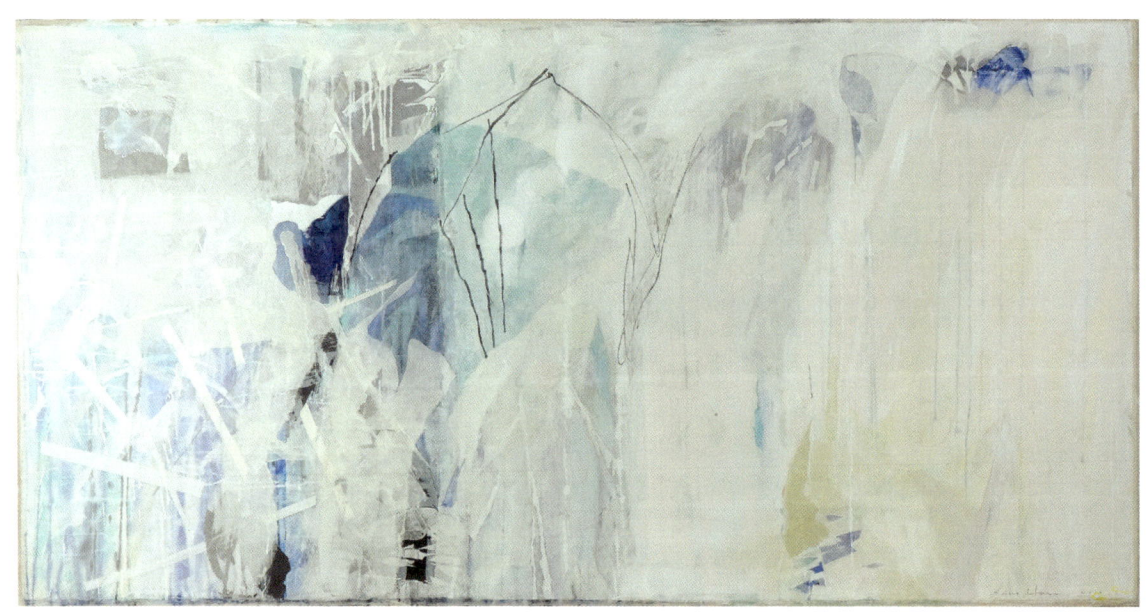

Verse · Blue with White | 2016
Paper and mixed-media on board
40 × 79 × 2 inches
Private collection

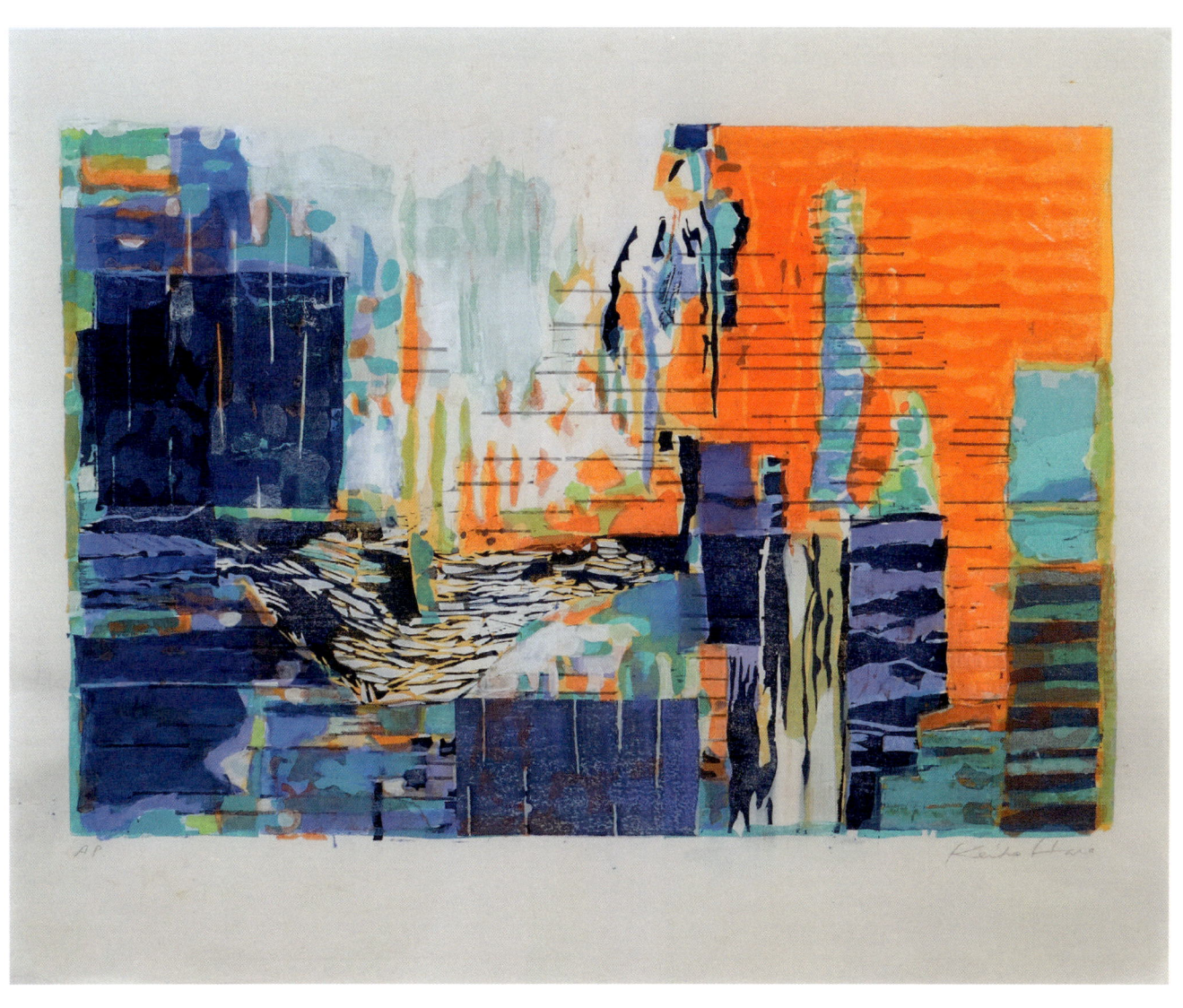

Verse · Ma and Ki · Memory | 2017
Mokuhanga print | Edition 15
12.5 × 18 inches
Private collection

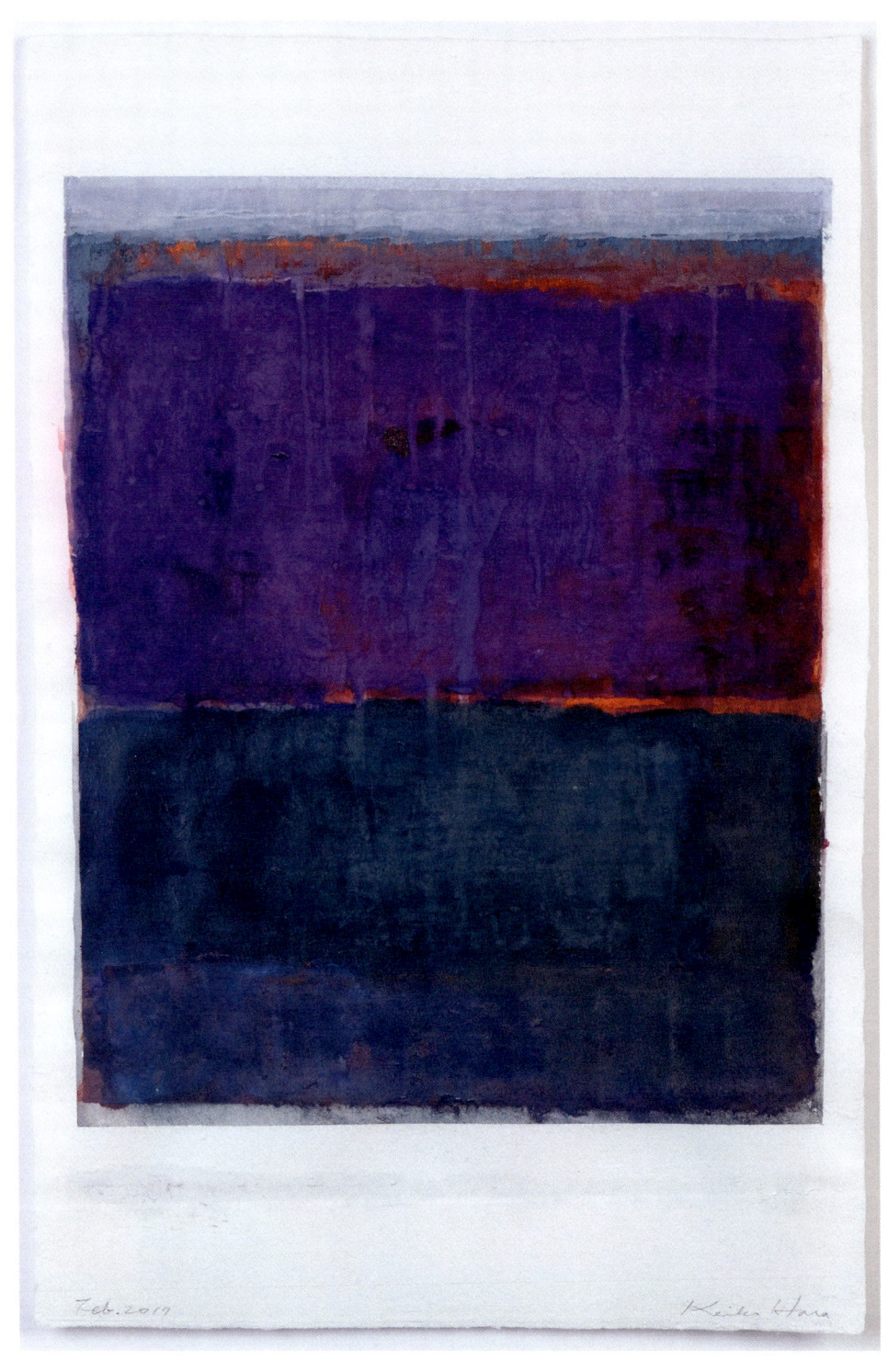

Verse R · Purple and Green | 2017
Work on paper
13.5 × 11 inches
Private collection

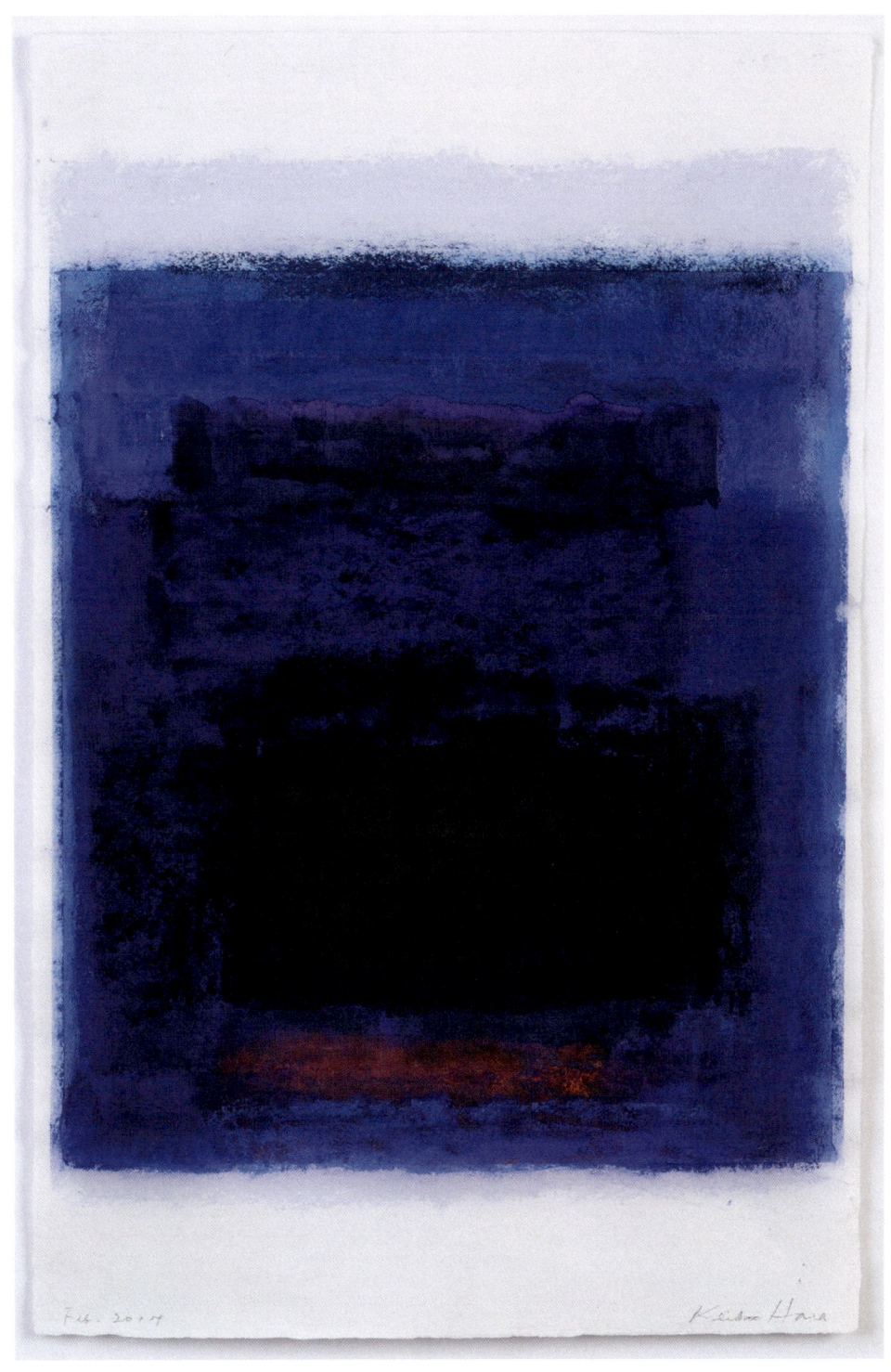

Verse R · Blue | 2017
Work on paper
13.5 × 11 inches
Private collection

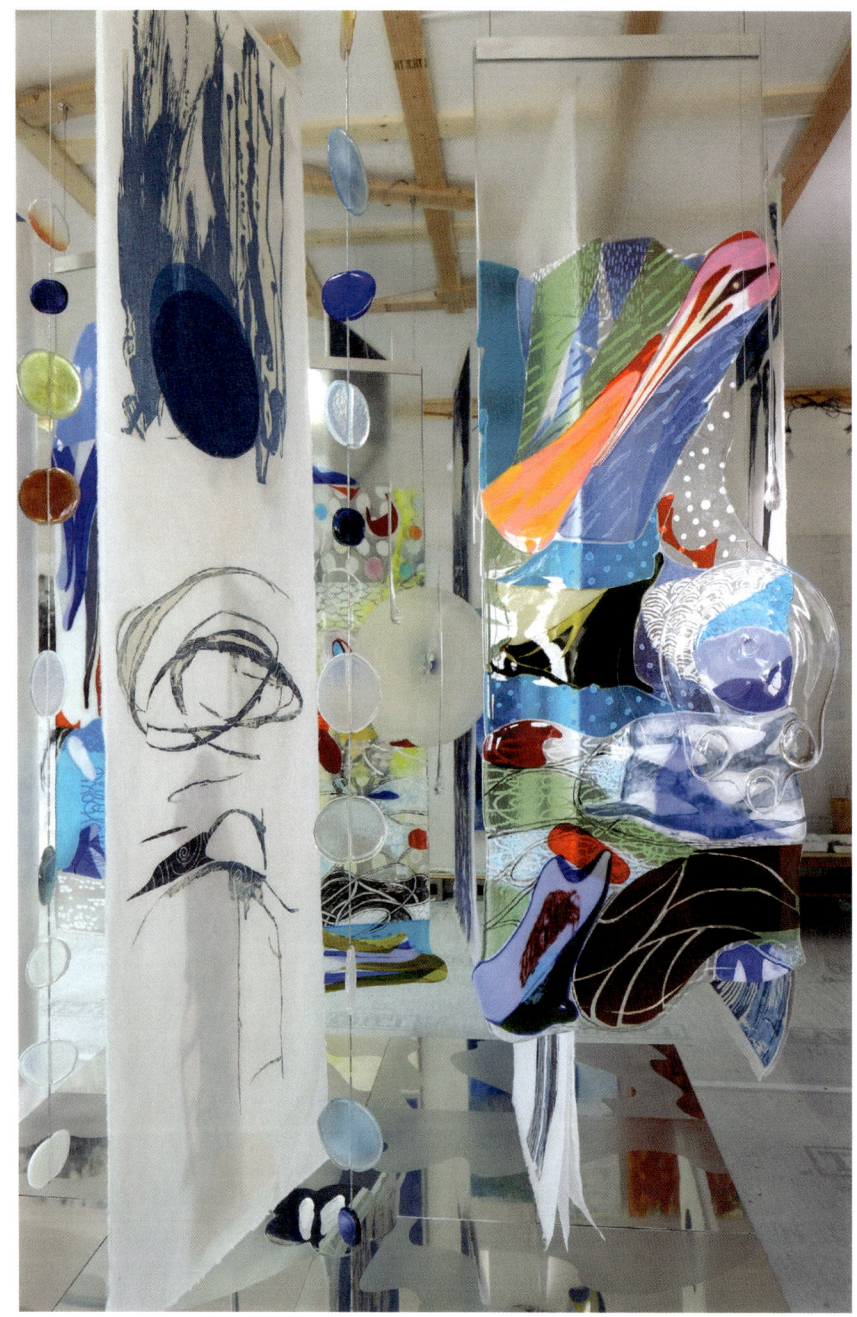

Current and facing page:

Topophilia · Red Shoes 1 | 2018

Multi-media installation

120 × 120 × 144 inches

Installation for the Bellevue Arts Museum

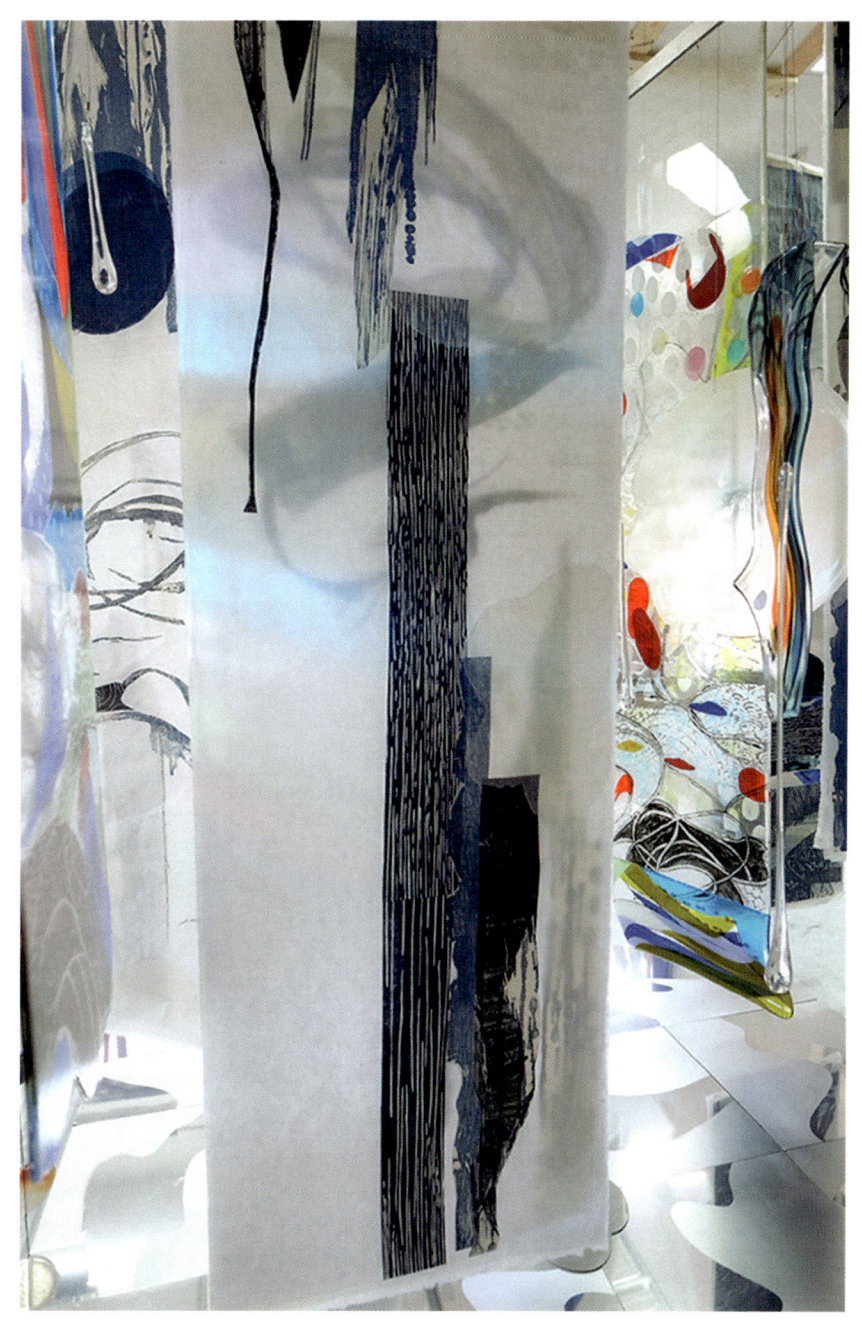

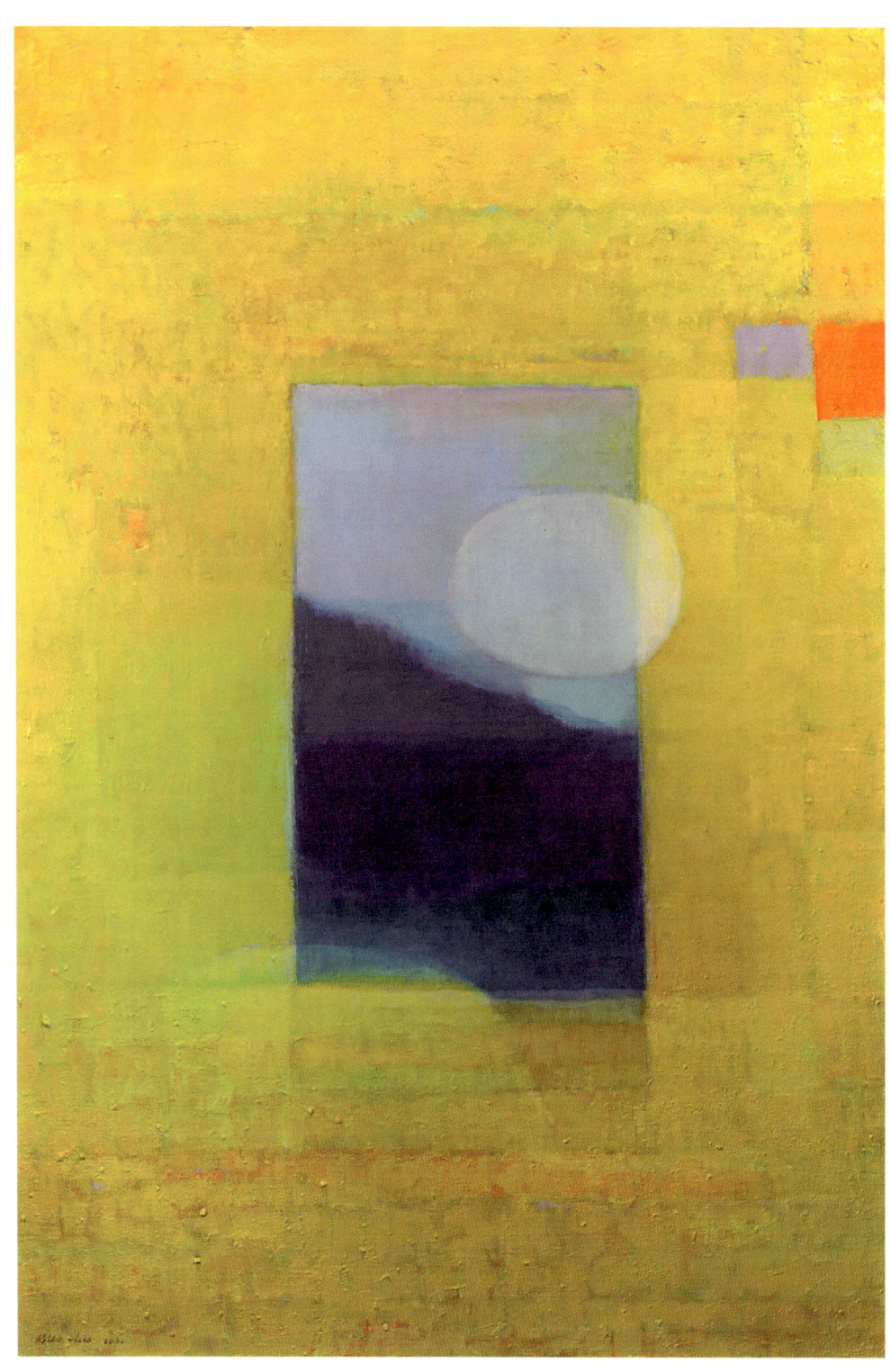

Verse · Sky and Field | 2020
Oil on linen | 53.5 x 38.5 inches
Private collection

Verse · Space in White | 2019
Gouache, graphite, and collage on paper
48.75 x 33 inches

Verse · Space in Blue | 2019
Gouache, graphite, and collage on paper
48.75 x 33 inches

Verse · Space in Green | 2019
Gouache, graphite, and collage on paper
48.75 x 33 inches

Verse · Space in Black | 2019
Gouache, graphite, and collage on paper
48.75 x 33 inches

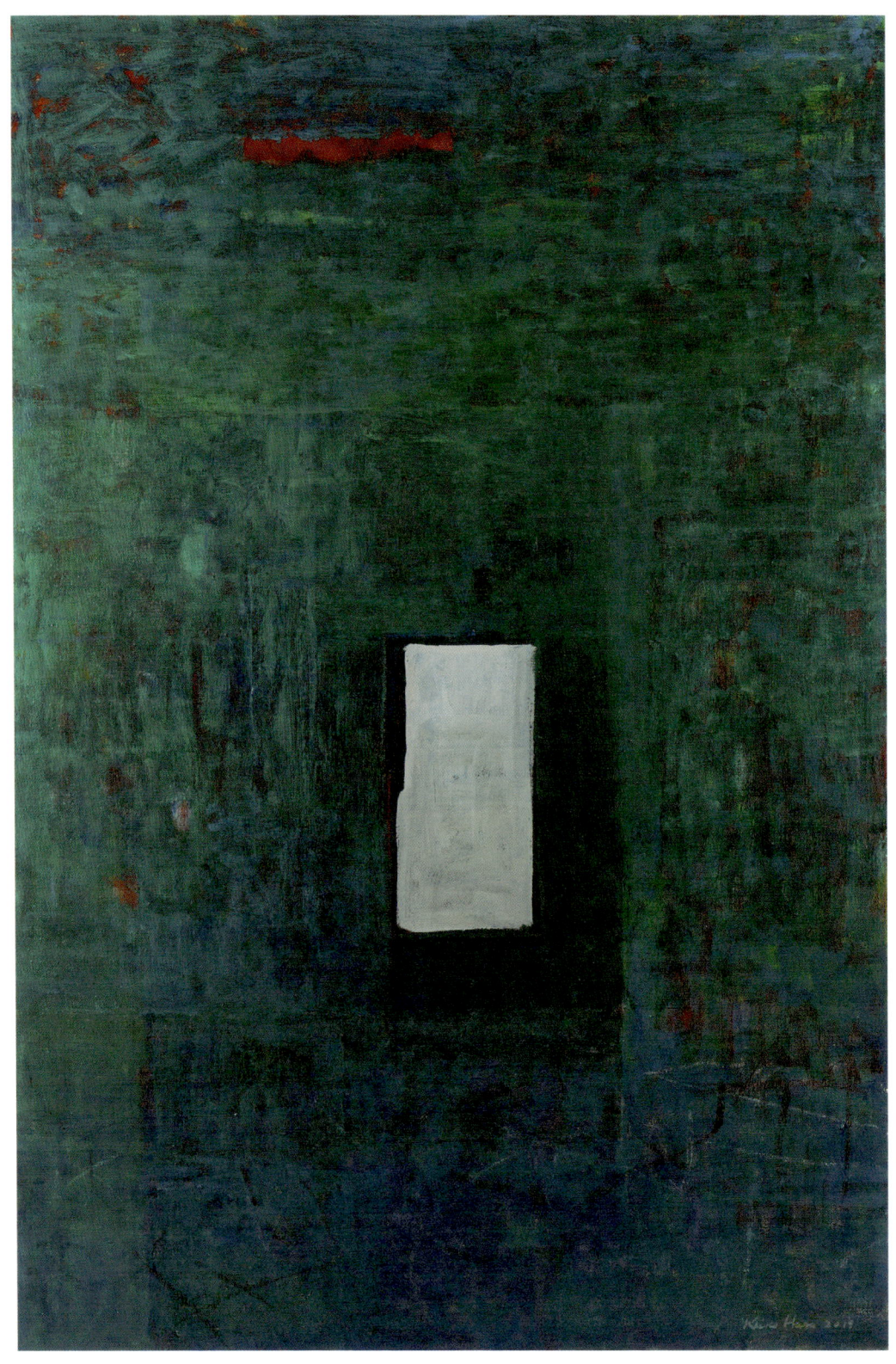

Verse · Voice in Silence | 2019
Oil on linen
53.5 × 38.5 inches

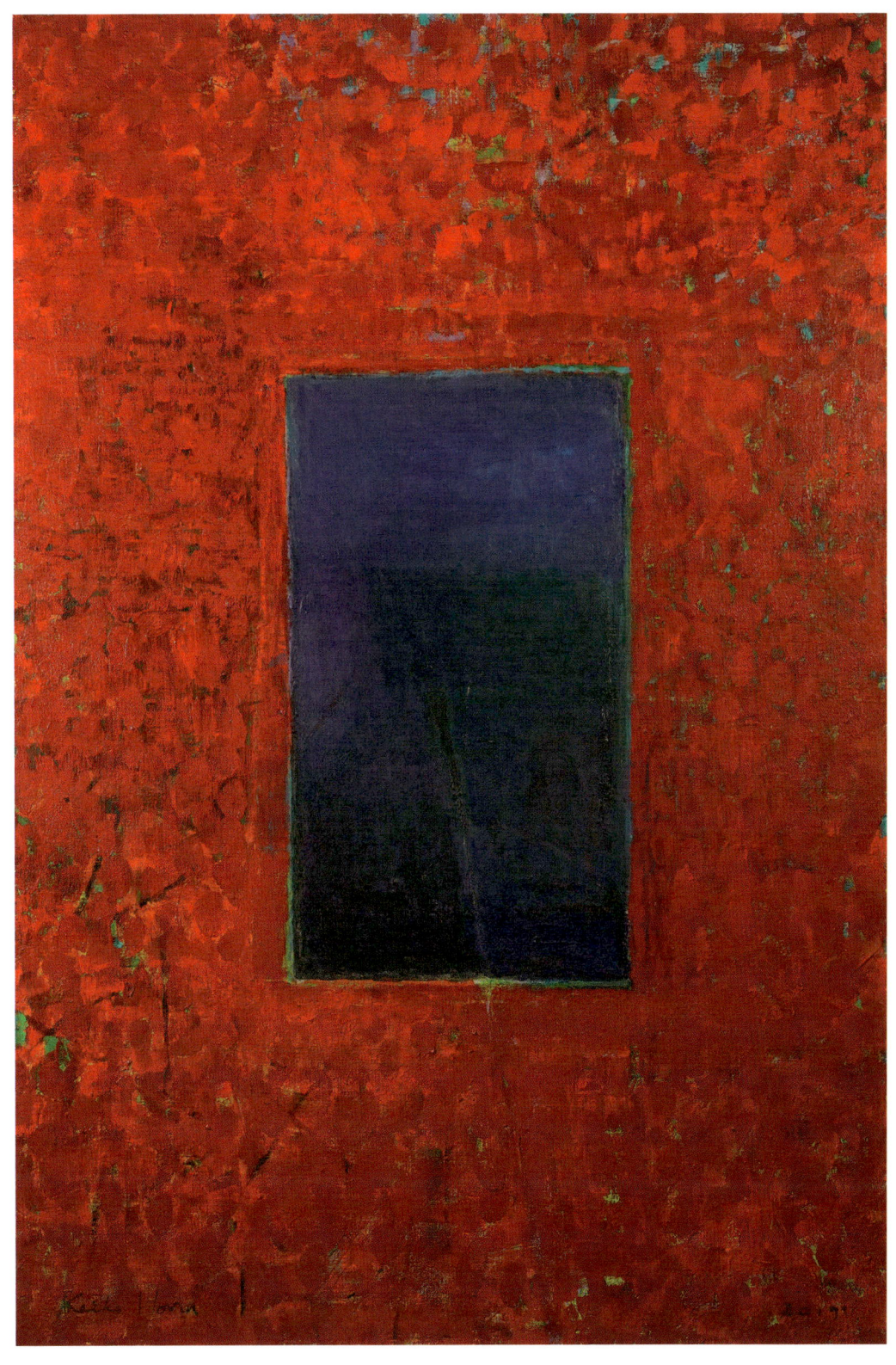

Verse · Voice in Red | 2019
Oil on linen
53.5 × 38.5 inches

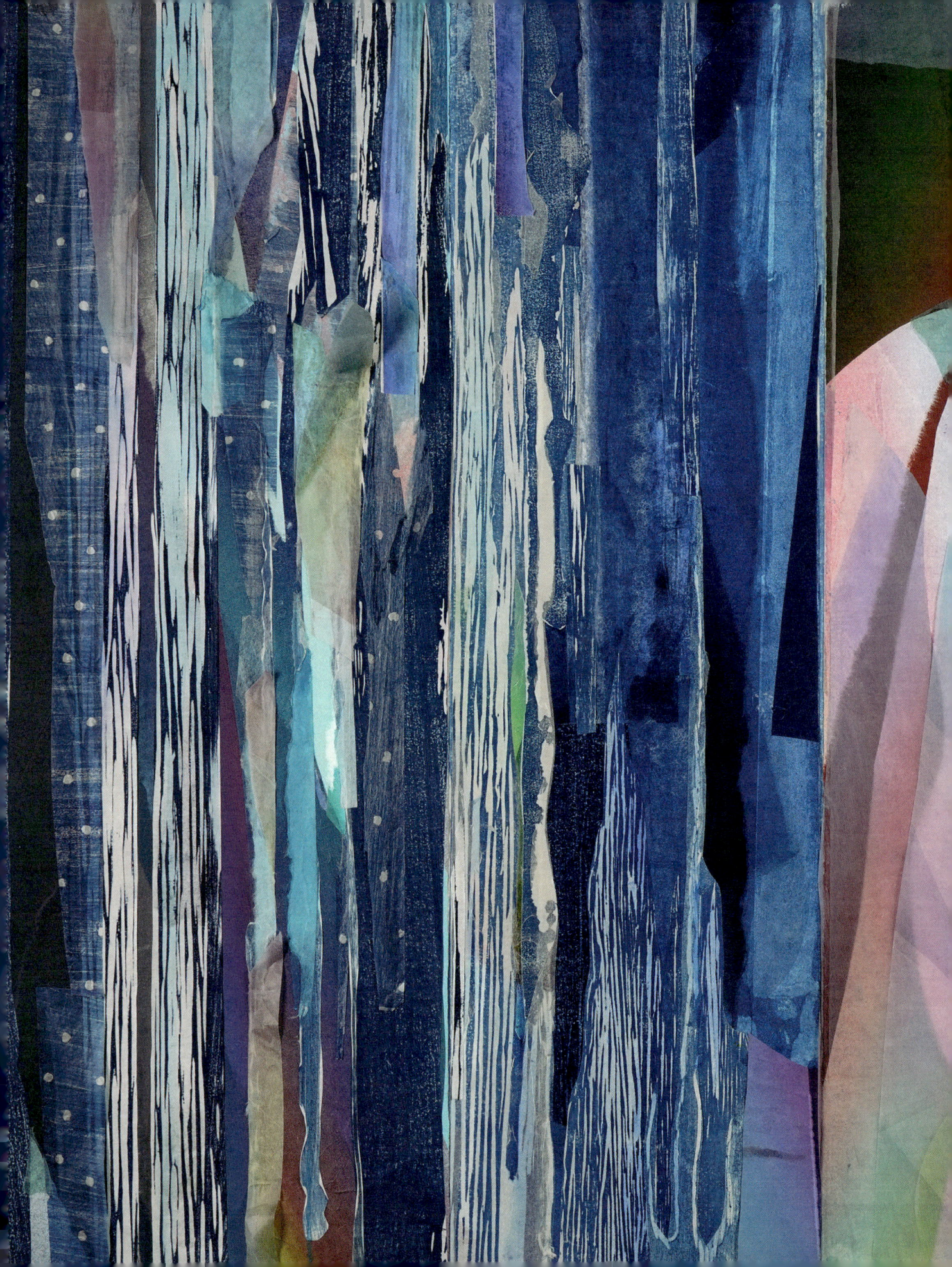

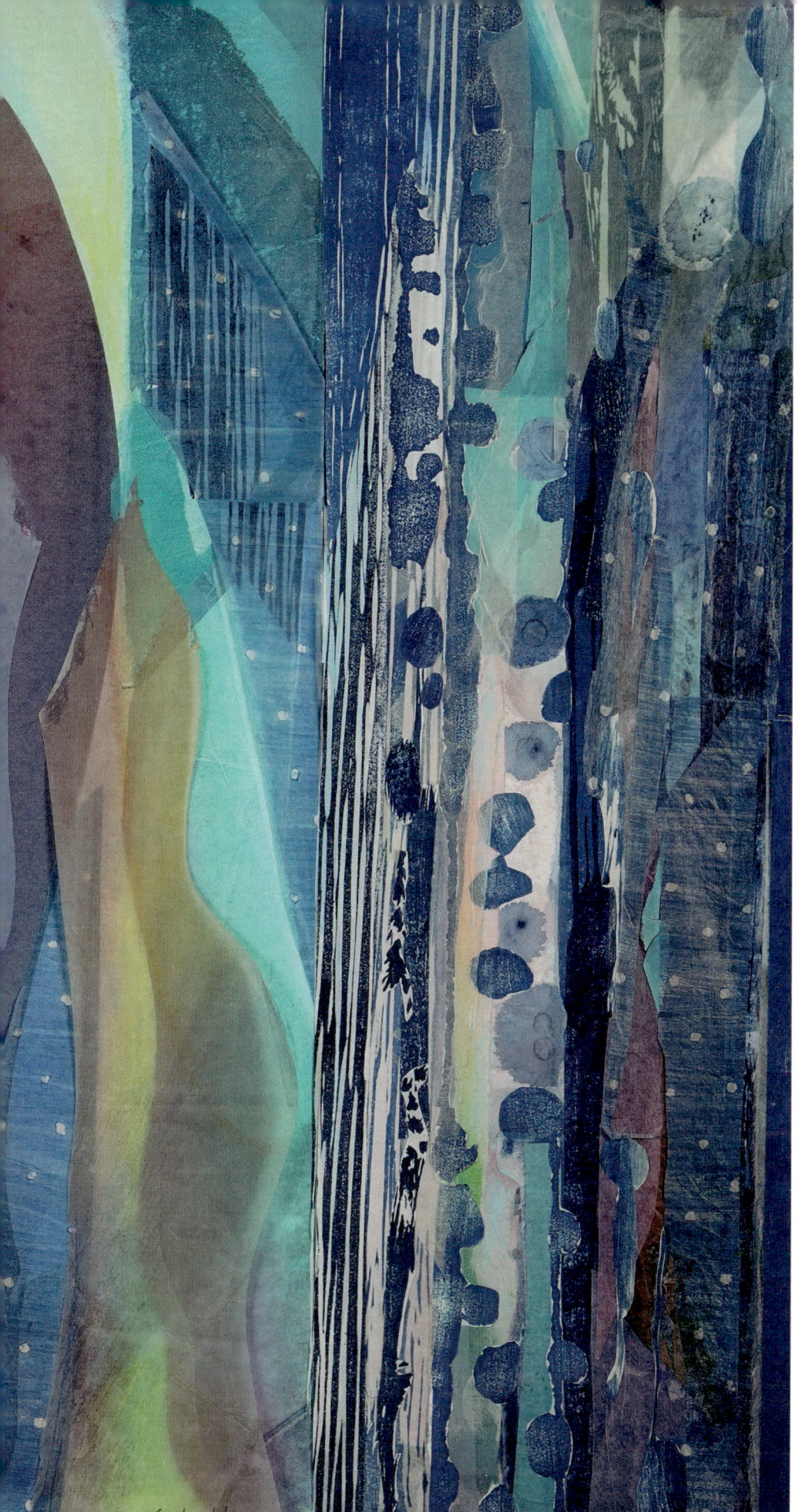

Verse · Space · Light 1 | 2019
Monotype with collage
30 × 41 inches
Private collection

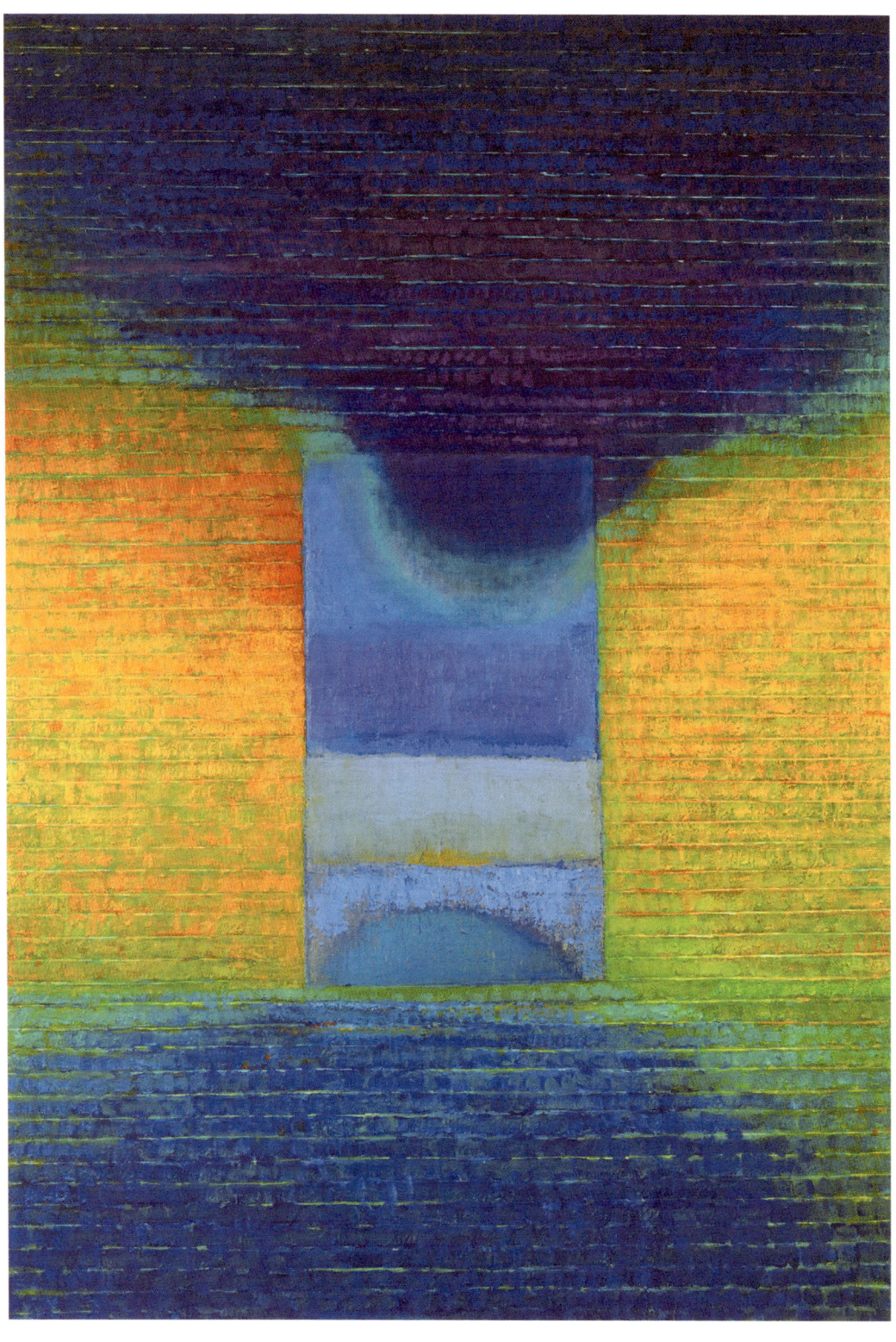

Space · Sky and Field | 2020
Oil on linen
76 x 54 inches

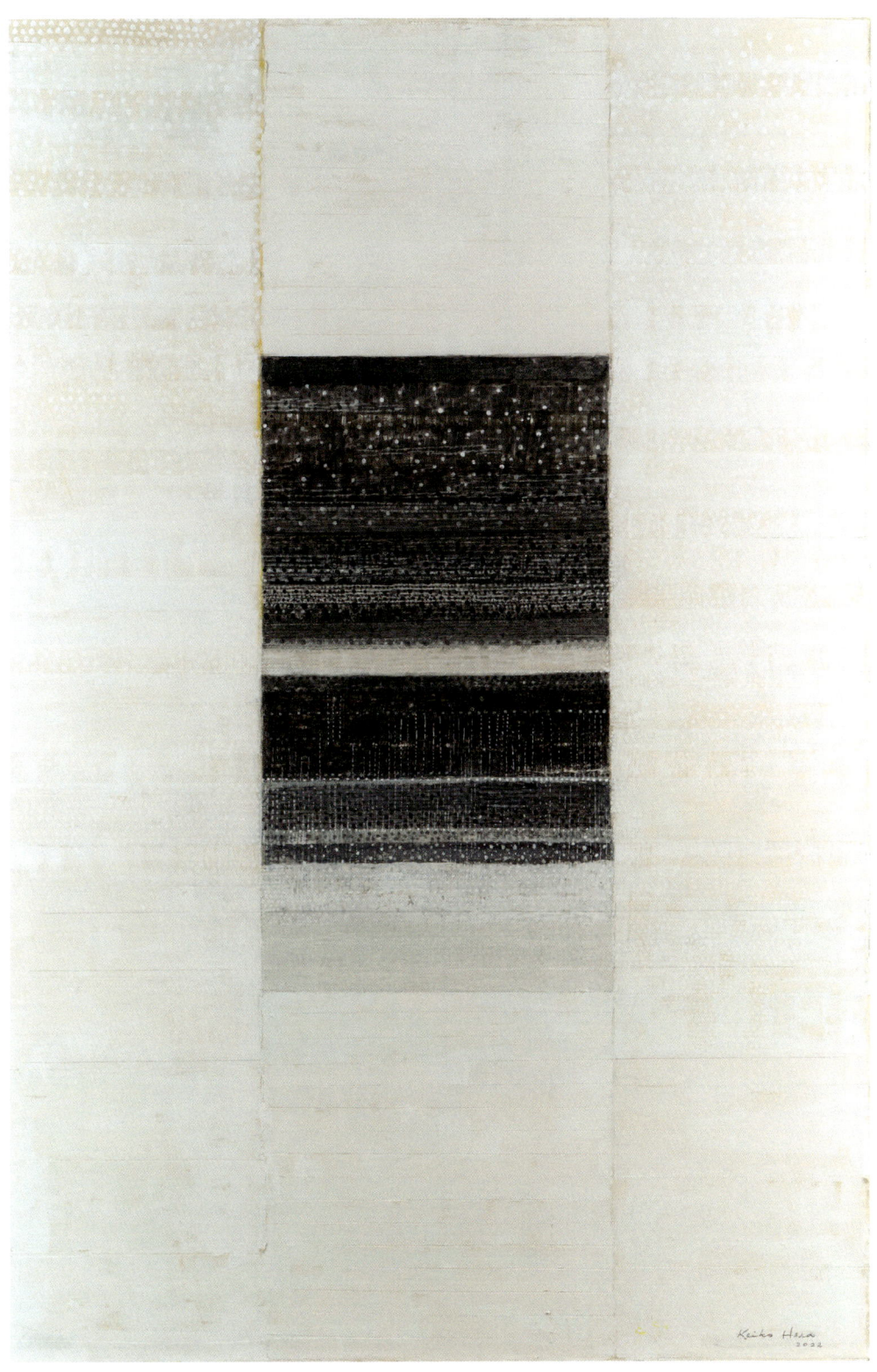

Verse · Space in Black and White | 2022
Water-based painting media, collage on washi paper mounted on panel
53.5 x 38.5 inches

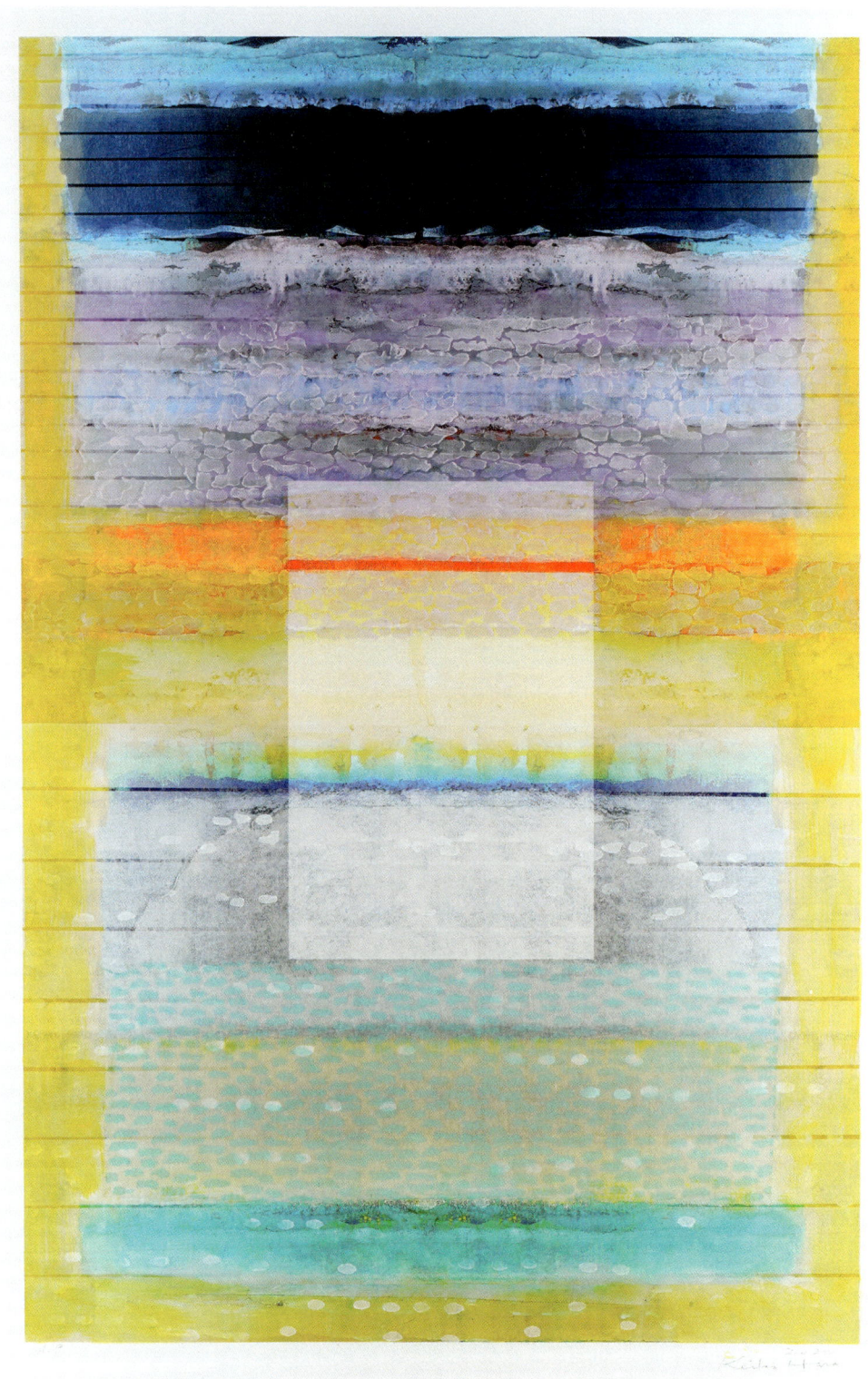

Verse · Space and Field | 2022
Mixed-media print with digital, silk screen, stencil, and woodblock
Printed with Susan Goldman, Lily Press
45.5 x 31 inches

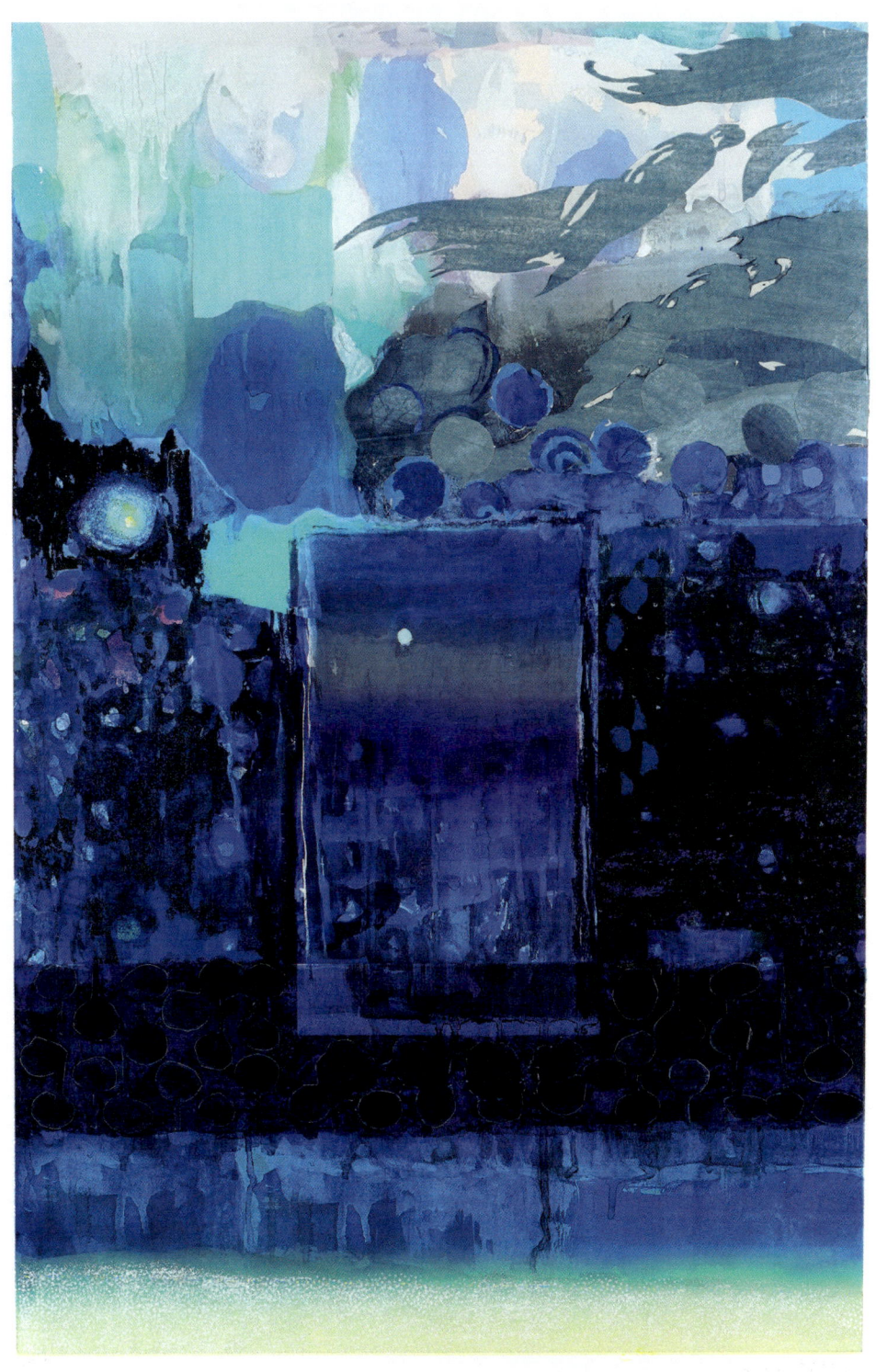

Verse · Space and Sea | 2022
Mixed-media print with digital, silk screen, stencil, and woodblock
Printed with Susan Goldman, Lily Press
45.5 x 31 inches

"I think getting older is fantastic because I have so much more to draw upon and use in brand new ways. Every day is something new."

— Keiko Hara

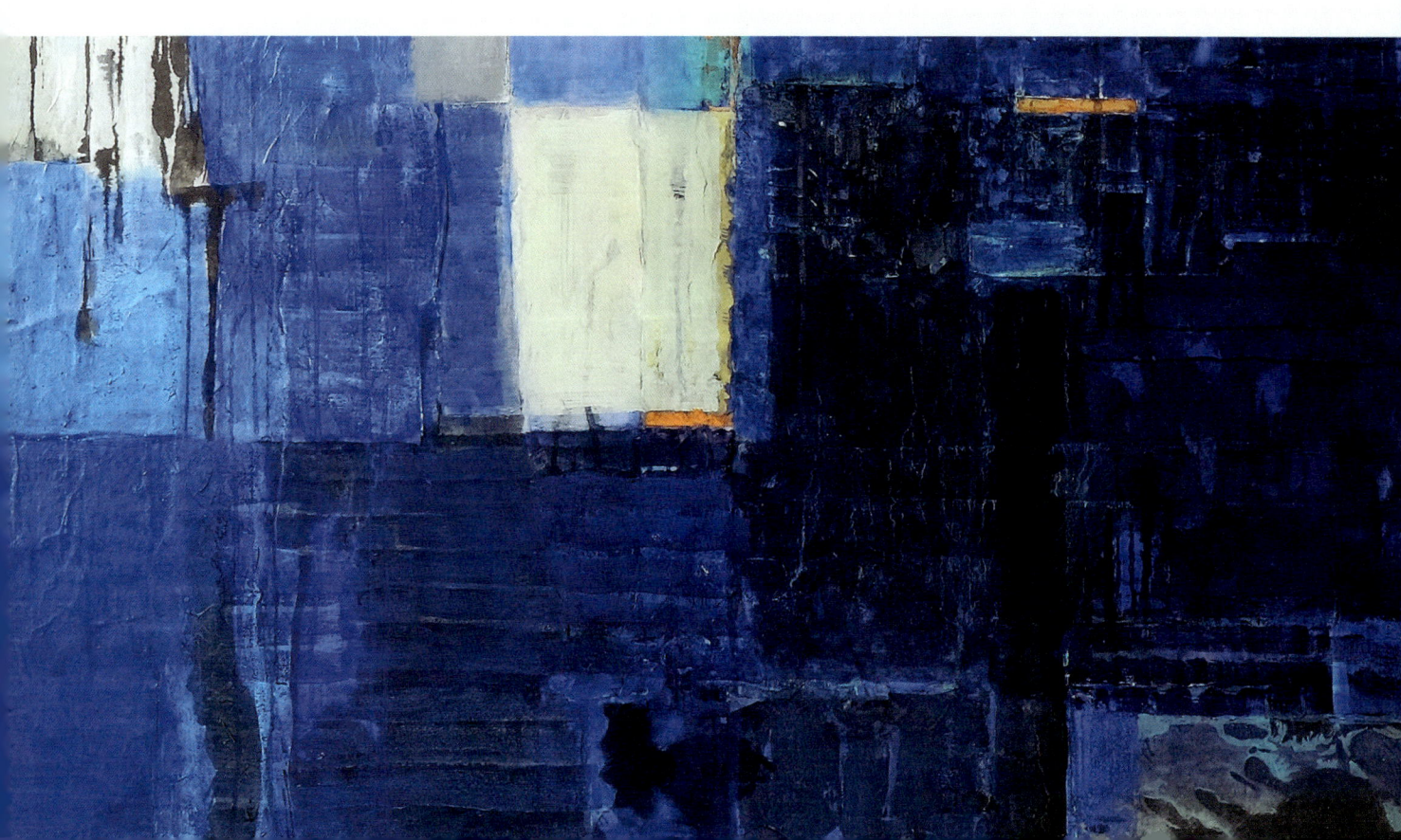

biography

education

1976 |
MFA, Printmaking, Cranbrook Academy of Art,
Bloomfield Hills, MI

1975 |
MA, Printmaking, University of Wisconsin,
Milwaukee, WI

1974 |
BFA, Painting, Mississippi State University for
Women, Columbus, MS

1966 |
Painting, Oita-Kenritsu Art College, Oita, Japan

1964 |
Painting and Drawing, Gendai Art School,
Tokyo, Japan

teaching

2006–Present |
Professor Emerita,
Whitman College, Walla Walla, WA

1985–2006 |
Whitman College, Walla Walla, WA

1980–1985 |
University of Wisconsin-River Falls, River Falls, WI

1978–1980 |
Carthage College, Kenosha, WI

grants, awards, and commissions

2020 |
Public Art Commission, ArtsWA, Vancouver, WA

2017 |
Artist in Residence, Pilchuck Glass Summer Program,
Stanwood, WA

2016 |
Public Art Commission, ArtsWA, Seattle, WA

2012 |
Mokuhanga Innovative Artist-in-Residence for
Mid-Career, Tokyo, Japan

2011 |
Research Teaching Fellowship, Associated Kyoto
Program (AKP), Doshisha University, Kyoto, Japan

2008 |
Public Art Commission, Regional Arts and Culture
Council, Portland, OR

2006 |
Public Art Commission, ArtsWA, Seattle, WA

2005 |
Pollock-Krasner Foundation Grant, New York, NY

2001 |
Invitational Public Art Grant, King County Art
Commission, Seattle, WA

1999 |
Northwest Academic Computing Consortium (NWACC)
Grant, Portland, OR

1997 |
Perry Summer Research Grant, Whitman College,
Walla Walla, WA

1997 |
Purchase Award, Portland Art Museum/Gilkey Center
for Graphic Arts, Portland, OR

1994 |
Fellowship Grant, Artist Trust, Seattle, WA

1991 |
Purchase Award, Oita Art College, Oita, Japan

1989 |
Artist-in-Residence at Centrum, Pacific Rim Cultural Connection Project, Washington State Centennial Commission, Olympia, WA

1987 |
Research Teaching Fellowship, Associated Kyoto Program at Doshisha University, Kyoto, Japan

1984 |
Selection Award, Philadelphia Print Center Exhibition, Philadelphia, PA

1983 |
Artist-in-Residence Grant, Artpark, Lewiston, NY

1976 |
First Prize, Michigan Print and Drawing Exhibition, Detroit Institute of Arts, Detroit, MI

selected solo exhibitions

2022 |
Keiko Hara: Four Decades of Paintings and Prints, Jordan Schnitzer Museum of Art WSU, Pullman, WA

2017 |
Keiko Hara: Recent Works in Painting, Print, and Glass, Foundry Vineyards Gallery, Walla Walla, WA

2016 |
Keiko Hara: Topophilia Ma and Ki · Memory, Kentler International Drawing Space, Brooklyn, NY

2015 |
Keiko Hara: Verse Ma and Ki · Memory, Perimeter Gallery, Chicago, IL

2014 |
Keiko Hara: Topophilia Ma and Ki, Perimeter Gallery, Chicago, IL

2013 |
Keiko Hara: Topophilia Ma and Ki, Perimeter Gallery, Chicago, IL

1981–2013 |
Keiko Hara Prints, Bainbridge Arts and Crafts, Bainbridge Island, WA

1981–2013 |
Keiko Hara Prints, Pendleton Center for the Arts, Pendleton, OR

2012 |
Works of Keiko Hara, Olympia Centre, Chicago, IL

2011 |
Keiko Hara: Works on Canvas and Paper and Installation, Perimeter Gallery, Chicago, IL

2010 |
Verses: Reflected and Reflecting, Public Art at the City Archives and Records Center, Portland, OR

2009 |
Keiko Hara: New Work, Perimeter Gallery, Chicago, IL

2008 |
Verse in Sesshu, COHJU Contemporary Art, Kyoto, Japan

2008 |
Keiko Hara: New Works on Canvas and Paper, Lorinda Knight Gallery, Spokane, WA

2007 |
Topophilia Imbuing, American University Museum at the Kazten Arts Center, Washington, DC

2007 |
Keiko Hara: New Paintings, Lorinda Knight Gallery, Spokane, WA

2006 |
Keiko Hara: Verse Imbuing, Walla Walla Foundry Gallery, Walla Walla, WA

2006 |
Keiko Hara: Imbuing in Monet, Perimeter Gallery, Chicago, IL

2005 |
Keiko Hara: Verses from the Sea, Center for Arts and History, Lewis-Clark State College, Lewiston, ID

2004 |
Keiko Hara: Seasons, Northwest Museum of Arts and Culture (MAC), Spokane, WA

2003 |
Keiko Hara: Painting and Works on Paper, Perimeter Gallery, Chicago, IL

2003 |
Keiko Hara: Works on Paper and Canvas, Perimeter Gallery, New York, NY

2002 |
Keiko Hara: New Works, Lorinda Knight Gallery, Spokane, WA

2001 |
Topophilia: Semaru Print Installation, Autzen Gallery, Portland State University, Portland, OR

2001 |
Keiko Hara: Recent Works on Canvas, Paper, and Glass, Foster/White Gallery, Seattle, WA

2001 |
Keiko Hara: New Works, Perimeter Gallery, Chicago, IL

2000 |
Paintings and Works on Paper, Lorinda Knight Gallery, Spokane, WA

2000 |
Topophilia: Semaru, Prichard Art Gallery, University of Idaho, Moscow, ID

1999 |
Topophilia: Departing, Foster/White Gallery, Kirkland, WA

1998 |
Verse: Semaru, Perimeter Gallery, Chicago, IL

1997 |
Topophilia: Hagoromo, Lorinda Knight Gallery, Spokane, WA

1997 |
Topophilia: Sumida River, Elizabeth Leach Gallery, Portland, OR

1996 |
Recent Works, Foster/White Gallery, Kirkland, WA

1995 |
Topophilia III: Quilt Works, Museum of Art, University of Oregon, Eugene, OR

1995 |
Topophilia V: 100 Gates, North Central Washington Museum Gallery, Wenatchee Valley College, Wenatchee, WA

1995 |
Keiko Hara's Recent Paintings and Prints, Perimeter Gallery, Chicago, IL

1994 |
Solo Exhibition, Perimeter Gallery, Chicago, IL

1994 |
Solo Exhibition, Sheehan Gallery, Whitman College, Walla Walla, WA

1994 |
Topophilia: 100 Gates, Tacoma Art Museum, Tacoma, WA

1992 |
Solo Exhibition, Perimeter Gallery, Chicago, IL

1991 |
Solo Exhibition, Mid-Columbia Art Center, Kennewick, WA

1990 |
Solo Exhibition, Perimeter Gallery, Chicago, IL

1990 |
Solo Exhibition, The Gallery 3286, Mississippi State University for Women, Columbus, MS

1989 |
Solo Exhibition, The Gallery, Cornish College of the Arts, Seattle, WA

1987 |
Solo Exhibition, Perimeter Gallery, Chicago, IL

1985 |
Solo Exhibition, Perimeter Gallery, Chicago, IL

1985 |
Solo Exhibition, Sheehan Gallery, Whitman College, Walla Walla, WA

1984 |
Solo Exhibition, Catherine G. Murphy Gallery,
St. Catherine University, St. Paul, MN

1982–1983 |
Solo Exhibition, Perimeter Gallery, Chicago, IL

1981 |
Solo Exhibition, Gallerie in Den Vierlander, Hamburg,
West Germany

1981 |
Solo Exhibition, Charles A. Wustum Museum of Fine Art,
Racine, WI

1976–1979 |
Solo Exhibition, Bradley Galleries, Milwaukee, WI

selected group exhibitions

2022 |
Focus on the Flatfiles: Between Worlds, Kentler
International Drawing Space, Brooklyn, NY

2022 |
*Unique Impressions, International Monoprint and
Monotype Invitational 2022*, Davidson Galleries,
Seattle, WA

2021–2022 |
Mokuhanga and Sumi: Woodblock Prints and Ink,
Gallery Ami-Kanoko, Osaka, Japan

2021–2022 |
Component Parts: Artworks Made of Multiple Elements,
Racine Art Museum, Racine, WI

2021 |
Black and Blue: Prints in the Time of COVID, Lily Press
in collaboration with Gallerie Myrtis, Baltimore, MD

2021 |
Music as Image and Metaphor: The Kentler Flatfiles,
Ohr-O'Keefe Museum of Art, Biloxi, MS

2021 |
*Music as Image and Metaphor: Selections from the
Kentler Flatfiles*, Bo Bartlett Center, Columbus, GA

2020 |
*Good Form, Decorum, and in the Manner: Portraits from
the Collections of Washington Print Club Members*,
American University Museum at the Katzen Arts Center,
Washington, DC

2019 |
Portrait: The Kentler Flatfiles in 58 Works, Kentler
International Drawing Space, Brooklyn, NY

2019 |
*Breaking Boundaries: International Contemporary
Mokuhanga Print Exhibit*, Foundry Vineyards Gallery,
Walla Walla, WA

2019 |
*Biennial Artist Book Exhibition: Construction/
Deconstruction*, Bend Art Center, Bend, OR

2018 |
BAM Biennial 2018: BAM! Glasstastic, Bellevue Arts
Museum, Bellevue, WA

2018 |
Mokuhanga: Impressions Past and Present,
Feigenbaum Center for Visual Arts, Union College,
Schenectady, NY

2017 |
*Keiko Hara: Fluid and Free Mokuhanga Style, A
Contemporary Approach*, Studio 7 Fine Arts,
Donkey Mill Art Center, Holualoa Village, HI

2016 |
*Mapping Spaces: Carte Blanche, Selections from the
Kentler Flatfiles*, Kentler International Drawing Space,
Brooklyn, NY

2016 |
Suitcase, Gallery 110, Seattle, WA

2016 |
Bend, Fold, Mutilate: Paper Takes Shape, Bainbridge
Arts and Crafts, Bainbridge, WA

2015 |
Nebulous: Abstract Works from RAM's Collection,
Racine Art Museum, Racine, WI

2015 |
From Artist's Eye, Museum of Northwest Art,
La Conner, WA

2015 |
705 Driggs: 27 Artists Working in NYC, Central
Connecticut State University Art Galleries,
New Britain, CT

2015 |
Washington Print Club 50th Anniversary Biennial,
American University Museum at the Katzen Arts Center,
Washington, DC

2015 |
Abstract American Mokuhanga, Sheehan Gallery,
Whitman College, Walla Walla, WA

2015 |
*Impressions: Selections from Stewart & Stewart, 1980–
Present*, Kalamazoo Institute of Arts, Kalamazoo, MI

2014 |
Artist In Residence Program Exhibition, International
Mokuhanga Conference 2014, 3331 Arts Chiyoda,
Tokyo, Japan

2013 |
*Impressions: Selections from Stewart & Stewart, 1980–
Present*, Gallery 72, Omaha, NE

2013 |
Mokuhanga Exhibition, Cullom Gallery, Seattle, WA

2012 |
Mokuhanga Artist in Residence Print Exhibition,
Mokuhanga Innovation Laboratory (MI-LAB) Gallery,
Tokyo, Japan

2010 |
*Someday My Prints Will Come: Wisconsin Printmakers
in RAM's Collection*, RAM's Charles A. Wustum Museum
of Fine Arts, Racine, WI

2010 |
Japanese Prints and Works on Paper,
Thos. Moser Studio, New York, NY

2010 |
Abstract Art, Perimeter Gallery, Chicago, IL

2009 |
The Arts: A Celebration, The Anacortes Arts Festival at
the Port Invitational Exhibition, Anacortes, WA

2009 |
Love, Let Me Count the Ways, Washington Print Club
20th Biennial, American University Museum at the
Kazten Arts Center, Washington, DC

2008 |
Border Crossings, Kyoto International Cultural Center,
Kyoto, Japan

2008 |
A Sense of Place, Mid America Print Council Invitational
Exhibition, University of Nebraska, Lincoln, NE

2008 |
Three Artists from Brooklyn, New York, Art Forum JARFO,
Kyoto, Japan

2007 |
*Visions: Selections from the James T. Dyke Collection of
Contemporary Drawing*, Arkansas Arts Center,
Little Rock, AR

2007 |
*Visions: Selections from the James T. Dyke Collection of
Contemporary Drawing*, Naples Museum of Art,
Naples, FL

2007 |
In Circulation: Works on Paper, Luther W. Brady
Art Gallery, The George Washington University,
Washington, DC

2007 |
Cultural Evolution and Diffusion, Albrecht-Kemper
Museum of Art, St. Joseph, MO

2006 |
Print Types, Ashford University, Clinton, IA

2005 |
East Meets West: The Contemporary Asian Aesthetic,
Racine Art Museum, Racine, WI

2004 |
Cultural Evolution and Diffusion, The Print Consortium,
Kansas City, MO

2004 |
Mixed-Media Print Invitation, Rental/Sales Gallery,
Seattle Art Museum, Seattle, WA

2004 |
American Relief Prints, University Place Art Center,
Lincoln, NE

2004 |
Mark My Word: Text, Code and Literary Allusion,
Museum of Northwest Art, La Conner, WA

2004 |
Impressions, Jundt Art Museum, Gonzaga University,
Spokane, WA

2003 |
New Prints 2003: Autumn, International Print Center
New York, New York, NY

2002 |
Sensory Experience Portfolio, Southern Graphics
Council Conference, New Orleans, LA

2001 |
Gallery Space, Bellevue College, Bellevue, WA

2000 |
Sumida River, Stadium Exhibition Center, Seattle, WA

1999 |
"Japonisme" and Japanese Printmaking,
The George Washington University, Dimock Gallery,
Washington, DC

1999 |
Contemporary Collaborations, Sheehan Gallery,
Whitman College, Walla Walla, WA

1999 |
Graphica Creativa '99, 9th International Print Triennial,
Jyvaskyla Art Museum, Jyvaskyla, Finland

1998 |
The Artist Trust Grant Recipient Exhibition,
Chase Gallery, Spokane, WA

1998 |
Regional Women Printmakers, Kittredge Gallery,
University of Puget Sound, Tacoma, WA

1998 |
Blue Mountain Artists, Simon Edwards Gallery,
Yakima, WA

1998 |
Japanese Contemporary Printmaker, Atrium Gallery,
University of Connecticut, Storrs, CT

1998 |
Contemporary American Prints, Addison/Ripley Fine Arts,
Washington, DC

1998 |
Color Print USA, National Invitational Print Portfolio
Exhibition in 50 US States, University of Iowa Museum
of Art, Iowa City, IA

1998 |
Japanese/American—The In Between, Art Gym,
Marylhurst College, Marylhurst, OR

1997 |
Northwest Experimental Printmakers, Art Gym,
Marylhurst College, Marylhurst, OR

1997 |
International Print Art Exhibition, Portland Art Museum,
Portland, OR

1997 |
The Best of Chicago, Gallery V, Columbus, OH

1997 |
Abstraction Painters, Center on Contemporary Art,
Seattle, WA

1996 |
Beyond the Rock Garden, Wing Luke Asian Museum,
Seattle, WA

1995 |
The National Print Art Invitational Exhibition, Elizabeth
Leach Gallery, Portland, OR

1995 |
*Interior Idioms: The Idiosyncratic Art of Eastern
Washington*, Seafirst Gallery, Seattle, WA

1994 |
Graphic Legacy, National Museum of Women in the
Arts, Washington, DC

1994 |
Group Exhibition, Seafirst Gallery, Seattle, WA

1994 |
Group Exhibition, Brendan Walter Gallery,
Santa Monica, CA

1992 |
Auction of Mailboxes, Archives of American Art, Smithsonian Institution, Washington, DC

1992 |
Group Exhibition, One Illinois Center/Metropolitan Structure, Chicago, IL

1992 |
Group Exhibition, Brendan Walter Gallery, Santa Monica, CA

1991 |
Group Exhibition, Bellevue Arts Museum, Bellevue, WA

1991 |
Group Exhibition, Centrum, King County, WA

1991 |
Collaboration in Print: Stewart & Stewart Prints, 1980-1990, Detroit Institute of Arts, Detroit, MI

1991 |
Landmark Editions: A Decade of Contemporary Prints, Katherine E. Nash Gallery, University of Minnesota, Minneapolis, MN

1990 |
Works on Paper and Canvas—Multi-Cultural Perspectives, Governor's Invitational Exhibition, Washington State Capital Museum, Olympia, WA

1986 |
Contemporary Screens, Contemporary Arts Center, Cincinnati, OH, traveling exhibit organized by the Art Museum Association of America

1986–1988 |
Outside Japan, Museum of Art/WSU, Pullman, WA

1986–1988 |
Works on Paper, Perimeter Gallery, Chicago, IL

1985 |
The Print Club Selects, Philadelphia, PA

1985 |
Off and on the Wall Dimensional Paper, State University of New York, New Paltz, NY,

1985 |
Off and on the Wall Dimensional Paper, Pennsylvania State University, Middleton, PA

1984 |
Philadelphia 60th Print Club Exhibition, Philadelphia, PA

1984 |
International Art Exposition, Chicago, IL

1984 |
National Dimensional Paper Works, Baltimore, MD

1984 |
Paper Works with Wood, Plum Gallery, Kingston, MD

1983 |
Wisconsin Painters and Print Exhibition, Madison Art Center, Madison, WI

1983 |
Printed by Women, A National Exhibition of Prints and Photos by Women, Port of History Museum at Penn's Landing, Philadelphia, PA

1982 |
One of a Kind Printmaking USA, England

1982 |
Electronic Art Exhibit, Honeywell Co., Minneapolis, MN

1981 |
Midwest Company Art, Pillsbury Gallery, Minneapolis, MN

1979 |
Philadelphia 55th Print Club Exhibit, Philadelphia, PA

1979 |
18th Annual International Invitational Print Show, New York, NY

1978 |
Madison Invitational, Madison, WI

1977 |
Group Exhibition, Benjamin Galleries, Chicago, IL

1976 |
30th American Invitational and 20th National Print Show, Brooklyn Art Museum, Brooklyn, NY

1976 |
Michigan Print and Drawing Show, Detroit, MI

bibliography

2022 |
"WSU Schnitzer Museum showcases new exhibitions,"
WSU Insider, Pullman, WA

2022 |
"On View, Keiko Hara: Four Decades of Paintings and
Prints," by Lauren Gallow, LUXE Interiors + Design,
Pacific Northwest, luxesource.com

2017 |
"Japanese Arts and Artists Flourish in Walla Walla,"
Union Bulletin, Walla Walla, WA

2013 |
"Review: Keiko Hara/Perimeter Gallery," Chris Miller,
New City Art, Chicago, IL

2013 |
"Art Exhibition Surpasses Language and Tradition,"
Cecilia Garza, *Bainbridge Island Review*,
Bainbridge, WA

2009 |
"Keiko Hara: Juxtaposition to the Character to Surface,"
Sylvia Krzystofek, *Art Talk*, Chicago, IL

2008 |
"Border Crossings: Painting for a New Era,"
Robert C. Morgan, Exhibition Essay, Kyoto, Japan

2008 |
International Community House and COHJU
Contemporary Art, Kyoto, Japan

2007 |
*Visions: Selections from the James T. Dyke Collection of
Contemporary Drawings*, Townsend Wolfe,
Washington, DC

2007 |
"Keiko Hara: Sense of Place," Dorothea A. Dietrich,
American University Museum at the Kazten Arts Center,
Washington, DC

2006 |
"Keiko Hara's Springtime, Shreds of Language,"
Robert C. Morgan, Perimeter Gallery, Chicago, IL

2006 |
"Keiko Hara at Perimeter Gallery," Alan Artner,
Chicago Tribune, Chicago, IL

2005 |
"Keiko Hara Seasons," Lois Allan, Northwest Museum of
Arts and Culture (MAC), Spokane, WA

2004 |
"Making Her Mark," Sheri Boggs, *Pacific Northwest
Inlander*, Spokane, WA

2003 |
"Keiko Hara at the Perimeter Gallery," Lisa Stein,
ARTnews, Chicago, IL

2003 |
"Critic's Choice," Fred Camper, *Chicago Reader*,
Chicago, IL

2001 |
"Reflecting Her Heritage," Andrea Palpant,
Spokane Home and Life, Spokane, WA

2000 |
"The Art of Keiko Hara: Topophilia-Semaru,"
Gail Siegel, Prichard Art Gallery, University of Idaho,
Moscow, ID

1999 |
"Print Inside, Graphica Creativa '99," Jukka Partanen,
Jyvaskyla Art Museum, Jyvaskyla, Finland

1999 |
"Japonisme and Japanese Printmaking," Lenore D.
Miller, George Washington University Galleries,
Washington, DC

1998 |
"Creating the In Between," D. K. Row, *Oregonian*,
Sunday Arts and Books section, Portland, OR

1998 |
"Japanese American In Between," Terry Hopkins,
Marylhurst University, Marylhurst, OR

1998 |
"Color Print USA," Mark Pascale, Art Institute of
Chicago, Chicago, IL

1997 |
"Contemporary Printmaker in the Northwest,"
Lois Allen, Craftsman House, Spokane, WA

1994 |
"Graphic Legacy," Susan Fisher Sterling, National Museum of Women in the Arts, Washington, DC

1994 |
"No Discernible Path," Loly Anderson, *ArtWeek*, New York, Laguna Beach, Los Angeles

1992 |
"*Keiko Hara*," Peter Frank, *Vision*

1992 |
"Keiko Hara: Topophilia," Alan G. Artner, *Chicago Tribune*, Chicago, IL

1986 |
"Contemporary Screens," Virginia Fabbri Butera, Art Museum Association of America, San Francisco, CA

1983 |
"Printed by Women," Judith K. Brodsky and Ofelia Garcia, Port of History Museum at Penn's Landing, Philadelphia, PA

1976 |
"The 20th National Print Exhibition," Gene Baro, *Print Collector Newsletter*, New York, NY

selected public and private collections

Arizona State University Art Collection, Tempe, AZ

Arkansas Arts Center, Little Rock, AR

Art Institute of Chicago, Chicago, IL

ArtsWA's Public Art Collection, Olympia, WA

AT&T, Chicago, IL

Bellevue Arts Museum, Bellevue, WA

Chapman and Cutler, Chicago, IL

Charles A. Wustum Museum of Fine Art, Racine, WI

Council House-Johnson Wax Company, Racine, WI

Cray Research Co., Minneapolis, MN

Detroit Institute of Arts, Detroit, MI

Harborview Medical Center, Seattle, WA

Hood Museum of Art, Dartmouth College, Hanover, NH

IBM, Chicago, IL

Jordan Schnitzer Museum of Art WSU, Pullman, WA

Jundt Art Museum, Gonzaga University, Spokane, WA

King County Public Art Commission, Seattle, WA

Library of Congress, Washington, DC

MacMurray College, Jacksonville, IL

Marshall Field & Co., Chicago, IL

Microsoft, Seattle, WA

Milwaukee Art Museum, Milwaukee, WI

Muskegon Museum of Art, Muskegon , MI

National Gallery of Art, Washington, DC

Northwest Museum of Arts and Culture, Spokane, WA

Oita Art College, Oita, Japan

Piper, Jaffrey, and Hopwood Inc., Minneapolis, MN

Portland Art Museum/Gilkey Center for Graphic Arts, Portland, OR

Regional Arts and Culture Council, Portland, OR

SONY, Washington, DC

St. Paul Company, Minneapolis, MN

Tacoma Art Museum, Tacoma, WA

Vail Athletic Club, Vail, CO

Washington Art Consortium/Western Gallery, Western Washington University, Bellingham, WA

Whitman College, Walla Walla, WA

Worcester Art Museum, Worcester, MA

Yale New Haven Hospital, New Haven, CT

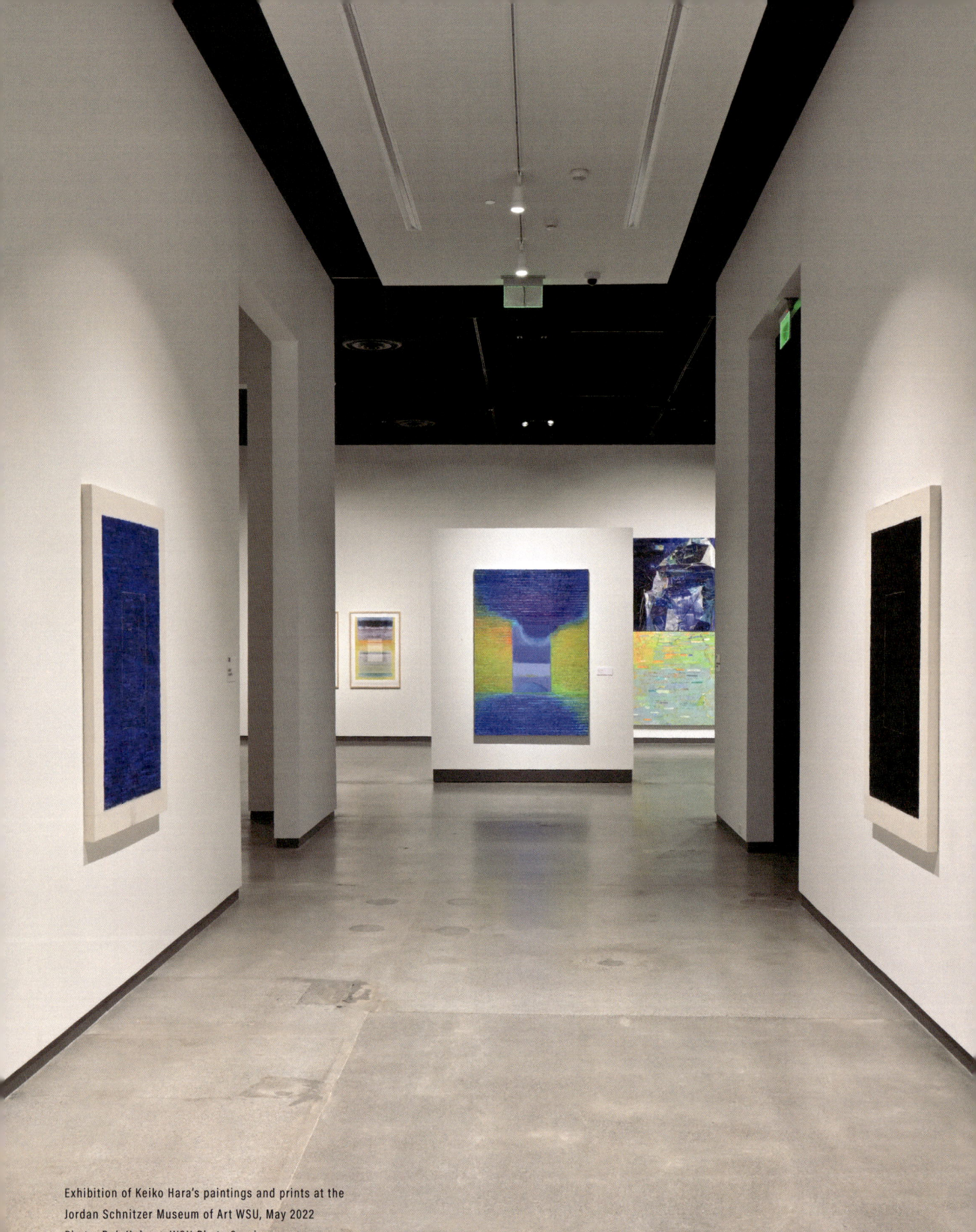

Exhibition of Keiko Hara's paintings and prints at the
Jordan Schnitzer Museum of Art WSU, May 2022
Photo: Bob Hubner, WSU Photo Services

checklist | works in
the exhibition

Image · Space | 1977–1978

Gouache and drawing media on
handmade washi paper

22 x 37 x 1.12 inches

Topophilia 1 | 1981

Lithograph on handmade gampi paper with collage
and machine stitching | Edition 20 (set of 12)

Published by Perimeter Press

24 x 36 inches each

Topophilia 2 | 1989

Mixed-media monoprint with intaglio, lithography,
and chine-collé

Published by Perimeter Press

22.5 x 15 inches

Private collection

Topophilia 7 · Grey | 1996

Ukiyo-e woodblock print with stencil and collage | Edition 20

Printed with Tadashi Toda in Kyoto, Japan

32 x 24 inches

Topophilia 7 · Blue | 1996

Ukiyo-e woodblock print with stencil and collage | Edition 20

Printed with Tadashi Toda in Kyoto, Japan

32 x 24 inches

Topophilia 7 · Green | 1996

Ukiyo-e woodblock print with stencil and collage | Edition 20

Printed with Tadashi Toda in Kyoto, Japan

32 x 24 inches

Topophilia 7 · Red | 1996

Ukiyo-e woodblock print with stencil and collage | Edition 20

Printed with Tadashi Toda in Kyoto, Japan

32 x 24 inches

Verse from Sea | 2002
Mokuhanga woodblock, stencil, and collage print
Edition 15 (set of 12)
10 x 20 inches each

Verse · Imbuing in Blue | 2003
Lithograph with chine-collé | Edition 25
Printed with Craig Cornwall at Trilobite Workshop
28 x 20 inches

Space · Kirameku in White and Blue | 2011
Oil on linen
84 x 216 inches
Collection of the Jordan Schnitzer Museum of Art WSU

Topophilia Ma and Ki in Memory | 2015
Oil and collage on canvas
142 x 288 inches

Verse · Space in Blue | 2017
Water-based painting media, collage
on washi paper mounted on panel
60 x 41 inches

Verse · Space in Black | 2019
Gouache, graphite, and collage on paper
48.75 x 33 inches

Verse · Space in Green | 2019
Gouache, graphite, and collage on paper
48.75 x 33 inches

Verse · Space in Blue | 2019
Gouache, graphite, and collage on paper
48.75 x 33 inches

Verse · Space in White | 2019
Gouache, graphite, and collage on paper
48.75 x 33 inches

Verse · Sky and Field | 2020
Oil on linen
53.5 x 38.5 inches
Private collection

Space · Sky and Field | 2020
Oil on linen
76 x 54 inches

Verse · Space and Sea | 2022
Mixed-media print with digital, silk screen, stencil, and woodblock
Printed with Susan Goldman, Lily Press
45.5 x 31 inches

Verse · Space and Field | 2022
Mixed-media print with digital, silk screen, stencil, and woodblock
Printed with Susan Goldman, Lily Press
45.5 x 31 inches

Verse · Space in Black and White | 2022
Water-based painting media, collage on washi paper mounted on panel
53.5 x 38.5 inches

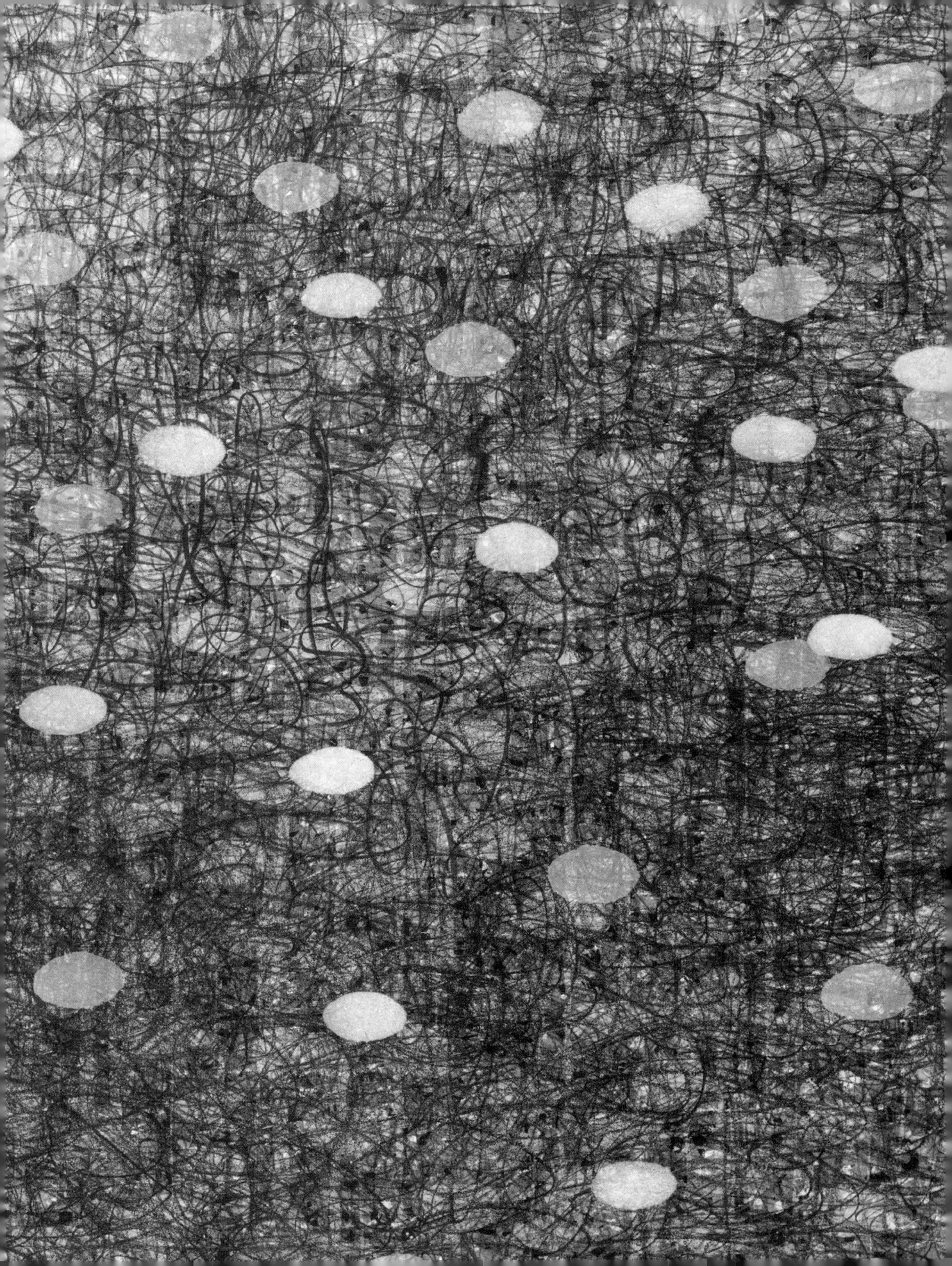

artist's acknowledgments

Keiko Hara

I would like to dedicate this publication to Ainslie and Keith Peoples in recognition of our friendship and their support of my art.

Ainslie's uncle was Tom Thomson, a well-known Canadian artist. She grew up around his paintings, which began a lifelong and profound love of art. I met Ainslie in 1976, during my first solo exhibition at the Bradley Gallery in Milwaukee, Wisconsin. She purchased one of my prints and visited me the very next day at 7:00 a.m. to see more artwork at my studio. Over cups of coffee, we looked and talked extensively.

In 1985, Ainslie moved to Washington, DC, to lead communication services at the American Red Cross. In the 1990s and early 2000s, she served on the board of the Washington Print Club (WPC), where she chaired the program committee. It was through the WPC that Ainslie met her husband, Keith Peoples. Since then, Ainslie and Keith have collected and supported my work. Sadly, Ainslie died on May 11, 2022, after enduring twenty years with multiple sclerosis.

I would also like to acknowledge Karen Johnson Boyd, an important art dealer and supporter who believed in me from the beginning of my career and exhibited my work through the Perimeter Gallery in Chicago. Along with director Frank Paluch and associate director Scott Ashley, the gallery provided me with the resources and support that made it possible to continue my work.

Finally, I am grateful to executive director Ryan Hardesty and the professional staff of the Jordan Schnitzer Museum of Art WSU as well as WSU Press for making possible this exhibition and publication. My art has connected me to wonderful friends, students, collaborators, and collectors. It has been the most enriching life experience. I would like to express my sincerest appreciation to you all. Thank you. —KH

Previous page
Verse · Space M-IV (detail) | 2006
Lithograph and stencil print | Edition 25
Printed with Craig Cornwall at Trilobite Workshop | 22 × 30 inches
Collection of the National Gallery of Art, Washington, DC

Following page
Verse · Space M e | 2007
Work on paper
22 × 15 inches
Private collection

author bios

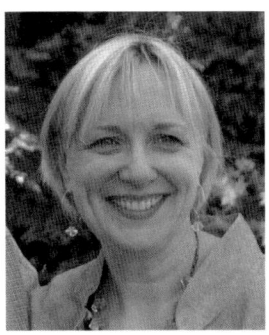

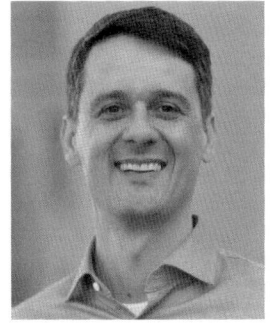

Linda Tesner is a fine arts consultant and independent curator in Portland, Oregon. She was the interim director and curator of the Jordan Schnitzer Museum of Art at Portland State University and formerly the director and curator of the Ronna and Eric Hoffman Gallery of Contemporary Art at Lewis and Clark College in Portland, Oregon, the assistant director of the Portland Art Museum, and the director of the Maryhill Museum of Art in Goldendale, Washington. She is the author of numerous exhibition catalogues and monographs and has a special interest in public art projects.

Ryan Hardesty is the executive director and curator of exhibitions and collections for the Jordan Schnitzer Museum of Art at Washington State University. Prior to WSU, Hardesty held a twelve-year tenure at the Northwest Museum of Arts and Culture in Spokane, Washington. Additional museum experience includes work with the Institute of Contemporary Art in Boston and the Fogg Art Museum in Cambridge, Massachusetts. His recent curatorial projects include exhibitions with artists Polly Apfelbaum, Jeffry Mitchell, and Marie Watt.

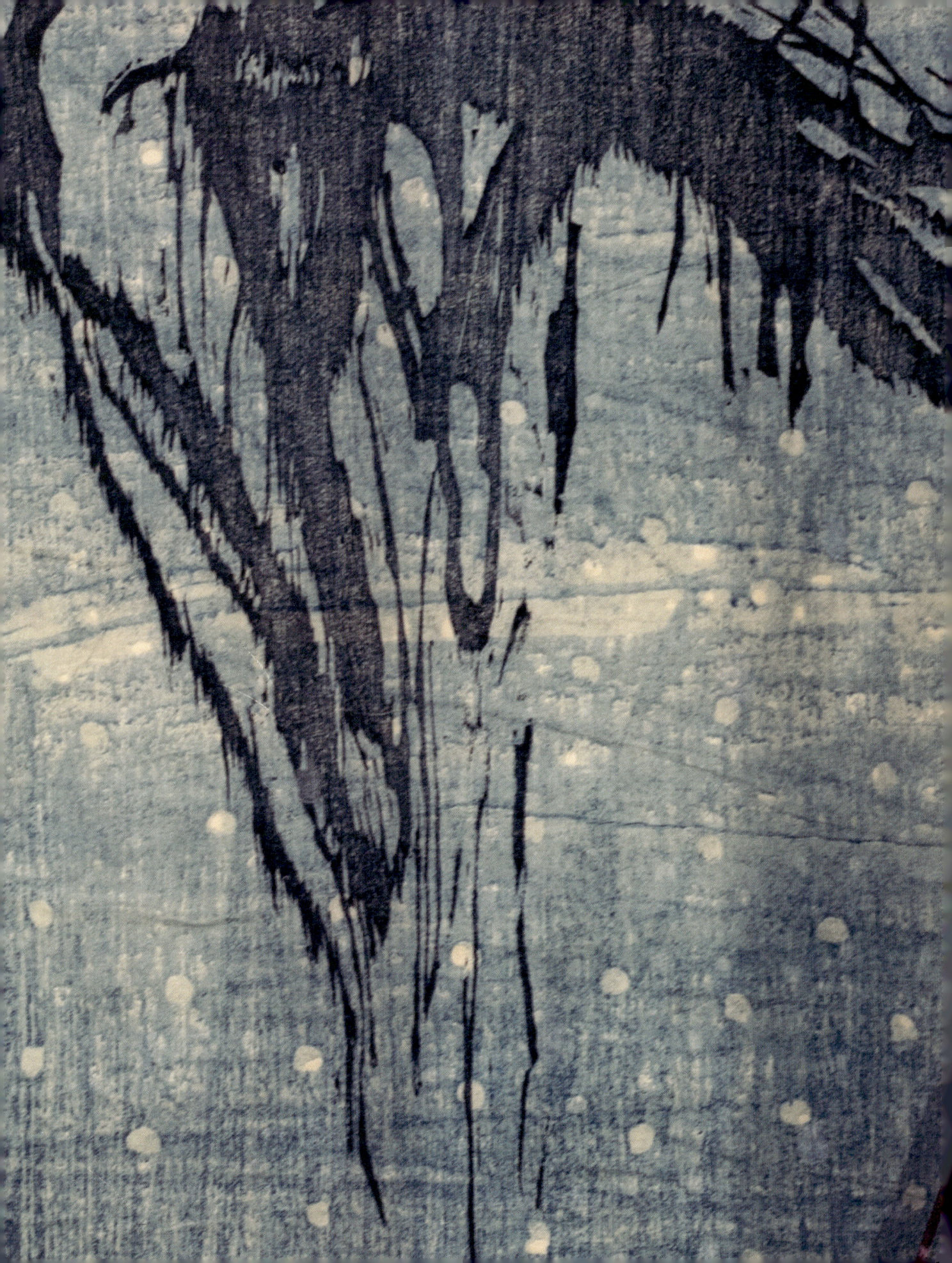